THE PATRIOT GAME

THE PATRIOT GAME

National Dreams & Political Realities

Peter Brimelow

KEY PORTER·BOOKS

Canadian Cataloguing in Publication Data

Brimelow, Peter, 1947–
   The patriot game

Bibliography: p.
Includes index.
ISBN 1-55013-001-3

1. Canada — Politics and government — 1980-1984.*
2. Canada — Politics and government — 1984-   .*I. Title.

FC630.B75 1986   971.064'6   C86-094492-1
F1034.2.B75 1986

Passage from *Two Solitudes* © 1957
Hugh MacLennan
reprinted by permission of Macmillan of Canada
A Division of Canada Publishing Corporation

Key Porter Books Limited
70 The Esplanade
Toronto, Ontario
Canada M5E 1R2

Text design: Michael van Elsen Design Inc.
Typesetting: Computer Composition
Printing and Binding: John Deyell Company
Printed and bound in Canada

86 87 88 89   6 5 4 3 2 1

Contents

For My Parents

Far off thou art, but ever nigh.
– Tennyson

THE PATRIOT GAME

A Note from the Author

This book's modest objective is to present a sort of General Theory of Canada.

I am a wandering WASP, having spent considerable portions of my life in three different countries. My qualifications for writing a book about any one of them are therefore inevitably vulnerable to attack from hostile natives. The obvious defense is to point out that there is a long tradition of insight by outsiders into a nation's character. De Tocqueville at twenty-six spent only nine months travelling in the U.S., and look what he produced: *Democracy in America,* still the most famous study of a much-studied subject. Goldwin Smith, whose 1891 book *Canada and the Canadian Question* is in many ways the model for the present work, was born in England and only came to Canada in mid life. There are important human reasons why outsiders can see, and even more to the point say, things that insiders cannot. On the other hand, Trotsky once wrote a book predicting Communist revolution in Britain and war with the United States. So you have to be careful.

In the course of this book, I am disrespectful of much that Canadians are nowadays encouraged to identify with their nationhood. Indeed, I argue that contemporary Canadian Nationalism is a fraud, designed primarily to benefit particular interest groups in Canada. Nevertheless, I want to emphasize that from an intellectual standpoint I approve of nationalism: I think that the nation-state is unshakeably based on the fundamentals of human nature. My objection to what now passes for nationalism in Canada is that English-speaking Canada's national culture is manifestly not limited to its political boundaries, but is held in common with the English-speaking world. Far from being disparaging, anyone with half an eye can see that this book's attitude to English Canada is in fact one of ardent, if perhaps unrequited, love.

This raises the question of my attitude to French Canada. One of the symptoms of pathology in Canadian politics is that any expression of affection for English Canada is automatically taken to imply anti-French "bigotry." I am not a Francophile, in the sense of being particularly drawn to French society and culture, and I do not make the usual pious noises on the subject. However, I respect the essential integrity of Francophone nationalism and take it seriously – more seriously, it might be claimed, than many Francophones have yet done (but I have faith in them). This, of course, is the reverse of the official Canadian posture. It was an impeccably pious bunch of federal and provincial politicians, for example, who nevertheless in Ottawa in November 1982 settled the impasse over patriation of the constitution by reaching an agreement secretly at night as soon as the Quebec delegation had gone back across the Ottawa River to Hull for dinner. I should have thought that Francophones might prefer a discriminating respect to an indiscriminate and ultimately hypocritical love. But of course the choice must be irritating.

The original version of this manuscript contained over a thousand footnotes, seriously testing the capabilities of my Perfect Writer word processing program and, when she first saw it, the expansive capacity of my publisher's eyes. Since this is a work of journalism, albeit hopefully of a somewhat *haute* type, all such footnotes have been judged unnecessary. I have some lingering regrets about this decision, partly because footnotes were helpful in indicating the further scope of arguments too complex to be compressed into the text and partly because of their intimidating effect. They remain in spirit. I have provided a selected bibliography.

Throughout this book, I have made heavy use of secondary sources. My argument is essentially one of synthesis, and I have deliberately quoted various luminaries to illustrate its components, although of course the conclusions are my own. These sources are quoted precisely because they are representative of conventional wisdom in Canada, not because they are necessarily good historians. No doubt for professional reasons, the good historians who have read the manuscript feel this should be made clear.

Actually, I am not without sympathy for any native indignation this book may inspire. It is almost as alarming to find yourself in print as to see yourself on film, particularly because of the element of necessary caricature. Saint-Just said no one can rule guiltlessly; equally, no one can write without giving pain. I sincerely believe, however, that no matter how shocking and unwelcome some of my observations may appear, they represent a reality that Canadians cannot indefinitely evade. The truth, it is reliably reported, shall set you free.

1

Canada on One Half-Sheet of Notepaper: A Diagnosis

Truth, even scientific truth, is merely a special case of the fantastic.

– Ortega y Gasset

One winter afternoon in late 1975, Joe Clark came to see me in the Toronto offices of the *Financial Post.* This was even before he became Joe Who. He was running for the leadership of the Progressive Conservative Party, but almost no one had noticed. Earlier that fall Clark had broken a previous appointment with me, pleading insufficient time to consult his economic advisors. Economics is a stigma you have to accept when you write for the *Financial Post.* Somewhat reluctantly, I began our rescheduled interview by asking him what he thought about the Economic Council of Canada's just-published report *Looking Outward,* which had recommended continental free trade and had therefore been widely denounced as advocating Canada's absorption into the U.S.A.

Clark immediately fell apart. Frankly, he said, he didn't know anything about economics – still – and his exhausting schedule wasn't helping. You see, he added, *"when I went into politics I had to choose between learning economics and learning French. And I chose French."*

Italics added.

Needless to say, I was completely disarmed. Still considering how I could possibly write up the incident without humiliating such a nice and obviously harmless man, I went off to the Middle East to do a *Financial Post* Special Report on the effects of the oil boom. The report won the Royal Bank/Toronto Press Club Award. Joe Clark won the Tory leadership.

Several morals can be extracted from this tale. One is the subtle, but in my opinion profoundly debilitating, cost of the French connection to English Canadian politics. Another is just how inexperienced Joe Clark was when he became Tory leader at the age of thirty-six. For a practicing politician to know nothing about what has historically been the central economic question facing his country may be less than surprising, although mildly ironic in Clark's case because of the starring role he has recently been playing as External Affairs Minister in the Mulroney government's effort to reach a free trade agreement with the U.S. But to be unable to talk his way around such a question is a shocking breach of professional standards. Inexperienced leaders do surface in other countries – witness President Carter – but generally only under unusual circumstances. They turn up in Canada with suspicious frequency.

In the early 1900s, Sir Wilfrid Laurier and others proclaimed that the twentieth century would belong to Canada. Some sixty years later, Pierre Trudeau held out the prospect of its becoming "a brilliant prototype for the moulding of tomorrow's civilization." But for some time now, Canadians have received such sentiments with quiet derision. In the mid-1970s, when Barry Bruce-Briggs and Marie-Josée Drouin interviewed Canadian businessmen for one of Herman Kahn's Hudson Institute futurological surveys, they found their opening question so often volleyed right back at them in inverted form that only at the insistence of Kahn, a professional optimist, was the title of their book converted from a wry interrogative into the emphatic protestation: *Canada* Has *A Future.* And that was when the Canadian dollar was just coming off its 1976 peak of $1.04 U.S. and Canada had been substantially spared the 1975-76 recession. More recently, the Canadian dollar has been below $0.70 U.S. and the recession of 1982-83 was far deeper and longer in Canada than in the U.S.A., where it was still the worst since World War II.

Historians and journalists have an understandable tendency to focus on what actually has happened and is happening. It is occasionally illuminating, however, to consider what could and should happen. A searing light is thrown upon the Canadian conundrum by asking one simple question: why is Canada poorer than the U.S.? From Walter Gordon in 1957 to Simon Reisman in 1985, semi-official estimates have placed Canada's standard of living at as low as 70% of the American level. Canadians seem to accept this, in their melancholy way, as a sort of law of nature. But it isn't. Canada's natural resources base is at least as good as that of the U.S., particularly per capita, its people are conveniently concentrated in a few large cities, and the climate they face is little more severe than the northern tier of U.S. states – the "Frost Belt." There is no disadvantage inherent in Canada's fundamental economic position that suitable policies, like free trade, could not correct. Moreover, Canada's population is homogeneous, without the Americans' intractable underclass problem, and Canada spends practically nothing on defense, preferring to freeload on the American effort. Without these serious financial burdens, its living standard should actually be higher than that of its larger neighbor.

Canada should be a second Switzerland (which is also, after all, a rather cold place). It should be an oasis of prosperity and civilization, what Ronald Reagan keeps calling a city on a hill. But instead Canada more closely resembles sluggish, querulous Britain. It has even developed some disturbing fiscal parallels with countries like Argentina and Uruguay, that at the beginning of the century stood on the threshold of development, only to diverge into ignominious Third World status.

This Canadian failure is tragic, but of course it is not truly a tragedy. Far worse things have happened to the other successor states of the British Empire. Even in purely economic terms, Canada's record has been passable by world standards. The real disappointment is in comparison to what might have been. For example, it now seems probable that Canada has missed the chance to develop its high-cost energy resources offered by the OPEC cartel's price hikes during the 1970s. The failure was entirely due to Ottawa's mismanagement; the price, however, will be paid mainly by the West.

The fundamental reason for this chronic underperformance is that – to appropriate the famous phrase used by Daniel Patrick Moynihan to explain the failure of American black families to work their way into the middle class – Canadian politics is embroiled in a tangle of pathologies. This book undertakes to unravel the skein.

One of Winston Churchill's methods of running Britain at war was to demand periodically from his cowering subordinates an account of what was happening in some area or another "on one-half of a sheet of notepaper." He found it concentrated their minds on essentials. Because my analysis of Canada will seem unfamiliar, disorienting and even fantastic to those accustomed to the more comforting conventional view, I have tried to compress the essential arguments into the outline below. This guide might also prove helpful to politicians unable to spare more time from their French lessons. I would like to point out to my fellow professional book reviewers, however, that it is not a substitute for riffling through the remaining pages in the usual way.

1. Canada is merely a geographical expression. For historical reasons, Canada has acquired the legal form of a nation-state, but it is not a nation. Culturally and even geographically, its Anglophone and Francophone communities are growing more separate each year.

(Throughout this book, I use "English Canadian" and the Ottawa neologism "Anglophone" interchangeably. Essentially, these are linguistic, not ethnic terms. They designate Canadians who belong to the English-speaking majority, not merely that fraction of the majority which is of British origin. Indeed, I shall argue that one symptom of the Canadian malaise is the recent official propaganda about Canada's "multicultural mosaic," which has had the effect of over-emphasizing the extent of non-British immigration and under-emphasizing its assimilation into the common English Canadian culture. Actually, it would probably be a good idea to import the term "Anglo," which the Americans have invented to distinguish between their similarly hybrid English-speaking majority and the Hispanic minority. But I figure there is a limit to what an author can expect readers to absorb.)

2. There are at least two and conceivably seven incipient sub-nations within Canada. By far the most important division is that between English and French Canada, but there are also lesser distinctions within English Canada: Ontario; the West, with or without British Columbia; the Maritimes, with or without Newfoundland; and the native-dominated North. All these divisions constitute political fault lines underlying the Canadian polity.

3. Within the Canadian framework, Quebec is emerging as a genuine nation-state. History does not move in straight lines. There is a cyclical rhythm to Francophone nationalism as well as a rising long-run secular trend. Canadian attention recently quite naturally has been fixated on the decline of organized separatism after its 1980-81 peaks. But this overlooks the fact that the last quarter-century of turmoil has left the Francophones in total institutional control of Quebec, which is now regarded by all segments of French opinion as their political expression. In Ottawa jargon, the *deux nations* concept – the idea that Canada should resolve its internal problems by making Quebec a French-speaking enclave within an English-speaking state – has triumphed posthumously over *une province comme les autres.* Quebec is in fact now being treated as a separate entity. But simultaneously Ottawa is trying to prolong Pierre Trudeau's fantasy and treat Anglophones and Francophones as if they had blended into one bilingual whole.

4. All of Anglophone Canada is essentially part of a greater English-speaking North American nation. Canada is a sectional variation within this super nation, just like the American South or Far West, but fundamentally shares the same culture.

5. Canada's political system is badly designed and seriously misrepresents Canadian reality. The most important flaw is lack of effective regional balance, which has allowed elements in Central Canada to dominate the country since Confederation. But specific institutional factors, for example the parliamentary system, are also responsible for many Canadian political characteristics that are conventionally attributed to Canada's unique (= unAmerican) political culture.

6. The political system and Canada's deep divisions, particularly linguistic, have facilitated the growth of an unusually large and powerful public class. This elite, which is the real Canadian Establishment, mediates across Canada's various divisions and invents policies that benefit itself and its clients. Examples of such policies are official bilingualism and the National Energy Program.

7. The Canadian public class has developed what Marxists call a "dominant ideology" rationalizing and justifying its power, and has been quite successful in imposing it as the Canadian conventional wisdom. This ideology, which basically amounts to the direct opposite of everything asserted above, can for practical purposes be identified with the federal Liberal Party, but it extends far beyond. An important radical mutation of the Liberal Ideology is Canadian Nationalism, the "patriot game" of this book's title.

8. Canadian politics are surprisingly volatile. The present political order is not particularly secure. The most obvious symptom of volatility, of course, has been the rumblings and grumblings along the regional fault lines. But political scientists have also found it significant that Canada, exceptional among the countries with a similar electoral system, has never evolved an unequivocal two-party system at the federal level. Instead, there have been repeated third- (and even fourth-) party insurrections. Moreover, although long influential in Canada, the Liberal Ideology only finally established its hegemony in the 1960s. During the sixteen years that Pierre Trudeau led the federal Liberal Party, Canada's official institutions and attitudes were revolutionized. The full ramifications of their new form have not yet been felt; they may well prove to be merely a transitional phase.

Part One

Canada and the Canadian Question Revisited

2

The Canadian Question

The undiscover'd country ...

– William Shakespeare

Almost exactly ten years after my conversation with Joe Clark, after he had lost the Tory leadership to Brian Mulroney and I had moved to New York, I staggered into my Manhattan apartment under the accumulated debris of a weekend in the country to find the red light of my telephone answering machine blinking dementedly. I couldn't think why. It made me feel vaguely uneasy – as if I'd been found out.

Perhaps I had. The calls were from Canadian radio stations. They wanted to talk about an editorial I'd written for the American financial magazine *Barron's* in celebration of Brian Mulroney's first anniversary as prime minister. I had found Mulroney's performance disappointing, particularly compared to Ronald Reagan's dramatic start as U.S. president in 1981-82, when he commanded nothing like Mulroney's massive majority. The Tory government's slippage in the opinion polls, I noted, had actually been faster than that following John Diefenbaker's very similar Tory sweep in 1958 – and *his* government had become a legend for its distressingly unCanadian collapse into chaos and hysteria. After Mulroney's triumph on September 4, 1984, many pundits like the *Toronto Star's* Richard Gwyn thought that he had, "almost certainly, made the Conservatives the majority party for the rest of the century." But now Gwyn was saying that he was amazed at ordinary Canadians' skepticism about Mulroney. It was no longer inconceivable that he would turn out to be, like Diefenbaker, a temporary aberration.

It's interesting to question why this American critique, disseminated throughout Canada via the CBC morning news and a summary in Toronto's *Globe and Mail,* attracted such attention. My analysis, after all, was hardly news to Canadians, even if felicitously phrased. Of course, Canadian sensitivity is a phenomenon of which American journalists are well aware. A classic comment came from Michael Kinsley of the Washington-based *New Republic* magazine, who noted that one of his proudest achievements as editor was the ruthless exclusion of all articles on three "subjects so fascinating that more people wish to write about them than read about them." These were: the Law of the Sea Conference, enthusiastic accounts of the people of China – and "Canada: Troubled Neighbor to the North."

> Now any slighting reference to Canada is bound to produce a flurry of anguished letters, most of them attached to manuscripts. On the other hand, so is any favorable reference to Canada, so it would be futile to add at this point that I think it's a lovely country and we're darned lucky to have it next door, especially considering the alternatives. Yet Canada is, for all its acknowledged merits, a nation of assistant professors, each armed with articles designed to "dispel misunderstanding." These literary missiles are aimed at the American media, ready to be fired at the slightest provocation. Those who are themselves transfixed by subjects like Canada and the Law of the Sea Conference (now there's a title) tend to see misunderstanding where there is actually judicious indifference.

Canadians I have consulted about this hypersensitivity cite, with their usual morbid glee, the national inferiority complex. Nothing in Canada is ever regarded as significant, they say, unless it is noted by someone outside. Maybe so. But I think that it's also an example of the way in which Canada, like certain obscure sea creatures, has evolved vital organs outside its skeletal structure, in this case south of the 49th parallel. Hundreds of thousands of Canadians subscribe to American magazines and millions watch American TV. The true nature of Canadian culture simply cannot be understood unless this fact is recognized. To paraphrase Kipling: what do they know of Canada, who only *Maclean's* (or the CBC) know? This is a natural and inexorable consequence of sharing a common language – and does not, therefore, apply to Quebec, which in this as in every other respect is a separate society. To English-speaking Canadians, however, an American rumination about Mulroney was an integral part of the process by which they were making up their own minds about the Tory government.

Brian Mulroney need not face the Canadian electorate again until 1989. A lot could happen in the interim. But he will not regain that first fine careless rapture, when, like Trudeau, he was credited by a relieved Canadian Establishment with creating a national party of government, representing all of Canada rather than just the embattled Central Canadian bunker to which the Trudeau Liberals had ultimately been compelled to retreat.

Close contact with any politician inevitably brings a certain amount of disillusion. But the Canadian cycle of ecstasy and excoriation is particularly acute. Mulroney is the third national leader to undergo the treatment in recent years, after both Pierre Trudeau and John Diefenbaker. Canadian prime ministers from Sir John A. Macdonald to Lester B. Pearson are on record as complaining that their mild-mannered country is "difficult to govern," a paradox in view of the deference to authority that is conventionally supposed to be part of both the Anglophone and Francophone tradition. In this sense at least, however, they seem to be right.

Like Ancient Greeks confronted with the Sphinx and its riddle, all these leaders have failed to answer what might be called "The Canadian Question" – to borrow the terminology of Goldwin Smith, Canada's most prominent Victorian intellectual. Smith's book *Canada and the Canadian Question,* which supplies the title of this chapter and the theme of the present study, appeared in 1891 at an earlier moment of debate about Canada's future.

Smith himself was a patrician English liberal, a product of Eton and Oxford like his contemporary William E. Gladstone, the great British Prime Minister and Liberal Party leader; he had taught both at Oxford and at Cornell before settling in Toronto. Characteristic of the era, Smith's liberalism was "classical" or what could now be called "libertarianism." It favored free trade and free markets, and opposed hereditary privilege and imperialism. It also appears to have been compatible with a number of distressing although eminently Victorian opinions on such questions as Roman Catholics and various lesser breeds without the law. On the other hand, Smith was a dedicated philanthropist – he left his Georgian mansion, the Grange, as the nucleus of what is now the Ontario Art Gallery complex – and Catholic and Jewish causes were among the many charities he supported generously and without discrimination. He was simply alien to the modern practice of public piety and private parsimony.

Smith argued that the Canadian state did not represent the social and political reality of the Canadian people – or more accurately peoples, since he regarded the Francophones as distinct and unassimilable. It took an almost impossible balancing act, he thought, to make it work at all. After arriving in Canada and finding it wanting,

Smith announced that its destiny manifestly lay with the United States. Naturally enough, this advice was not received with unmixed gratitude in Toronto. There was even talk of jail. Today, Canadian Nationalist historians – for example, Kenneth McNaught in his popular *Pelican History of Canada* – regularly pause to revile Smith's memory and jeer at his prediction, although paradoxically they are the intellectual heirs of his disapproval of the British Empire. But the fact is that in crucial ways Goldwin Smith's Question has proved unanswerable. Above all, he was right to insist that there was no one Canadian people. The Francophones have not been assimilated, but instead have proved an incessant and insoluble problem within Confederation. And the Anglophones have continued to develop along American lines. In addition, systematic government intervention in the Canadian economy in the name of Nationalism and other edifying political ideals has been accompanied by equally continuous complaints about the economy's poor performance – bearing out Smith's famous diagnosis that Canada was "rich by nature, poor by policy."

Canada in the 1980s is more than ever in a state of frozen crisis, in which its internal contradictions are suspended but not solved. Why this should be so constitutes the Canadian Question. Until it is resolved, Canada's course will continue to be – relatively speaking – difficult and disappointing.

The conventional response to Goldwin Smith's argument is that he was insensitive to the emotional reality of Canada, and therefore underestimated the willingness of Canadians to make compromises to keep the country together. Since the present work basically endorses Smith's view that Canada in its present form is an unnatural entity, this is a criticism that must be taken seriously.

It is true that Canadians are, generally speaking, a patriotic people. Properly understood, however, patriotism is an expression of a specific culture and set of values, not merely loyalty to a geographic area – what Quebec separatists call "mapism," to distinguish Canadian "Nationalism," as it became fashionable in the 1960s, from their own more flavorful variety. But in the nineteenth century and until well within living memory, the culture and values that Canada consciously expressed were British. Canadians regarded themselves as part of what Sir Charles Dilke called the "Greater Britain" beyond the seas. This Imperial patriotism was pervasive to an extent that is now completely forgotten. To give one quick example from the public schools: the Ontario Fourth Reader of 1910 had on its flyleaf a Union

Jack and the motto "One Flag, One Fleet, One Throne," opened with Kipling's "Children's Song",

> O Motherland, we pledge to thee
> Head, heart, and hand through the years to be!

and closed with his "Recessional" after four hundred pages of poetry selections like Browning's "Oh, to be in England," Thomson's "Rule Britannia," Scott's "Love of Country," Campbell's "Ye Mariners of England," Macaulay's "The Armada," Byron's "Eve of Waterloo," Tennyson's "Funeral of Wellington," Hemans' "The Homes of England" and Doyle's "The Private of the Buffs;" and prose extracts such as Russell on Balaclava, Southey on the death of Nelson, Froude on "The Elizabethan Seaman" and an essay from the *Atlantic Monthly* on the military impregnability of the British Empire. You got the definite impression, in short, that Britain mattered.

Goldwin Smith doubted the strength and endurance of this Imperial loyalty. Himself an anti-Imperialist, like the modern Canadian Nationalists, he was inclined to downplay the reality of the British connection. "If England ever has occasion to call on her children in Canada for a real sacrifice," he wrote, "she may chance to repeat the experience of King Lear." In this respect, Smith was utterly wrong, as two world wars demonstrated. In World War I alone, Canada put 625,000 men into uniform and suffered 61,000 dead. This was an heroic performance for a country of a mere eight million people.

After 1945, however, Britain effectively vanished from the geopolitical stage. Canada's Greater British patriotism was rendered obsolete, and the competing Liberal Ideology was able to fill the vacuum. Without the emotional content of the Greater British alternative, however, the issue of Canada's identity and its relationship with the United States becomes quite different. It must now be rephrased: does the Canadian Confederation, as reoriented by the modern Liberal Party and civil service establishment, express the culture and values of Canadians, both in terms of their own history and in the context of the wider English-speaking (or, for that matter, French-speaking) world?

Just as in the U.S., the political history of Canada is comprised of distinct eras in which one or other of the major parties was able to forge an electoral coalition that made it, for a time, the natural party of government. The first such coalition in Canada was put together around the time of Confederation in 1867 by the Conservative Party's Sir John A. Macdonald in alliance with Sir George-Etienne Cartier in

Quebec. Its ideology, at least in English Canada, was Greater British. Macdonald died in 1891 and, after a succession of short-lived Tory leaders, the Liberals came to power under Sir Wilfrid Laurier in 1896. They succeeded in establishing a second coalition that, with periodic adjustments, kept them in office for all but twenty-two of the next eighty-eight years.

The essence of the Liberal electoral strategy from the 1890s has been to unite the Francophone minority and divide the Anglophone majority. Typically, in that decade the party won most of Quebec's seats and sufficient Anglophone seats to form a parliamentary majority.

The Liberals' relative success in English Canada has been a fascinating example of what the Italian Marxist Antonio Gramsci called "hegemony." As Gramsci's biographer James Joll has described it, "the hegemony of a political class meant for Gramsci that that class had succeeded in persuading the other classes of society to accept its cultural values. If the ruling class is successful, this will involve the minimum use of political force. . ." Thus the "dominant ideology thesis" holds that by achieving ideological hegemony a social group can rule far longer and more effectively than the material basis of its power would suggest. Gramsci believed that a political party had to work to achieve ideological hegemony during the long periods of apparent quiet between political upheavals – a "passive revolution," or "war of position." This was a complex process requiring compromise and accommodation with other interests. By such a process, he argued, the Italian Liberals had been quietly working for power long before the Risorgimento and the unification of Italy.

Similarly, the Canadian Liberal Party has been able to persuade English Canada that preserving the Canadian Confederation and common morality itself requires continual concessions to Quebec. English Canada's British heritage has been systematically subverted. The national unity issue has been used as a club to beat down every other political concern – to the point where Anglophone Liberals in the 1979 federal election reportedly had the greatest difficulty persuading Pierre Trudeau's Quebec lieutenants that it would be necessary to address economic issues at all. The extraordinary result is that in Canada today, it is the Anglophones and not the Francophones who are the colonized group. Despite the proclamations of separatism's demise that constitute one of the regular rituals of Canadian life, the Francophones in Quebec are steadily acquiring the symbols and institutions of a nation. But the Anglophones have been giving theirs up equally steadily – and they have been prevented from following the political patterns of their cultural siblings, America and Britain. English Canada's induced passivity closely parallels that of the Anglophone minority in Quebec, which has been effectively shut out of provincial politics for over a hundred years. And in fact the Liberal Ideology to a considerable extent is the projection of internal Quebec concerns onto the national stage, so that Canadian politics in the Liberal era have been essentially those of a sort of Greater Quebec. (The Liberal hegemony is examined in loving detail later in this book.)

By the early 1980s, the material basis of the Liberals' hegemony was developing serious weaknesses. First, the party's persuasive powers in English Canada were obviously failing fast. It had won only one federal election outside Quebec since 1953; its victory in the 1980 election was based almost entirely on the votes of Francophones and carefully cultivated immigrant blocs in Ontario. In the two thousand miles of Western Canada between the Ontario line and the Pacific Ocean, the Liberals won only two seats in 1980, and one of those was from a Francophone enclave in Winnipeg.

Secondly, separatists had begun to stir not just in Quebec, where they controlled the provincial government, but in Western Canada, where the first separatist ever to be elected, Gordon Kessler of the Western Canada Concept party, won an Alberta provincial by-election in 1981. The spectre of Anglophone separatism provoked intense, alternating spasms of rage and denial in Central Canada. When Claude Ryan, leader of the Quebec provincial Liberals, ignored the party line and remarked that Western separatists had a better economic case than Quebec and might ultimately be a more serious problem for Canada, he was publicly rebuked by Pierre Trudeau. Eventually Alberta's Kessler was defeated in a provincial general election called partly to pre-empt the separatist threat, and the movement thereafter splintered into the faction-fighting typical of political insurrections at an early stage. But although once again ignored by Central Canadian opinion, which has a record of consistently underestimating regional and ethnic alienation, Western separatism remains a new and significant trace element in Anglophone politics.

Despite this weakening material base, however, the Liberals had been able to reinforce their hegemony by various ingenious expedients. One of them was an increasing reliance upon "Canadian Nationalism." In political terms, this meant an appeal to the Anglophone left, which had largely invented the modern theory of Canadian Nationalism in the 1960s to rationalize its perennial statist ambitions. In this case, the left was calling for the interdiction of established but unsuitable commercial and cultural liaisons between Canadians and foreigners, mostly Americans.

Canadian Nationalism has dominated Anglophone debate for nearly a generation. It appeared to have institutionalized itself after 1980, when the Liberals, under Pierre Trudeau, unveiled a series of far-reaching interventionist measures, notably the National Energy Program. But after the severe 1981-82 recession and the unexpected resurfacing of the heresy of free trade with the U.S., this looked much less likely. It would be unwise, however, to disregard the Nationalists. Their continuous complaints about betrayal, impotence and general injustice are central to their polemical technique. For example, the 1972 federal election inaugurated an earlier quantum leap in nationalist legislation. But the pre-election book of essays published by *Maclean's,* then in a particularly nationalistic mode, contained such plaintive titles as "Are We Watching the Sun Quietly Set on Canada?" and "The Short Life and Premature Death of Canadian Nationalism." In reality, Canadian Nationalism serves the interests of influential groups in Canada and it will not go away soon. The tragedy is that it has amply borne out the analysis made by the noted Canadian economist Harry G. Johnson way back in 1961: "Far from contributing to the growth of a stronger, more independent, and identity-conscious nation, Canadian Nationalism as it has developed in recent years has been diverting Canada into a narrow and garbage-cluttered cul-de-sac."

Along with their newfound Nationalist ploy, the Liberals had developed a crucial political asset in the shape of the emerging alliance of civil servants, educators and assorted media and political hangers-on – a social group that had appeared throughout the Western world with the development of the welfare state, and that had become sufficiently powerful to assert class interests of its own. In the U.S., Irving Kristol had named this faction "the New Class," pointing out that it benefitted directly from the expansion of government activities. But the Canadian New Class was peculiarly powerful. Apart from anything else, given the two countries' populations (24.3 million versus 226.5 million) the concentration of federal government employees in Ottawa was three times as large as that in Washington, D.C. (100,294 versus 345,456), just as the Canadian capital loomed relatively twice as large (717,978 versus 3,045,399). The Canadian civil servant is therefore that much less exposed to the rude populace, and that much more inclined to develop a corporate identity than his American counterpart – who has not been slow.

In Canada, in addition, because of the stubborn ethnic and regional particularisms over which Ottawa presides, the Canadian bureaucrat would not be far wrong in thinking that only the federal civil service remotely approaches the bilingual, bicultural ideal to which the country has been officially committed. Like the Prussian Army, the Ottawa bureaucracy can regard itself as the true repository of official national values. Similarly, the only true "Europeans" in the European Economic Community, notoriously, are the employees of the European Commission in Brussels. Such features of recent Canadian history, as the struggle over energy policy and the much advertised Canadian predeliction for government intervention in the economy cannot be properly understood without allowing for the role of this able, assertive, self-conscious and self-confident faction.

Popular journalism has accustomed Canadians to regard a selective cross-section of their business world as "the Canadian Establishment," imbued with exciting if intangible power and privilege. But given the way Canada actually functions, this is rather like explaining American society in terms of the Daughters of the American Revolution and the Episcopalian Church. It is the interlocking New Class that really constitutes Canada's Establishment, with the civil service playing a vital underpinning role and the Liberal Party acting as its political arm. I have therefore rescued this term from its previous inaccurate use. Throughout this book, "Establishment" means Canada's true governing elite.

For example, Canadian civil servants have regularly metamorphosed and entered politics openly as Liberal cabinet ministers. Two of them, Mackenzie King and Lester Pearson, eventually became prime ministers. Both Liberal politicians and, even more significantly, key members of the Ottawa press corps, frequently move in the opposite direction, into the bureaucracy. Civil servants have also invaded the outside world by inventing and staffing "Crown corporations" to perform various commercial and cultural activities, the most important example perhaps being the Canadian Broadcasting Corporation. There are even some slight signs of hereditary caste developing, with son following father (Skeltons, Pearsons). Even the federal Liberal leader John Turner, although supposedly a representative of the business community, is actually the son of a former Tariff Board chief economist and grew up in Ottawa.

The Liberal hegemony's greatest success, however, has been its successful subjugation of considerable sections of the Tory party. This, of course, is the hallmark of a dominant ideology: years earlier the Tories' British Imperial version of Canada was accepted by many more French Canadians than it is now fashionable to remember.

A decisive victory in the Liberal hegemonic emergence occurred when the Tories were persuaded to endorse the Liberals' Official Languages legislation in the 1960s. This effectively removed bilingualism from politics, preventing Anglophone distress from finding expression – and cutting the Tories off from a natural source of support.

Since then, the Liberal hegemony has continuously distorted Tory politics. It played a vital role in the 1983 Tory leadership race. In their book *Contenders,* Patrick Martin, Allan Gregg and George Perlin report that Joe Clark, born in Alberta and representing an Alberta riding, admitted he now felt "distinctly uncomfortable" with his fellow Westerners and had "no rapport" with them. He said that "in many ways" the right-wing Peter Pocklington was "the quintessential Alberta candidate." Martin, Gregg and Perlin commented admiringly: "The trouble was that Clark had transcended his roots. His national outlook no longer jibed with the regional view of his local constituents." But this is merely a laudatory way of saying that Clark had replaced one set of regional values for those of the Central Canadian Establishment and the Liberal ideological hegemony that protected it. Clark's attempt to impose those values on a restive party caused him to become one more victim of the Canadian Question.

Clark's goal, as Martin, Gregg and Perlin have described it, was to build a "modern, moderate, Quebec-oriented party." At the Tory leadership convention in 1983, Clark deliberately stayed on the ballot after he saw that he could not win – largely to ensure that Brian Mulroney, from Quebec, would defeat John Crosbie, from Newfoundland,

> . . . a unilingual Anglophone whose attitude toward Quebec, in Clark's opinion, reflected a fundamental misunderstanding of that province . . . Crosbie's inability to speak French was only one part of his problem with the Quebec issue. In consciously choosing not to make the effort to learn French he appeared, in the eyes of Francophones and those concerned with finding an accommodation in French-English relations, to show that he did not care about the issue, or at the very least that he did not understand it . . . *He did not seem to understand that his words challenged the fundamental concept of Canada as a political community.* (Italics added.)

The Liberal hegemony strikes again. In order to conform to this so-called "fundamental concept of Canada as a political community,"

Clark, stripped of emotive phraseology, had sought to keep the Tory party on the left, preoccupied by the French-English question and disproportionately influenced by Quebec – a carbon copy of the Liberals in the Trudeau years, and certainly not responsive to the examples of Ronald Reagan and Margaret Thatcher. Clark believed that Mulroney would follow the same course. By contrast, John Crosbie was disqualified because "as a Newfoundlander, he knew little or nothing from his own experience" about French-English relations. But this could be said equally well of the vast unilingual majority of English Canadians. If Joe Clark was right about Mulroney, the leadership of English-speaking Canada's main political expression had been deliberately passed to a man who would focus on essentially alien concerns.

Mulroney's biographers, Patrick Murphy, Rae Chodos and Nick Auf der Maur, have written: "If in [the leadership convention of] 1976 the issue for the Tories was expressed as 'Can we elect a bilingual Quebecker as leader?' in 1983 Mulroney was able to force the party to rephrase it as 'How can we not?' "

This is a rather romantic description of the 1983 convention, which was actually determined by the anomalous presence of large numbers of Francophone instant Tories. Under the convention rules, Quebec, which in the 1980 federal election gave the Tories a mere 10.5% of their total vote, provided somewhere up to three times that proportion of the delegates. The Tory party was practically non-existent in many Quebec ridings, and delegate selection a farce. Had Quebec been absent, or even proportionately represented, the convention almost certainly would have selected John Crosbie.

But the authors' claim suggests the astonishing power of Liberal hegemonic ideology. The Tories supposedly felt that for both practical and moral reasons they had to turn to Quebec's candidate. Neither of these contentions, as a matter of fact, was defensible. It was perfectly natural for Anglophones to want a representative leader, and as it turned out the Tories would have won the 1984 election without any seats from Quebec. And beyond that, it was chilling evidence of the weakness of the Canadian political system. Only through submitting to an almost unknown and quite atypical leader could the party of the majority come to power. The only solution Mulroney could offer to the party's problems, which were ultimately those of Canada, were personal, charismatic – and therefore temporary.

3

"A Hybrid Bicultural Monstrosity"

If some countries have too much history, we have too much geography.

- Mackenzie King

I don't even know what street Canada is on.

- Al Capone

"Whoever wishes to know what Canada is, and to understand the Canadian question, should begin by turning from the political to the natural map," wrote Goldwin Smith. Geography is destiny in Canada, with a little help from demography and one or two other more conventional considerations. Any discussion of Canada must begin with a quick trot through its peculiar but ineluctable realities.

Gallia est omnis divisa in partes tres . . . Caesar famously divided Gaul into three parts: Canada is divided into ten provinces and two federally administered territories. But the inhabitants of Canada's provinces come in distinct clumps, separated from each other by formidable natural barriers and closely linked to similar settlements across the border to the south. There is an Atlantic coastal clump, in the provinces of Prince Edward Island, New Brunswick and Nova Scotia, with the island of Newfoundland a special subclump; a Central Canadian clump, in the provinces of Quebec and Ontario; a prairie clump, in Manitoba, Saskatchewan and Alberta; and, beyond the Rockies, a Pacific coast clump in British Columbia.

It's worth emphasizing that even by North American standards, Canada is breathtakingly vast. With 3.8 million square miles, it forms the second-largest state in the world, compared to 8.6 million for the Soviet Union – which is very similarly situated in the cold latitudes of the northern hemisphere – and a mere 3.0 million for the continental U.S., which has an additional half-million square miles or so in Alaska.

Canadians take this for granted. But sheer size poses a more serious political problem for their country than they generally recognize. Human communities are centrifugal in tendency. It has been the exception rather than the rule for the great overseas possessions of the European imperial powers to retain political unity after independence. Spanish America has undergone perhaps the most spectacular fragmentation, but there are many other examples – even proverbially lucky Australia suffered a secession crisis in the 1930s. In the U.S., regional or "sectional" rivalry has been a notoriously important and often dominant political theme. A similar torsion is continuously if quietly at work in Canadian politics.

According to the 1981 census, there are a mere 24 million Canadians in Canada's enormous area and it has become something of a cliché to note that most of this number live within 100 miles of the U.S. border, leaving a vast and scarcely populated northern hinterland. Canada is actually a sort of horizontal Chile. I've always felt, not altogether whimsically, that this linear simplicity contributes to the vertigo many Canadians seem to feel when they contemplate their southern neighbor. "Too many roads!" a young Canadian woman once exclaimed to me as we were driving through the urban sprawl of Washington, D.C. She was disoriented by the proliferation of expressways and their annoying habit of heading in directions other than the east and west of her homeland. Canada is a long, mostly English-speaking python of a country, stretched out from coast to coast along the top of the U.S. The bulge in its throat is the still-undigested lump of more than 6 million French-speakers, overwhelmingly centered in the province of Quebec, but with an aftertaste of some half-million or so lingering on in eastern Ontario and northern New Brunswick.

English-speaking Canada is a surprisingly new development. It began in one of history's overlooked tragedies: the northward movement of some 60,000 American Tories, deprived of their country and virtually all the compensation for looted property promised by the 1783 Treaty of Paris, which ended the American War of Independence. *Vain faith, and courage vain* was Lord Macaulay's epitaph on earlier Royalist refugees from the English Civil War. Whether this fits the "United Empire Loyalists," whose descendants in Canada today are estimated to number some 3,500,000, is one of the finer points to be considered in this book.

Of course, some parts of the U.S. were settled fairly recently, but from a solid base on the eastern seaboard, where the states are named after Tudor and Stuart monarchs and noblemen. New York City began life in 1626 as New Amsterdam. It was already 167 years old when what is now Toronto, the largest city in English Canada, was founded by Lieutenant-Governor John Graves Simcoe, former commander of the loyalist Queen's Rangers of New York. He and his wife turned back from a winter jaunt because she saw wolf tracks in the snow where a busy midtown subway station now stands. A bear once attacked a coach horse in the grounds of Goldwin Smith's house, the Grange. The Canadian West is positively raw. Most prairie cities were grassland until late last century. John Diefenbaker, who only died in 1979, recalled in his memoirs waking one morning in 1904 as a boy newly arrived in Saskatchewan to find his home surrounded by Indians in war paint. (This being the Canadian, not the American frontier, the Indians were only looking for an escaped lunatic, but there was real fear of an Indian uprising on the Prairies that year.) One of the favorite stories of William A. Rusher, columnist and publisher of William F. Buckley's conservative *National Review* magazine in New York, concerns his visit to Banff National Park in the 1950s, when the guide pointed out the route of the first explorers, the first road, the first house and then – coming out of the door to collect his morning mail – the first settler.

Under any circumstances, the institutions of so young a society could hardly be regarded as fixed. But in fact quite radical political changes have been imposed upon English Canada in its short life.

French Canada, as usual, is different. Agents of the French crown founded Quebec City in 1608, so long ago that they automatically built a wall around it. It is now the only such fortified city in North America, although the name Wall Street is a reminder that Manhattan's Dutch settlers were once moved by the same considerations. Passing into the Great Lakes and the Mississippi valley, French fur traders established claims to a remarkable proportion of the North American interior, in a great arc from Idaho to Louisiana. But this justly renowned feat obscures the true nature of the colony of New France: devoutly Catholic, highly centralized, authoritarian, wholly without any tradition of self-government, deeply suspicious of its necessary but unpoliceable minority of peripatetic fur-trading *coureurs de bois* and *voyageurs,* and above all stable – even static.

After 1759, when the British captured Quebec City and effectively ended France's imperial role in North America, the French Canadian settlers were left behind, clinging stubbornly to the banks of the

St. Lawrence. And there they have remained ever since. A not-uncommon case is that of Finance Minister Marc Lalonde, Pierre Trudeau's lieutenant and architect of the National Energy Policy: his family farmed on Ile Perrot near Montreal for nine generations; he was the first Lalonde ever to go to university. This combination of immobility and assiduous government – there were thirty-six censuses between 1666 and 1760 alone – has meant that, as Colin McEvoy and Richard Jones remark in their *Atlas of World Population History*, "French Canadians are one of the best recorded populations in the world." But the rootedness that delights demographers can confuse compatriots, particularly when their background is as different as that of Canada's Anglophones.

Canada's demography has other implications. Unlike the U.S., the majority of Canadian Anglophones are still of British Isles' descent – perhaps 40% of the entire population of Canada, with another 5% part-British. But, particularly on the Prairies, there are substantial concentrations of Anglophone Canadians originating in central and eastern Europe, including, for example, over half a million Ukrainians. Some arrived as anti-Communist "Displaced Persons" in the aftermath of World War II. Most have tended in recent years to vote for the opposition Progressive Conservative Party. However, the blocs of southern Europeans that have developed more recently, mainly in Toronto where there are now for, instance, over 300,000 Italians, have become Liberal or NDP bastions.

In the last twenty years, moreover, Canada has been experiencing a wave of new immigration similar to but proportionately even heavier than the one that has broken over the U.S. And, as in the U.S., this has coincided with a dramatic change in official policy. The effect has been to reduce the numbers of immigrants from "traditional" countries and greatly increase Third World immigration. In 1980, for example, only 29% of Canada's 142,439 immigrants had their previous residence in Europe, including just 13% from the British Isles. Some 5% came from the West Indies, and over half from Asia. If continued, this policy will certainly end the Caucasian homogeneity which to the casual observer most strikingly differentiates Canadian from American cities. The Liberal Party made great efforts to secure the allegiance of these immigrants, with some success.

Reinforced by recent immigration, Roman Catholics now make up some 47.3% of Canada's population, although of course they are still outnumbered two-to-one among the Anglophones alone. Protestants are down to 41.2% of Canada's total. (About 1.2% of Canadians are Jewish and 1.5% Eastern Orthodox; some 7.4%, mainly in the West, sternly told the census takers they had no religious preference.) In Canada, Roman Catholics have tended to vote for the Liberals, and Protestants for the Progressive Conservative Party. Until quite recently, both parties elaborately balanced their tickets with every permutation of religious and ethnic affiliation. But about the time Pierre Trudeau became Prime Minister in 1968, sectarian consciousness seems, at least overtly, to have vanished from politics. One curious feature of Canadian public life since then is that Catholics have been somewhat over-represented in the top ranks of government, relative to their numbers in the population at large. The last two leaders of both principal parties, supplying between them the last four Canadian prime ministers and leaders of the opposition, have been Catholics, as have the last two governors-general.

The religious issue may not be quite so deeply asleep in Canada as unwary politicians assume, however. The defeat of Ontario's long-lived Progressive Conservative provincial government in 1985 was at least partly because it had outraged its traditional supporters by proposing, with the agreement of the other parties, an education reform scheme that many believed would accord special privileges to Catholic schools.

The Liberals could choose to be complaisant about these features of Canadian demography, but other trends were working against their electoral coalition. One such trend, paralleling U.S. developments, was the steady shift of the balance of Canada's population away from the East, the Liberal stronghold, and towards the West, the Conservative bastion. In 1901, in approximate numbers, the four Western provinces constituted only about 10% of Canada's population, Ontario around 40%, Quebec 30% and the Maritime provinces 20%. By the 1980s, in contrast, the Western provinces' proportion had risen to about 27%, and Vancouver had become Canada's third-largest city. For the first time, the West had topped Quebec, which had just over 26%. Ontario had some 36%, and the Maritimes had declined to below 10%. (Only about 66,000 Canadians, 0.3% of the total, live "North of 60," in the federally administered Yukon and Northwest Territories.)

Even more ominous from the Liberals' point of view was the gradual reduction in the relative size of Canada's Francophone component. For over a hundred years, this had remained steady at around 30% of the overall population. But after 1950, Francophones began to lose ground. By 1976, they were below 26%, by 1981 they were at 24.6% and there are estimates that by the year 2000 they could be down to 21%. This trend is a direct attack upon the foundation of

Canada's current political order. It also helps account for the urgent tone of Francophone nationalism in Quebec.

Much of what was to become the Canadian Question was implicit in a laconic sentence carved on a rock overlooking the Pacific eleven years before the Americans Lewis and Clark made the second overland crossing of the continent. The rock was in what was to become British Columbia, and the inscription on it was made by the son of a New York Tory family who was then working as a young partner in the Montreal-based North West Company. It read: "Alexander Mackenzie, from Canada, by land, the twenty-second of July, one thousand seven hundred and ninety-three." Four years earlier the author, Alexander Mackenzie, had canoed down the river later named after him and reached the Arctic Ocean.

For what Mackenzie meant by Canada was Ontario and Quebec, or Upper and Lower Canada, as the settlements 3,000 miles behind him on the shores of the Great Lakes and the St. Lawrence were then officially described. The self-governing colonies of "British North America" that agreed to Confederation in 1867 chose to call themselves the "Dominion of Canada," but the biblical reference usually cited ("He shall have dominion also from sea to sea, and from the river unto the ends of the earth." Psalms 72:8) was a distinct exaggeration. Although Canadian publicists often advance the "Fathers of Confederation" as a local substitute for the U.S. "Founding Fathers," a glance at the 1866 London Conference group portrait reveals that these bewhiskered eminences came only from Ontario, Quebec and the now-minor Maritime provinces of Nova Scotia and New Brunswick. There were no representatives of British Columbia involved in the negotiations, Prince Edward Island and Newfoundland had withdrawn at an earlier stage, and the Prairie provinces – Alberta, Saskatchewan and Manitoba – had not yet been politically organized and were virtually unpopulated by Europeans. What these "Fathers" made was a local deal, designed largely to settle local conflicts rather than to solve the problems of governing a subcontinental state, and they naturally took the title of the dominant partner. The other provinces were acquired gradually over the next few years, with the exception of Newfoundland, Britain's oldest colony, which resisted Confederation until 1949. In an important sense, Mackenzie's words are still accurate. All the additions remain hinterlands, overshadowed by what Westerners call the "East" and Maritimers, more accurately, "Central Canada."

There was a fair amount of resistance to Confederation, particularly in the Maritimes, and British officials had to do a lot of behind-the-scenes kicking and cajoling. Canada, in fact, was an early example of the Colonial Office's obsession with decanting its regional responsibilities into neat federations, ostensibly to make them more viable. It is salutary to reflect that, after the apparent successes of Canada, Australia and South Africa, all subsequent efforts ended in failure.

The strained relationship between Central Canada and the rest of the country is crucial to this book. In terms of the way the Canadian political economy works, it need only be noted at this stage that much Canadian public policy serves to concentrate rents from a resource-based economy in Central Canadian hands. A case in point is Canada's protectionism. This was originally developed under Sir John A. Macdonald, and rationalized, in combination with railway subsidies, as a nation-building "National Policy." But the immediate beneficiaries were the manufacturers of Central Canada. The establishment of manufacturing industry has always been regarded as a Good Thing in Canada. This is partly because of the enthusiasm of the manufacturers themselves, who obviously have a vested interest, and partly because of the Canadian elite's distaste for being what they always describe as "hewers of wood and drawers of water." For the owners of unmatched forests and flowing waters, who might very well be most profitably employed in hewing and drawing, this is obviously somewhat capricious. Moreover, it is not completely reasonable: the *New York Times* can hardly be expected to print in northern Quebec. Nevertheless, it is long established: Goldwin Smith deplored both the phrase and the attitude ("It is not obvious why the producer of raw materials should be deemed so much beneath the factory hand.") back in 1891.

If Canada is considered a closed economic unit, the most efficient place to put a factory usually turns out to be the population centers of Ontario or Quebec. However, with free trade, a location like Chicago often offers significant economies. The cost of the tariff, therefore, is borne by the consumer, who has the choice of buying the dearer Ontario product or the Chicago product plus customs duties, which may make it uncompetitive. He might be consoled with the argument that he is supporting a home industry, albeit at the expense of whatever else he might have supported with the money that might have remained in his pocket. But if that consumer is a Prairie wheat farmer whose money is earned selling into world markets, and the industry is in distant Ontario or, worse, in Quebec, the consolation is that much less likely to be accepted.

In which case, Central Canadian politicians have to think of something else. Under the Liberals in the twentieth century, this something else turned out to be a combination of emphasizing the good deeds the federal state performs locally, paying pensions, unemployment benefits and other subsidies, and elevating Canadian Nationalism as a goal in itself. Ottawa has made a much-publicized commitment to redistribute income and equalize living standards across Canada. In effect, this amounts to a Second National Policy comparable to Sir John A. Macdonald's high-tariff National Policy in the nineteenth century. Interregional transfer payments constitute the single most striking difference between the Canadian and U.S. federal budgets. These transfers and the Liberal ideological hegemony are complementary aspects of a policy that has had the effect of keeping the hinterlands in thrall.

The centralization of Canada's institutions, both public and private, is a historic complaint of non-central Canadians. But it has its amusing side-effects. When I began writing for the *Financial Post*, Canada's main financial paper, an editor struck the expression "Hogtown" out of one of my stories. He explained that it was no longer used as a sobriquet for Toronto, where the *Financial Post* and the rest of the Canadian media are very firmly based, and of which he was very much a representative citizen. He added kindly that I was probably trying too hard for a Canadian tone. I had just moved from Winnipeg and knew perfectly well that "Hogtown" was among the natives' friendlier names for Toronto, but, as a new employee, was too discreet to say so. In 1982, the year Canada's constitution was officially "patriated," the federal government spent some time inducing a reluctant Yellowknife, capital of the Northwest Territories, to accept $60,000 worth of fireworks for a special celebration on July 1, the 115th anniversary of Confederation, although at that time of year in those latitudes there is no night. Also in 1982, Prime Minister Pierre Trudeau scheduled three televised "fireside chats" on the economy. He appeared at 7:30 in the evening in Montreal, Ottawa and Toronto, but that meant a rush-hour 5:30 in Alberta, and an impossible workday afternoon 4:30 in British Columbia. A true Québécois, Trudeau had never been west of Toronto when he became prime minister in 1968, according to Christina McCall-Newman in *Grits: An Intimate Portrait of The Liberal Party,* and since entering federal politics, he and Western Canada had never gotten along. Still, on this occasion the Liberals had an excuse. Chatting any later in the East would have put Trudeau in conflict with the World Series on the American border stations.

And at such moments of truth, Canadian politicians have no doubts about the cultural identity of their flock.

Central Canada, of course, was always bound to loom large in federal politics. Sixty percent of Canada's population still lives in the 600-mile strip of lowlands from Quebec City, to Windsor, Ontario, the southern edges of the provinces of Quebec and Ontario.

The Canadian political system, however, puts a peculiar weight on numbers. The system stems from the 1867 British North America Act, by which the British Parliament enacted the Confederation agreement reached by Canadian politicians and colonial officials, and in which is specified the objective of "a constitution similar in principle to that of the United Kingdom." Technically, Canada is a constitutional monarchy, with the Queen represented by a governor-general. Its supreme legislature is the federal House of Commons in Ottawa, to which 282 members are elected from equal-sized districts ("ridings"). The government, headed by the prime minister, is by custom drawn from the legislature, where as a practical matter it must maintain a working majority. An election must be held at least once every five years.

A fundamental flaw in this system is that it does not provide for the reflection of regional differences at the federal level. In the House of Commons, the values and wishes of the peripheral communities can be swamped by the vote of the Central Canadian majority. By contrast, the American Founding Fathers, who constituted a much broader cross-section of interests, allowed their different regions a voice at the center through the institution of a powerful Upper House, or Senate, to which each state was entitled to elect two senators regardless of population.

There is an Upper House in the Canadian Parliament, a Senate to which appointments are made on a regional basis by the prime minister and remain valid until the age of seventy-five. But it has become virtually a rubber stamp of the party in power. So nominal is its role as a representative of the regions that Joe Clark was able to name Lowell Murray, his 1979 campaign chairman, to an Ontario seat in the Senate, although Murray was a Maritimer and had to be persuaded to buy a condominium in Ottawa, a city he disliked, in order to meet the requirement that Senators own property worth at least $4,000 in "their" province.

The main residual function of the Senate is to relieve a regular embarrassment caused by the ethnic polarization of Canadian politics: one region or another often does not elect enough members of parliament to fill its traditional number of seats in the cabinet which in Canada, although not in other parliamentary democracies, is expected to contain representatives of all regions. Thus the cabinet in the short-lived Tory government in 1979 contained Quebec senators because there were only two Tory MPs from the whole of that province. The succeeding Liberal cabinet employed Western senators for a similar reason. This punctiliousness, however, is purely cosmetic. In the last analysis, there are very few restraints on the power of a parliamentary prime minister and his government, once elected. His own backbenchers can be suborned, and regions that foolishly return opposition MPs ignored.

This was probably not what the Fathers of Confederation had in mind. Unlike the Declaration of Independence, the BNA Act did not reason from general principles and it was far from a comprehensive document, but it did attempt to combine a stronger central government, which the spectacle of the just-completed Civil War to the south seemed to recommend, with a federal system, which local pride and contemporary politics demanded. The working-out of these essentially contradictory goals has been a source of continuous fascination to Canadian politicians. The men who negotiated in 1867 had been brought up in the British tradition – many were in fact immigrants, mainly from Scotland – and federalism was an unfamiliar creature to them. Moreover, in a graphic version of an argument often used about the U.S. constitution, they manifestly did not anticipate subsequent developments, either political, technological or social. They made, for example, no provision for independent Canadian diplomatic representation, or, hardly surprisingly, for the regulation of broadcasting. They could not be expected to foresee that the provinces would wish to expand their social welfare function far beyond their taxation powers, so that the federal government now shares its revenues with them ("cooperative federalism").

The regional checks and balances in Canada's political system are conventionally said to be provided by the governments of the component provinces. But what they provide is more like blockage than balance. Unlike the U.S. constitution, the BNA Act did reserve for the federal government all powers not expressly designated otherwise. However, the provinces have always had considerable authority. In 1946, the Canadian delegation to the United Nations even found themselves unable to sign the draft Declaration of Human Rights, because in Canada civil rights are a provincial responsibility. A

similar jurisdictional dispute has greatly complicated Brian
. Mulroney's efforts to negotiate free trade with the U.S.

The provincial governments went through a phase of partial
eclipse during the Depression and World War II, when emergency
conditions accentuated the federal government's role. Subsequently,
however, they reappeared as very real forces on the Canadian scene
and in the lives of their residents, partly as a by-product of Ottawa's
institutional appeasement of every recent Quebec government's
Francophone particularism. This is in diametrical opposition to the
trend in the U.S., where the states have steadily ceded power to the
federal government – over which, however, there is strong and continuing regional control. In Canada, both levels of government were
growing, with little reference to each other, although Pierre Trudeau's periodic ritual summit meetings with the provincial premiers
began to be auditioned for the role of official point of contact. To
adapt Stephen Leacock's phrase, the Canadian political system appeared to have flung itself on a horse and ridden madly off in all
directions. After Pierre Trudeau's return to power in February 1980,
he grabbed for the reins.

The National Energy Program, which had the (temporary) effect of
boosting Ottawa's revenues and economic power, was of course one
aspect of this grab. Another was Trudeau's "patriation" of the constitution, frequently called "repatriation," although this obscured the
fact that Canada's constitution was of British origin anyway. The
Fathers of Confederation had made no provision for amending Canada's constitution. Technically, it could only be done through an Act
of the Imperial Parliament at Westminster, the supreme legislature of
the Empire, which had authored the thing in the first place. As
Canada evolved into complete independence in this century, Ottawa
gradually acquired more sovereign functions, but it was never able to
persuade the provinces to accept an amending formula. Quebec in
particular was suspicious that any amendments might be directed at
its ability to promote the "French fact" in the province through
legislation so, technically, the ability to amend Canada's constitution
remained vested in Britain.

There was, as it happened, no urgent pressure to amend the
constitution. It might have continued being regarded as one of history's charming anachronisms, a demonstration of the value of monarchs and mother countries in removing a bone of contention from
among the quarreling pups. The Liberals, however, always have been

zealously uncharmed by such symbols, and Trudeau invested enormous political capital in a prolonged struggle to eliminate this one. He succeeded, and it is now within a Canadian government's power to amend the constitution, although the effort involved might well prove prohibitive.

But the process of patriation itself was used as an opportunity to alter the constitution in several key respects. Ostensibly, this was pursuant to promises to "renew federalism" made during the campaign against the Parti Québécois' 1980 referendum on sovereignty-association. But all the provinces reacted with great hostility. At length a compromise was reached in which Ottawa retreated from some centralizing goals. Certain aspects of public policy were entrenched, however, notably bilingualism, and a "Charter of Rights and Freedoms" was added. The Parti Québécois objected strenuously to the whole process, and the new constitution clearly does pose a legal threat to much of its nationalist legislation restricting the use of English. More subtly, the constitution represents a break with the British tradition of common law, custom and precedent, and greatly enhances the power of the judicial branch. Potentially, this is a most significant development. Even with the best of intentions, it is the political equivalent of DDT: aimed at immediate problems, its long-term consequences may well turn out to be unpredictable.

The fact that Ontario and Quebec in tandem can govern Canada has naturally concentrated Ottawa's mind on English-French relations. Since Confederation, whether innocently or by design, these had been characterized by a form of benign neglect, with Francophones building up their own institutions in Quebec and the Anglophones running commerce and, basically, federal affairs. Although there had been a Francophone prime minister as early as Sir Wilfrid Laurier in 1896, French remained such a rarity in the House of Commons that even as late as 1956, when two Quebec MPs broke into it during a heated exchange in the debate on the controversial pipeline bill, it was noted as an index of how extraordinary passions had become. (There are now elaborate simultaneous translation facilities.)

However, particularly after 1960 when the Quebec provincial Liberals under Jean Lesage finally ended the long-lived Union Nationale regime and presided over the "Quiet Revolution," it became obvious that something was stirring in Quebec. The response was a new official synthesis on the federal level. A Royal Commission on Bilingualism and Biculturalism was appointed by Lester Pearson in 1963, and many of its recommendations were embodied in Trudeau's

Official Languages Act of 1969. The reformed official philosophy, closely identified with Prime Minister Pierre Trudeau, was that now all of Canada was to be the homeland of both Anglophones and Francophones. Among other implications, this meant that the federal government had to be prepared to offer its services in both official languages everywhere in the country.

The concept of a bilingual and bicultural society is an interesting and intricate one. But although fundamental to contemporary Canada, it is very rarely discussed in principle there. René Lévesque, then leader of the PQ, described the state it envisaged as a "hybrid, bicultural monstrosity," and said it could never work. But bilingualism immediately became an article of faith for the Canadian Establishment. Opposition Leader Robert Stanfield imposed the policy on his mutinous Progressive Conservative Party, and in 1972 even withdrew the Tory imprimatur from a prominent opponent of bilingualism, Leonard Jones, the Mayor of Moncton, New Brunswick, who won the PC federal nomination in his home town. (He was elected anyway, as an independent.) French blossomed by decree on road signs, cornflakes boxes and government offices from coast to coast, quite regardless of the language spoken locally. Nevertheless, Lévesque's objection to the Liberal panacea still has to be reckoned with.

4

The World the Liberals Made

Canadian Questioner: *What do you think of a country that has no flag?*

Mort Sahl: *Well, it's a start.*

Canada did indeed have a flag in 1961 when the above exchange occurred, as opponents of the Liberals' intention to adopt a new one ceaselessly protested. It had the Red Ensign, with Britain's Union Jack in the upper quarter and the badge of Canada's coat of arms in the fly on a red background; originally authorized for Canadian-registered ships and flown proudly enough by the Royal Canadian Navy in the closing days of World War II (when it was the third-most powerful fleet in the world), it had been informally accepted for general use. And on occasion Canadians flew the Union Jack itself.

The bitter House of Commons' debates that preceded Prime Minister Lester Pearson's successful imposition of the now-famous *Gules on a Canadian pale argent a maple leaf of the first* are for many reasons much more remote from contemporary Canada than the less than twenty years that have actually elapsed. The Maple Leaf flag itself did catch the optimistic mood of English Canada in the period of Expo 67 and Canada's centennial celebrations, and it is now seen everywhere, adopted even by its erstwhile opponents, although the passage of time has if anything increased their distaste for the federal Liberals.

Flags are like that. Flying the Stars and Stripes in the American South does not necessarily mean that the social attitudes expressed during the desegregation controversies of the 1950s by flying the Confederate battle flag have been renounced, and it can mean quite the opposite. Poems can be similarly transmuted, which is what Auden meant when he commented on the death of W.B. Yeats:

> Now he is scattered among a hundred cities
> And wholly given over to unfamiliar affections.

Quebec, of course, is different. Although appeasement of the French province was to be one of the benefits of the change, today the elegant Quebec provincial flag, blue with a white cross and four white *fleurs de lis,* one in each quarter, is more widely favored there.

But the long months of debate were not the absurdity the media designated them at the time. For one thing, the final design was better than the original. For another, symbols matter. Canadian Nationalists tend to dismiss all opposition to the removal of "colonial trappings" as irrational by such tricks as linking it with what Toronto Nationalist writer June Callwood in her ultraorthodox *Portrait of Canada* describes as the "quivering rage" of the aging John Diefenbaker, who most often raised the issue in his declining years as a back-bencher. But in fact this resistance stemmed from a view of Canada as part of "Greater Britain" that had long been an internally consistent if debatable Canadian ideal. In the flag debate, moreover, the Tory Opposition was expressing English Canada's inchoate suspicion that something was being done to it. And it was.

Cut, as they say, to Ottawa's Parliament Hill on the morning of July 1, 1980, the 113th anniversary of Confederation. This was the day when "O Canada" was to be proclaimed the official national anthem. Both the words and music of "O Canada" had been written one hundred years earlier by two French Canadians, one of whom subsequently immigrated to Boston. The Liberals passed legislation in 1963 establishing its primacy over "God Save The Queen," but finding the right English version, according to June Callwood, had taken seventeen years and fourteen government bills.

A choir assembled on Parliament Hill to sing the national anthem before a vast holiday crowd. A dispute over which national anthem should take precedence, the English or the French one, was resolved with typical Canadian ingenuity. The choir was divided in half and sang both versions simultaneously. The platform party, which included Governor-General Edward Schreyer and Prime Minister Trudeau, sang in the language of choice. Those who preferred the English lyrics used song sheets. The crowd, moved and bemused, sang the French version or one of the many English versions, as it pleased.

The official English translation is now:

O Canada! Our home and native land!
True patriot love in all thy sons command.
With glowing hearts we see thee rise,
The True North strong and free!
From far and wide, O Canada, we stand on guard for thee.
God keep our land glorious and free!
O Canada, we stand on guard for thee,
O Canada, we stand on guard for thee.

(National anthems, like gift horses, should not be looked in the mouth, and Canada's after all does have a pretty good tune, sharing some bars with "The March of the Priests" from Mozart's *Magic Flute.*)

The first point to notice is that this national anthem contains no reference to the Queen. Yet Canada is still nominally a monarchy and the Queen is still head of state. Pierre Trudeau once said he expected to be the first president of Canada, although abolition of the monarchy was not a priority "at this time." His government continued the Liberal tradition of a stealthy campaign of attrition against the emblems of monarchy. In 1977, for example, it eliminated the technical convention that Canadian diplomats were accredited in the name of the Queen, and later it attempted in an early draft of its constitution reform to have the governor-general, who is appointed by the prime minister, open and dissolve Parliament in his own right rather than as the Queen's plenipotentiary. National symbols are not innate. If they are to play a role in a people's life, they need constant care and feeding – which is why Ottawa wanted to force on Yellowknife the $60,000 Centennial firework festival described in Chapter Three. Its attitude to the Canadian monarchy, by contrast, has been like that of the urchin secretly urinating on some shrub in the hope that it will die.

There can be no doubt that this is having an effect. For instance, *The National Deal,* the standard popular account of the post-1980 constitutional struggle written by Robert Sheppard and Michael Valpy of the *Globe and Mail,* contains simply no reference to the monarchy in its index at all – although one Canadian constitutional expert, Eugene Forsey, maintained that vestigial references in the

Constitution document as drafted meant that the monarchy has been inadvertently "entrenched."

However, outside of the intelligentsia, the House of Windsor has proved to have unexpectedly deep roots in English Canada. This has been known to produce the paradoxical result that British journalists covering a Royal tour in Canada focus in their stories home on the Anglophone elite's tacit republicanism (SHOCK! HORROR!), while their Canadian colleagues from that elite are reporting the visit's surprisingly (to them) popular success. After some nasty controversies such as that over the proposed removal of "Royal" from the title of the Royal Canadian Mounted Police, the Liberals under Trudeau clearly decided against open confrontation. The former national anthem, "God Save The Queen," still has shadowy official standing as something called the "royal anthem," just as the Union Jack hung in the House of Commons alongside the Maple Leaf – for a while.

The second point about the national anthem that will occur to observers is: why not just translate from the French? A literal rendition of the first French verse reveals the answer:

> O Canada! Land of our ancestors,
> Your brow is wreathed with glorious garlands.
> For your arm knows how to carry the sword,
> It knows how to carry the Cross;
> Your history is an epic of the most brilliant exploits;
> And your courage, blended with Faith,
> Will still protect our homes and rights,
> Will still protect our homes and rights.

Although most English Canadians don't realize it, what French Canadians have been singing all these years is an explicit hymn to Francophone ethnic particularism, which is blandly identified with "Canada." It specifically emphasizes the integral importance of the Roman Catholic faith to the Francophone nation, although there are some Francophone Jews and even a historic mini-community of Francophone Protestants in Canada, let alone (of course) the Anglophones. It extols the efficacy of action – including, in the past, violence – to defend "our rights," which in Canadian history has become a code-word for Francophone collective interests within the state.

So the comedy on Parliament Hill that June Callwood describes becomes a microcosm of Canada today. The Anglophones, confused and divided, dutifully try to sing a national anthem which, perhaps partly because of what Callwood calls the "long and serious consideration" given the words "in the hope of avoiding offense to women, racial minorities or atheists," has been essentially stripped of content. The Francophones sing what they sang all along, a paean of praise to themselves which by implication excludes everyone else. This resolution is duly hailed as a triumph of "typical Canadian ingenuity." Other terms might come more readily to mind. Concession has masked conflict, and the resulting cacophony is ignored. Individuals and nations can perhaps live with contradictions for years, but English Canada now poses a new question to Mort Sahl: what do you think of a country that doesn't know what its own national anthem says?

The sturdy Francophones, of course, can hardly be blamed for this situation. It could not have occurred if the Anglophone majority had not been deeply divided. The flag debate was basically a continuation, cunningly phrased, of the longstanding quarrel among Anglophones about the British connection. The Francophones, although much cited by advocates of the Maple Leaf, were actually less exercised, regarding the whole matter as an alien affair. And the apotheosis of "O Canada" has been achieved long after the separatist anthem "Gens du Pays" has eclipsed it among Francophones, who anyway nowadays tend to waive their aboriginal rights to the traditional sobriquet of *Canadiens* in favor of *Québécois*.

This Anglophone quarrel has been echoed in every British colony. A particularly acrimonious version of it took place in Australia, where one of the first priorities of Prime Minister Gough Whitlam's Labor government when it came to power in 1972 after twenty years in the wilderness was to replace "God Save the Queen" with "Advance, Australia Fair." Since it is clear to everyone except Australians that an inexorable fate has marked "Waltzing Matilda" to be Australia's musical destiny – it makes a *magnificent* slow march – this was always a fairly quixotic gesture. But it appeared more so when on closer examination "Advance, Australia Fair" was itself found to contain verses of Greater British loyalism typical of the Victorian Empire at its zenith.

Nevertheless, Australia did not reject its youthful caroling, unlike English Canada. For there was a Canadian song exactly equivalent, also written by a Scottish immigrant – "The Maple Leaf Forever" – dating from the Confederation year of 1867. Once well-known, it is now hardly ever heard: "properly consigned to the dustbin," as Pierre Berton, a leading Nationalist publicist, said primly in his best-selling book, *Why We Act Like Canadians*. This is its scandalous opening verse and chorus:

In days of yore, from Britain's shore,
Wolfe, the dauntless hero, came,
And planted firm Britannia's flag
On Canada's fair domain.

Here may it wave, our boast and pride,
And joined in love together,
The Thistle, Shamrock, Rose entwine
The Maple Leaf forever!

The Maple Leaf, our emblem dear
The Maple Leaf forever;
God save our Queen, and Heaven bless
The Maple Leaf forever.

This song was certainly beyond earthly help after its direct reference to the undeniable but unmentionable Conquest of 1759, although there were various efforts at bowdlerization, even including the insertion of a Gallic lily amid the entwining flora in the seventh line. And no one ever proposed that there should be simply a different French version. Language barriers apparently offer only one-way shelter in Canada.

The practical effect of such self-abnegation by (or more accurately on behalf of) English Canada is limited, because it is directed at the symptoms of Francophone discontent, rather than at the continuing restlessness within Confederation which is its cause. However, it has its resonant moments. The Liberal governments of Louis St. Laurent and Lester Pearson, for example, decided with the abruptness characteristic of this form of political neurosis that the term "Dominion" was next for the dustbin. "It is unfortunate that Canada chose to call itself a Dominion in 1867," Yale's Professor Robin Winks, an American academic exponent of the Liberal *Weltanschauung,* wrote in an essay in the *Wilson Quarterly.* "Domination is what the debate [between French and English Canada] has been all about. . . ." As usual, all efforts to point out that "Dominion" (as ex-Canadian diplomat John W. Holmes said in his 1980-81 University of Toronto Bissell Lectures) was "completely misinterpreted as a badge of colonial shame" and that both "the term and the status" were a unique Canadian contribution to the world were brushed aside. But obviously neither "kingdom" nor "republic" could be substituted without embarrassment. Another typically ingenious solution evolved, which neatly confirmed the pivotal role of the Canadian bureaucracy. On Canadian official documents, "Dominion of Canada" has been replaced by "Government of Canada/Gouvernement du Canada." In Canada, *L'état, c'est eux.*

The new flag and the new anthem were part of the triumph of Liberalism. The twentieth century was once commonly said to belong to Canada, but it turned out to belong to the federal Liberal Party. Modern Canada is the creation of the Liberal Party, and it made it in its own image, even more thoroughly than Sir John A. Macdonald succeeded in doing, when he organized the Confederation of Britain's North American colonies on the basis of a common loyalty to the Crown that was best expressed by his Conservative Party. Even after Brian Mulroney's victory, the Liberal presence is to the Canadian consciousness what the New Deal is to the American, except that there has not subsequently been an Eisenhower overlay, let alone a Reagan countermine. The Liberal hegemony also began rather earlier, at least by 1921, and quite arguably in 1896. Its cultural consequences have been immense. When Canadian publicists talk about Canada or the interests of Canada, when *Toronto Star* Ottawa columnist Richard Gwyn throughout his valuable and highly successful Trudeau biography, *The Northern Magus,* refer unguardedly to "we" and "us," it is crucial to know that they are invariably talking about Canadian Liberaldom and its necessities, often without realizing it. "The 1968 election was our last joyous collective experience together," Gwyn, at the time himself an Ottawa bureaucrat, remembers fondly. "We'd dreamed the impossible dream. . . We called it, in 1968, Trudeau-mania. Really, it was Canada-mania." But only 45% of Canadians voted for it.

After World War I, Canadian Liberals even produced what the late Donald Creighton, perhaps the dean of Canadian historians, used to call the Authorized Version of Canadian history. Charles Taylor has perceptively identified this in his book *Radical Tories* as a Canadian variant of the Whig interpretation of history which at one time dominated British intellectual life, a "new Liberal version of Canadian history [with] Mackenzie King as its spiritual godfather and a host of academics, journalists and civil servants as its prime mythologists." Like the work of the British Whig historians, this version ratified certain desirable present-day trends and drew an unmistakeable political moral at the cost of a little distortion. An important premise was that Canada was to be viewed, not as part of a Greater Britain, but rather as a colony heroically struggling free from Imperial thrall.

This premise has not been easy to establish, given that Britain has spent most of this century dismantling its Empire with unprecedented enthusiasm, and that, as John Holmes pointed out in his Bissell lectures, "our history was in fact an extended exploration of the difficulties of reconciling freedom of action with shared policy-making in an association which we wanted to maintain in our own interests." But that old Canadian ingenuity comes to the rescue again. "If Britain declared war, Canada was automatically at war as well (which is what happened at the outbreak of World War I in 1914)," Professor Winks told his *Wilson Quarterly* readers in aghast tones. "Surely one of the truest tests of independence is whether a people can decide for themselves whether to go to war." The exquisite nature of this point can only be appreciated in the light of the fact that Canadian governments indeed effectively could make this decision, since they had exclusive powers over taxation and the raising of troops – and anyway, pro-war sentiment in Canada was overwhelming.

"Wow, we're free!" said a grade-six student at an Ottawa elementary school on April 17, 1982, after a celebration of the patriated constitution's formal proclamation at which, according to the authors of *The National Deal,* the principal had handed out government-supplied flags and decals and made his pupils sing "O Canada!" in English and French. The Liberals' authorized version of Canadian history had sanitized this complex internal quarrel, and was transmitting its version to a new generation. All these students had been taught to believe the story about Canada's long fight to get "free."

The Liberal Party's dominance of Canada in the twentieth century was like the feat of a circus stuntman riding two horses at once. In essence, the party was in the mediating business. Its survival depended upon its ability to manipulate the Anglophone and Francophone communities and keep them galloping in harness together. But it fully represented neither, as was obvious even in 1980 from its generalized electoral atrophy in English Canada and its displacement by the Parti Québécois in head-to-head contest at the provincial level in Quebec. The horses were steadily drifting apart. It would require ever-louder shouts and blows from the rider to force them together again.

The Liberals developed from a nineteenth-century alliance between the Francophone anti-clerical *rouges* faction in Quebec and the predominantly Presbyterian and Methodist "Clear Grits" of Anglophone Ontario. The Grits were basically a Canadian expression of the contemporaneous radical movement in Britain, which was strongest among non-Anglican "Nonconformists," particularly in the "Celtic fringe." The Canadian nickname derived from a type of sand favored by immigrant Scottish stonemasons for making mortar, and the first Liberal prime minister of Canada (1873-78) was in fact an immigrant Scottish stonemason, Alexander Mackenzie, born in 1822 in Dunkeld, Perthshire. A century later, under Pierre Trudeau, the Liberals were still a coalition between Francophone and Anglophone tendencies, each with their own political agenda.

Public life in English-speaking Canada has never been distinguished by acute ideological sensitivity. "I have no politics, I am Canadian," said George McCullagh, a prominent Liberal and the publisher of the Toronto *Globe and Mail,* in 1938. "We say the other fellows are corrupt" was the only answer a Canadian farmer back in the reign of Queen Victoria could come up with when Goldwin Smith questioned him on the difference in principle between his party and its opponents.

Nevertheless, successive Anglophone Liberal leaderships in the twentieth century were connected by a consistent ideological and emotional thread. They were systematically on the left of their party and their community. This tradition has been all the more tenacious for being cherished in private, so as not to disconcert a less enlightened Canadian public. The disastrous consequences of behaving otherwise were so deeply seared into the Liberal soul during the years of Conservative hegemony in the period after Confederation that traces of it persisted long after the Liberal hegemony had triumphed. At that time, differences between left and right in Canada tended to center on the British connection. In the general election of 1891 and 1911, the Liberals allowed themselves to become associated with schemes for continental free trade. The Tories immediately portrayed this as an attack on the unity of the Empire preparatory to a political merger with the U.S., and the Liberals went down to shattering defeat. In the general election of 1917, the Tories under Sir Robert Borden once again made Imperial loyalty the issue by campaigning on the question of conscripting Canadians for the holocaust in Europe; the troops already there were volunteers, and Francophones were not volunteering in proportion to their numbers in the population. Again, the Liberals were destroyed in English Canada, and a group of Western Liberals decamped altogether to form a Union Government with Borden.

As Liberal leader in 1926, Mackenzie King arguably achieved a technical victory over the British connection when he salvaged an otherwise-hopeless general election, at least in part, by inventing the ingenious charge that the Governor-General, Lord Byng, was improperly interfering in Canadian affairs. But nevertheless, in the 1930s the anti-Imperial neutralist mandarins who dominated the Department of External Affairs and who formed a key Liberal sub-group, resentfully knew they were powerless to keep Canada out of a European war involving Britain: "the loyalties of too large a number of our people are too deeply engaged," one of them wrote. When World War II broke out, Mackenzie King maneuvered between the Canadian communities with his usual deviousness and kept his party in power. But as late as 1948, with an avowedly anti-Imperial Labour government firmly established in London, and the heart of the Empire, India, already ripped out, King rejected at the last minute a sweeping free trade agreement negotiated in secret with the U.S., apparently fearing another 1911 catastrophe at the polls.

King's techniques of public caution and obfuscation were also applied by the Liberals to the economic issues that increasingly came to dominate English Canadian public debate, partly as an antiseptic substitute for politics, as the twentieth century wore on. In 1935, it was Conservative Prime Minister R.B. Bennett who proposed bold New Deal-type interventionism as a solution for the Depression. Mackenzie King equivocated, and preached classical nostrums like free trade. Bennett lost. This outcome was a closer parallel with the U.S. situation than meets the eye. In the U.S. presidential election of 1932, the incumbent Republican president Herbert Hoover had developed a more interventionist platform than that advocated by his Democratic challenger Franklin D. Roosevelt; Roosevelt, like King, subsequently presided over vast increases in government activity similar to that espoused by his defeated opponent.

Caution and obfuscation remained important Liberal techniques under Trudeau. In the general election of 1974, it was the Tories under Robert Stanfield who supported wage and price controls à la Richard Nixon, and the Liberals under Pierre Trudeau who opposed them, ostensibly on theoretical grounds, but basically for fear of labor union reaction. Stanfield lost, too. And then in 1975 the Liberals introduced their own controls. Similarly, the Liberals under Trudeau never campaigned much in a general election on the issue of Canadian economic Nationalism or public ownership, even counting the enigmatic references by Trudeau when his victory in 1980 was already assured. The Liberals' relative caution in office was a source of constant frustration to socialist and Nationalist ideologues. This convenient vagueness helped explain the continued presence in the Liberal ranks of various business community mascots like Ed Lumley, Trudeau's Minister of Industry, Trade and Commerce, and John Turner, the former finance minister and Trudeau's ultimate successor. But they were clearly an endangered species.

For there can be no doubt about what was lurking in the hearts of the Liberal leaders. They were men of the Left. Particularly where the Imperial connection was concerned, this could take an acutely personal form. For example, Mackenzie King privately adulated his late grandfather, William Lyon Mackenzie, who spent some years in exile and disgrace after leading a farcical insurrection in Toronto in 1837 that Liberal interpretation historians view as nobly anti-colonial, but that actually had much more in common with the British Reform Bill and Chartist agitations about the extension of the franchise. When King was made a member of the British Order of Merit, he gloated secretly in his diary that his chief motive in accepting the honor was to hang it beside a framed copy of the notice proclaiming a price on his grandfather's head.

In the House of Commons during World War II, John Diefenbaker unerringly hit this nerve by attacking King for including references to his grandfather, along with Leonidas and the Spartans at Thermopylae and King John and the Barons at Runnymede, in lectures on champions of liberty prepared for the edification of the Canadian Army. In his speech Diefenbaker said his own great-grandfather had taken up arms to follow Mackenzie. He had followed him as far as the Detroit River, across which Mackenzie had escaped and where Diefenbaker's great-grandfather had to stop – because the arms he bore were in the local militia, which was pursuing Mackenzie in the name of the Crown. King completely lost his self-control and had to be called to order by the Speaker.

"It was usually forgotten by Liberals later," Christina McCall-Newman points out in *Grits*,

> but when he was elected leader in 1919, King was seen as a progressive young man .... At that leadership convention, he wrote for the party platform a boldly progressive statement on social security. *Realpolitik* kept him from realizing the ideas contained in that platform for many years, but he continued to regard himself as a reformer, and was crafty enough to try systematically to head off any threat from the left such as that posed by the farmer's movement in the 1920s and the Co-operative Commonwealth Federation, the social democratic party founded in 1933.

Some sixty years later, after a period of decline and fall under the prime ministership of Louis St. Laurent (1948-57) and the takeover and the reconstruction of the Anglophone party by the left-leaning Toronto-based "New Guard," when the Liberals had become indisputedly Canada's ruling class, "to be called right wing in the Liberal Party was to be beyond the pale. No matter how prosperous, power-hungry, or self-engrossed Liberals became, they always liked to think they were progressive."

It was a long march for the Liberal left. Some reasons for their success can be generalized from J.L. Granatstein's neat analysis in *The Ottawa Men* of the ultimate victory won by the neutralist Liberal mandarins of External Affairs. Canadians favoring the Imperial connection with Britain, he wrote, ". . . were less well organized because they were the majority, certainly among English-speaking opinion makers." Moreover, he adds, for this majority,

> the Canadian situation was also difficult because the French Canadians were unhappy with any automatic commitment to the Imperial cause, whatever it might turn out to be. So too were many other Canadians who felt scant allegiance to Britain. Therefore the relatively few English Canadian neutralists, because they were articulate and because they used their bases in the universities and the churches as rostrums, had disproportionate influence and became a political force to be weighed and considered.

And the secretive habits of a conniving minority are not easily discarded. In early 1983 the *New York Times'* Michael T. Kaufman, reporting on an attempt by the New Democrats to block the entry of the Parti Québécois into the social democratic Socialist International, observed that

> . . . the Liberal Party, while not a member of the Socialist International, has many leading members who regard themselves as Social Democrats. Mr. Trudeau himself has maintained close and cordial ties with such leaders of the Socialist International as Willy Brandt of West Germany, Olof Palme of Sweden and Bruno Kreisky of Austria. One official of the New Democratic Party said there were "obviously key people in his Cabinet who we know are socialists though we'd never admit that publicly."

Neither would they.

Underlying the success of the Liberal left, and considerably facilitated by it, was one of the more extraordinary developments in the intellectual history of the twentieth century: a profound change in the meaning of liberalism. This occurred more or less simultaneously in Canada, the U.S. and throughout the English-speaking world. It amounted to a Reversal of Beliefs comparable to the famous Reversal of Alliances or "Diplomatic Revolution" that so excited the chancelleries of eighteenth-century Europe. Quite suddenly, classical liberalism was abandoned by the parties and social groups originally espousing it. Instead, the same parties and social groups came to favour the more statist, interventionist, mixed-economy complex of attitudes describing itself in the U.S. as "liberalism," a.k.a. "social democracy" or (daringly) "socialism" in Europe and Canada. In the U.S. since the late nineteenth century, the Democratic and Republican parties have simply changed sides on issues like free trade, now doubted by the former and defended by the latter. In Canada and Britain the picture is confused by the emergence of strong, avowedly socialist parties, but both the Canadian Liberals and their much-reduced namesakes in Britain have also turned their coats. Thus the dispossession of classical liberalism has been so complete that it has even been deprived of its name. Survivors from the classical liberal era, like Nobel Prize-winning economist Friedrich von Hayek, much to their disgust, have been driven to seek shelter under the hastily invented word "libertarianism," which many Canadian editors either still do not recognize or confuse with libertinism.

This transformation has not been completely clean. Individuals and odd beliefs can still be found attached to the parties from which the rest of their fellows have been wrenched. Both the grass-roots Democrats in the U.S. and the Liberals in Canada still retain a residual libertarianism on such social issues as pornography, and in certain civil liberties, such as questions of police procedure. As Pierre Trudeau told the 1978 Liberal policy convention: "The Liberal tradition has two parts to it. On the one hand, we have to protect the individual against the State so that the individual may remain free, master [of his] own destiny. But on the other hand, and this is of course an aspect of equal importance from the point of view of Liberal ideology, the State has to intervene to protect the weak members of society, minorities, those who need protection from the State against stronger forces than themselves."

Much depends on interpretation, of course, but it is notable that an omniscient "we" have to protect the individual and, implicitly, decide when he needs restraining. And from a logical point of view, the

Liberal tradition's "two parts" are ultimately incompatible. This rapidly shows up in practice, particularly when the intervening Canadian State meets those freedoms pertaining to economic life, an area where the Liberals have become completely insensitive. Trudeau himself illustrated the contradiction when as Justice Minister in 1967 he simultaneously introduced proposals to decriminalize bestiality and homosexuality and to impose new restrictions on the sale and ownership of firearms, already practically exterminated in Canada. Many Americans would applaud this combination, but it is a theoretical inconsistency, because in the name of preventing violence that is already illegal, it curtails the liberty of law-abiding gun-owners, just as Prohibition banned alcohol because it was linked with brawls, drunken driving and other social ills. It makes the value judgement that fetishism is fine only if you want a sheep, not a Smith & Wesson. One person's obscenity is another person's right to bear arms. "The state has no place in the nation's bedrooms," said Trudeau in a much-applauded phrase. But the state had a place everywhere else.

To some extent, the Reversal of Beliefs can be explained as a rationalization of naked self-interest. It made it easier for the Liberals to appeal to what Christina McCall-Newman has described as their "bedrock vote. . . . a coalition of minorities." The Liberals' standard operating procedure is almost an exact parallel of what critics of the American New Class allege is its cultivation of dependent "client" constituencies with taxpayers' money. Reversing Beliefs was also handy when patching over Canada's regional rifts. Sir John A. Macdonald's high-tariff National Policy has been criticized by historians, who think it was a convenient rationale for measures like protectionism and railway subsidies that were favored by key supporters, and they regard its economic effects as either nugatory or negative. Much the same can be said about the "Second National Policy," the bewildering variety of subsidies and incentives orchestrated by Ottawa in the 1960s and '70s to stimulate development in the peripheral regions. If you have convinced yourself that economic growth is not best left to market forces but always requires government direction, it is easier to justify what might otherwise appear a crude attempt to bribe the regions to shut up about federal trade policies that benefit only Central Canada.

But a party founded on this sort of minority "bedrock" is inevitably permeated by another theme: alienation from the culture of the majority, in this case, English-speaking Canada. The "leaders" attracted from the Anglophone majority to such a party tend to be individuals who themselves are disaffected from their own community. This may be for reasons of family history, like Mackenzie King, or because of ideology and local particularism as with Skelton, Pearson and the anti-Imperialist bureaucrats of External Affairs; or from feelings of sheer guilt. Personal psychology may well be a better explanation than political philosophy. Brooding on this phenomenon in the U.S. scene, the conservative American columnist Joseph Sobran invented the useful word "alienism" to describe it, arguing that it was clearly the mirror image of "nativism," the political tendency to favor the indigenous and established.

In nineteenth-century Canada, this alienism rendered classical liberalism irresistibly appealing to the party of the "outs." As preached by the British Liberal leader W.E. Gladstone, it had a deliciously anti-Imperialist tone – Gladstone was a Victorian dove, repeatedly attempting to withdraw Britain from colonial entanglements and even advocating Home Rule for Ireland. And a doctrine that attacked state power in principle was very convenient for a party of minorities in a state controlled by the majority, particularly at a time when state action like the National Policy was widely seen as essential in making Canada into a unified and British nation, rather than allowing North American gravitational forces to prevail. (On purely economic questions, it is probably also significant that by the time Sir Wilfrid Laurier was citing Gladstone while building his electoral coalition in the 1890s, the British elder statesman had become much more collectivist than in his early years.) In the twentieth century, however, Britain has quite suddenly vanished from the Canadian scene. The U.S.A. has largely occupied the role of cultural mentor to the majority. Protest against the majority culture has therefore refocused on it. Suddenly, those natural North American gravitational forces appear ominous. The idea that the role of government should be strictly limited looks less attractive.

In Canada, as in all the English-speaking world and perhaps the West at large, the party of the left is inevitably the party of disaffection from the prevailing bourgeois order. This is true no matter how assimilated and bourgeois its leaders may appear to be. Even when parties of the moderate left have been in power for generations, as in Canada, the same underlying dynamic is still at work. These parties remain essentially an anti-cultural force.

The idea that the party of the left is opposed to the existing culture is not new. American conservatives, after all, have been croaking darkly for years that much contemporary American liberalism is motivated by guilt and alienation from the society and is ultimately self-destructive. "Liberalism is the ideology of Western suicide," said

James Burnham in his seminal *Suicide of the West.* Nor is the idea an exclusively partisan perception: Gramsci would have agreed that the task of the left is to persuade the "West" – the bourgeois world – to disarm itself by accepting the legitimacy of revolutionary (or at least progressive) values.

The anti-cultural stance of the parties of the left also helps explain the sharply differing emotions with which intellectuals in various parts of the English-speaking world view the concept of patriotism and the nation-state. In Britain, nationalism has not been fashionable among intellectuals for most of this century. Particularly since 1918, almost everyone has agreed that what the World War I poet Wilfred Owen called "the old lie," *dulce et decorum est pro patria mori,* was indeed a lie. There was almost unanimous support among the British elite for Britain's entry into the European Economic Community, despite the explicit supranational ambitions of the Treaty of Rome and its negative implications for national sovereignty. Even the Labour Party's left wing, which did oppose entry, chose not to express its objection in nationalist terms, and was uncomfortable in the presence of those right-wing Tories like Enoch Powell who did. The status of nationalism in the U.S. is complicated by various factors, including the profound national self-absorption and the resultant difficulty in grasping that other nations exist at all. But here too, the anti-American tone of the domestic left has become a standard complaint of their opponents, typified by former U.N. Ambassador Jeane Kirkpatrick's attack on the "San Francisco Democrats" ("They *always* blame America first") at the Republican national convention in 1984. The disrepute into which the concept of nationalism has fallen among the English-speaking intelligentsia in this century is all the more striking because of the way it has blossomed everywhere else in the world, even in the former colonies where nation-states had never previously existed and where there are often no homogeneous national groups to which it can be applied.

But not in Canada. There nationalism is still respectable and it is possible to hear progressive Anglophone intellectuals like Professor Stephen Clarkson in his *Canada and the Reagan Challenge: Crisis in the Canadian-American Relationship* (itself a classic of post-1980 Nationalist hubris) wax lyrical about the value of national identity and culture as a "spiritual legacy" or, more prosaically, as a "social glue." The public class which in Britain united in favor of integration with an adjoining continental polity appears in English Canada to be equally united in opposing it, or anything remotely resembling it.

The reason for this contrast is simple. Britain and the U.S. are both sufficiently large that they appear to be culturally self-sustaining. In either country, opposition to the concept of nationalism is an attack on the majority culture. Canada is smaller, and the majority culture is more obviously underwritten by links with the rest of the English-speaking world, particularly the U.S. Assertions of "Canadian Nationalism" have the effect of attacking those links with the U.S. and Britain and hence attacking the majority culture.

Naturally, all of this has been extremely confusing for the Conservatives, the party of the Canadian Anglophone majority. Much of their history has been devoted to attacks on the U.S. that are superficially similar to expressions of Canadian Nationalism but were in reality part of a defense of the old majority culture and its Greater British nature. With the abrupt implosion of Britain after World War II, the Conservatives' traditional position was completely undermined. Their consequent disorientation and demoralization has been a key element in their eclipse.

Moreover, the Canadian Nationalism currently fashionable among Canada's elite is discernibly ersatz. It is based on what would be a contradiction in terms for any true nationalism: a denial rather than an affirmation of the underlying cultural reality. Both these points will be expanded later.

The other partner in the Liberal order is Quebec. The Francophone horse in the Liberal team has been galloping along equally preoccupied, paying little attention to the emotional travail of its fellow. For the Francophones of North America, there is a good chance that the era of Pierre Trudeau will in retrospect turn out to have been a second New France, claiming a vast but illusory empire extending this time to the Arctic, the Pacific and to the Atlantic coast of Newfoundland rather than to the Mississippi and down to the Gulf of Mexico, but equally devoid of the political reality of a French-speaking population. But this is not yet apparent. Under Brian Mulroney, "French power" is enjoying an Indian summer.

In the last years of Pierre Trudeau's prime ministership, amid almost total abjuration of comment by Anglophone politicians and press, the traditional symbols of ethnic balance in Canadian federal politics were silently abandoned. When the Liberal cabinet gathered after the federal election of 1980, as reported in *The National Deal*,

> ... an unusually high number of ministers (14 of 33) crowding into the formal photograph were French Canadian, holding such key posts as justice, energy, health and welfare, regional economic

expansion, transport and communications. The finance minister was a dour and remote Cape Bretoner [Allan MacEachen] but the two ministers of state were Quebecers. The key patronage posts – supply and services, postmaster general, and regional economic expansion – were all held by Francophones.

Sheppard and Valpy attributed this development to the tactical requirements of the imminent referendum battle in Quebec. But in fact it was part of what Christina McCall-Newman described as "a minor revolution," which in twenty years had transformed Ottawa from "a resolutely English town" to one where "French was in use everywhere." In 1983, when Sheppard and Valpy's book was in the stores and the separatist spectre was supposed to have been exorcised, the Francophone contingent of Trudeau's 36-member cabinet had risen further, to 16 or 44% as opposed to their 25% of the population at large. This included twelve of the top eighteen ministers ranked in official order of precedence. Despite the fact that the Prime Minister was himself French, the finance ministry, formerly an Anglophone preserve, was held by Francophones on and off after 1977. Francophones had occupied no fewer than two and sometimes all of what McCall-Newman regards as "the four key Cabinet posts" (Prime Minister, Finance Minister, Justice Minister, Health and Welfare Minister) continuously since 1968. Symbolically, when Queen Elizabeth II came to Ottawa to proclaim Canada's new patriated constitution in 1982 and thus bury the last relic of Greater Britain, the only Canadian signatories of the formal document were both Francophones, Pierre Trudeau and André Ouellet, Minister of Consumer and Corporate Affairs, who was present in his capacity as Registrar General (Minister of Justice Jean Chrétien also signed although there was no technical reason for him to do so).

This Francophone drive into Canada's federal politics has distinct parallels with the Afrikaaner takeover of South African public life in the years following the Nationalist Party victory in 1948, a development which was also assisted by the developing post-Imperial trauma of the local English-speaking community. But there is a difference. Afrikaaners make up two-thirds of South Africa's white population. Francophones are only one-quarter of Canada's. Their influence in Canada has been magnified – leveraged, to use the language of corporate finance – to the maximum extent. Not even the political skill of their most successful generation of leaders since the Conquest can maintain their present level of power indefinitely.

So omnipresent are reminders of what is sometimes called the

"French Fact" in Canada, emblazoned from coast to coast on whatever signs, notices and airwaves the federal government can compel or cajole to be bilingual, that it is hard to recognize that it was not always so. Well within living memory, Canada was officially and unquestioningly regarded as an English-speaking country, in which a French-language minority happened also to reside. As late as 1942, Mackenzie King was able to get along with only one French Canadian cabinet minister for a period of some five months without exciting adverse public comment. Despite their Quebec base, the Liberal governments of both King and Louis St. Laurent refused on the grounds of expense to print in both languages the official documents and the checks issued to the public under the various public welfare schemes. The latter practice was only begun in 1962. King built his entire political career and the modern Liberal Party on what Christina McCall-Newman called "the major Liberal shibboleth: you stick with Quebec no matter what, and should you quarrel with French Canadian Liberals, never do so in public." But in 1937, when a Francophone civil servant tried to run his department in French, King thought he was mad.

"The nation would pay dearly for these sins of omission and commission by its leaders," sighed Professor Granatstein, reporting this incident in *The Ottawa Men*. But this reflects the guilty sensibility of contemporary English Canada, after a sort of dialectical Death of a Thousand Cuts that has lasted for nearly two generations. By a succession of steps, each apparently as reasonable as the last, English Canadians have been induced to abandon and forget their original position, which was that Canada was English-speaking with a French community allowed to function internally in French, much like the Celtic minorities of Britain and France or the historic Spanish-speaking community of New Mexico. There was nothing atrocious about this position. On a world scale of majority attitudes to minorities, it was distinctly amiable. It oddly resembles in principle the policy adopted by successive Quebec provincial governments towards Anglophone Quebeckers, and was considerably less stringent in practice.

And, although it is now unpopular to say so in Quebec, the traditional Anglophone position was obviously accepted by French Canadians, at least to the extent that their leaders felt themselves able to make public statements on the subject that would be utterly unimaginable today. "I am an Englishman who speaks French," Sir George-Etienne Cartier, Quebec co-founder with Sir John A. Macdonald of the Conservative alliance that achieved Confederation and ruled Canada for a generation, was in the habit of saying in the 1850s. "I am British to the core," Liberal Prime Minister Sir Wilfrid Laurier told a banquet organized for him by the Lord Mayor of London during his visit to Britain for the Diamond Jubilee of Queen Victoria in 1897. Even if these professions were totally hypocritical – and Laurier did systematically obstruct the late-Victorian enthusiasm for a more formal union of the British Empire – they would still reveal something about the tenor of debate in Canada, and what French Canadians were then prepared to tolerate. In fact, however, they reflected a precise and quite unservile conception of the duties and rights of a French Canadian as a British subject. As Laurier said in the House of Commons in 1918:

> I am a Canadian first, last and all the time. I am a British subject by birth, by tradition, by conviction – by the conviction that under British institutions my native land has found a measure of security and freedom it could not have found under any other regime. I want to speak from that double standpoint, for our policy is an expression of that double opinion.

But it takes nerve to look a minority member in the eye and tell him that at a given point his language and his community must yield to the official language and the national community. And yet it must be done constantly, because the natural pressures inherent in such a relationship will rapidly destabilize it unless the majority can continue to set the moral agenda. Sometime this century, English Canada lost its nerve.

Perhaps this was not surprising. Even American politicians have since World War II begun to compromise the traditional U.S. policy of assimilation, and have permitted Hispanic immigrants to vote without speaking English, and allowed a measure of bilingualism in the public schools, although the politics of some Hispanic groups are clearly revanchist. In Canada, where French was already more institutionalized, the Anglophone leaders were correspondingly much more susceptible. Although John Diefenbaker led a bitter-end resistance in the late 1960s to the legislation that formally established the principle that Canada was a bilingual state, his own Progressive Conservative government (1957-63) had been positively anxious to curry a little favor in Quebec through apparently harmless concessions. Diefenbaker began the simultaneous translation of parliamentary debates in 1958, and the printing of bilingual welfare checks in 1962. He remained proud of these feats, somewhat inconsistently, to the end of his life.

As the Anglophones retreated, the Francophones advanced. But their movement was not simply opportunistic. They were also impelled by the seismic upheaval in Quebec society that led to the so-called Quiet Revolution in the 1960s. The effect on federal politics was in fact only one of the consequences of *La Révolution Tranquille*. This development is discussed more fully in chapters ten and eleven, but it basically involved the sudden and dramatic end of the conservative, rural, deeply Catholic Quebec which had been a seemingly immutable feature of the Canadian landscape for two hundred years.

The Francophone Liberals' position in Quebec was never as secure as outsiders assumed. As a group, they have been unmistakeably under great nervous stress. This was most obvious on the provincial level. Historically, according to a study done by Conrad Black and Peter White in 1971, the provincial Liberals in Quebec could rely on much of the 20% of the total Quebec electorate who were non-French, but they could never be sure of more than a bilingual reformist minority among French voters – amounting perhaps to another 20%, or one French vote in four. Another 20% was said to be "nationalist" and 20% "Conservative" (in a general sense, that is, since the provincial Tory party merged with the Union Nationale in 1935). Finally, about 20% of the electorate was "floating." Federally, of course, all these factions usually came together and Quebec presented a united front. If the wind was in the right direction, however, this could easily disintegrate – as happened in 1958 and again in 1984.

Contrary to advertisement, the reforms the Francophone federalists talked English Canada into in the late 1960s did not prevent the election of a separatist government in Quebec. Although the PQ lost its 1980 referendum, the proportion of Francophones voting in favor was so close to half, despite everything Ottawa could do, that there were some claims that the proposition had in fact won a bare majority – and hence a moral victory – among them. In 1981 the PQ, in winning re-election, decisively increased its share of the French vote to 57%, up from 47% in the previous provincial election. Even in 1985, after bitter internal dissension, it received about half the Francophone vote.

Francophone Liberals had been able to dismiss earlier Francophone nationalists as primitive rustic chauvinists, in the grip of a priesthood that the Liberals regarded with the subtle skepticism that only sophisticated Catholics can fully achieve. And indeed important nationalist theorists often were priests, like Abbé Lionel Groulx (1878-1967). But this new separatism was especially powerful among students and Quebec's progressive intelligentsia, the very groups upon which the Liberals have normally depended, and it professed socialism, the opium of the intellectuals to which the Liberals themselves were attracted. In the small pressure cooker of French Quebec, this kept the Francophone federalists and their children under a continuous and debilitating social stress. In the late 1970s Marc Lalonde was heard to complain that English Canadians seemed unaware of the abuse he and his fellow French Canadian federalists had endured from their separatist peers, who considered them sellouts to a party controlled by Anglophones.

English Canadians, to be fair, were not regularly informed of the specifically Francophone nature of the Trudeau takeover, any more than they were encouraged to think about the implications of bilingualism. The Liberals habitually ran completely separate federal election campaigns in French and English Canada. According to McCall-Newman, in 1974 the Quebec Liberals took from the national campaign only the party's Maple Leaf logo ("a logo that said implicitly the flag is Liberal, the country is Liberal, we're the government Party") and a worker was reprimanded for booking a Francophone cabinet minister to speak in an Ontario riding. This proved quite effective in convincing each community that the party was at heart its very own.

But the high cost to the Francophone federalists of the resulting isolation, discipline and institutionalized deception was perhaps the characteristic that they had most in common with their fellow conniving minority, the Anglophone Liberal left. Explaining the Trudeau government's extraordinarily forceful reaction to the kidnapping crisis in 1970, when a form of martial law was invoked to deal with what turned out to be a handful of separatist terrorists, the then-Minister of Industry, Trade and Commerce, Jean-Luc Pepin, said:

> I cannot swear it, but I think we were thinking about ourselves. We ourselves were a very small group, Trudeau, Pelletier, Marchand, Lalonde, Chrétien, myself and a few people in the civil service, say, fifty all told .... And we were bringing off a revolution. We held the key posts [in Ottawa]. We were making the civil service, kicking and screaming all the time, bilingual. We were a well-organized group of revolutionaries, just like them, but working in a different way, of course.

Of course.

Diefenbaker's slim victory in 1957 was the Tories' first experience in office for twenty-two years, and a good example of the Canadian elite's propensity for losing touch with its workers and peasants. Diefenbaker, a Western populist, had won the leadership of his party over prolonged protest from its regular management in Central Canada. He had been completely discounted by the Liberal Establishment and by informed opinion in Canada at large. Bruce Hutchison and other prominent Liberal-linked journalists had reportedly even offered odds after the leadership convention that chose Diefenbaker that the next election would reduce the Tories to sixteen seats. For U.S. Embassy officials in Ottawa, none of whom came remotely close to forecasting the election result, "it was like a bunch of guys from Mars had taken over," according to the veteran Ottawa correspondent of the Chicago *Tribune* to whom they turned in desperation for information on Canada's new rulers. The following year, Diefenbaker did it again. He called a general election in which he eradicated the Liberals from the Prairies, apparently for good, won an astonishing 50 of Quebec's 75 seats, and piled up an overall total of 208 seats to the Liberals' 49, the greatest sweep in Canadian political history.

Diefenbaker's election constituted the beginning of the Liberals' first major crisis in the modern era. Despite his peculiar flaws, by the mid-1960s they had been unable to re-establish themselves in power in Ottawa with more than a minority government, basically because of his appeal to Anglophones. Simultaneously, there was further trouble on the Quebec front: a rejuvenated Union Nationale had defeated the provincial Liberal government in 1966, and Quebec nationalism was on the move again in its new and improved separatist and socialist form, affecting the very progressive Francophones upon whom the Liberals had traditionally depended.

Things looked black for the Liberal Party. Canada, however, was not to be deprived of its services just yet. For the Liberals responded to their converging troubles with a master stroke so brilliant that for much of the next two decades their position would appear again impregnable, and Canadian conventional wisdom would once again hold that they were the country's invincible, imperturbable party of government.

They invented Pierre Trudeau.

5

Trudeauism: The Highest Form of Liberalism

His political fate will likely be the political fate of Canada.

– Kenneth McNaught, 1966

The principate of Pierre Elliott Trudeau extended over nearly sixteen years, disturbed only by a few months of Tory minority government. These were eventful years for Canada, and in retrospect will almost certainly prove to have been decisive ones, although their full significance is only beginning to be recognized.

Pierre Trudeau was too much of a professional politician to be described as a good man, nor, it can be argued despite much publicity to the contrary, was he a particularly clever or even wise one. But he was a great man, perhaps the very greatest that Canada has produced in this century. Twice, during the FLQ crisis in 1970 and again after the Parti Québécois election victory in 1976, he held the country together by the sheer strength of his personality. By the time he left office in 1984, Canada's Confederation to a very considerable extent could best be analyzed in terms of his peculiar predilections.

The irony was that Trudeau's greatness was quite different from that predicted by his early admirers. It did not adorn the Canadian state as they expected, but instead exposed its deficiencies. When he resigned there was another bilingual, bicultural Quebecker ensconced opposite him in the House of Commons as leader of the Progressive Conservative Party, and this development has been urged by Trudeau's admirers as evidence of his success in transforming even the darkest corners of Canada. But in fact it was an indication of the extent to which he had distorted Canadian politics to answer the Quebec question. Not even he could do so indefinitely; imitators like Brian Mulroney will find the answer correspondingly more difficult to give.

61

In 1968, as the time approached for Justice Minister Trudeau to be the anointed leader of the federal Liberal Party, hysteria overcame Canada's incestuous media elite. Peter C. Newman, in the nationalist *Toronto Star*, ventured the following assessment:

> His intelligent, skull-formed face (which might have been carved in alabaster to commemorate some distant war of the crusades) is a pattern of tension, subtlety, unrest and audacity. He is a man who both in his physical presence and intellectual discourse manages to maintain a detached view of his environment, yet at the same time give an impression of being responsive to the play of political forces around him. Unlike the unreconstructed political dinosaurs of the Liberal Party who still occupy most of its positions of power, Trudeau is an agent of ferment, a critic of Canadian society, questioning its collected conventional wisdom. He mistrusts rhetoric, has only disdain for pomposity, and longs for contemporary fulfillment through experience.

But there was always an element of conscious myth-making in the Canadian media's coverage of Trudeau. The truth was that the "unreconstructed political dinosaur" who actually led the Liberals, Lester Pearson, clearly approved of his candidacy, as did the dinosaur heading the powerful Liberal left, Walter Gordon. Pearson's reign had not enhanced his reputation with ordinary party members, and he was unable to announce his choice as successor quite as baldly as King and St. Laurent had done before him. But it was obvious that he was systematically building up Trudeau, by bringing him into federal politics in 1965, by making him his own parliamentary secretary in 1966 and then justice minister in 1967, by orchestrating constitutional, legislative and party happenings to ensure his prominence, and finally by resigning in 1968 at the moment best calculated to benefit him and inconvenience his rivals. At various times afterwards, Pearson admitted his role, and the other candidates had no doubt they were up against what one of them, the young John Turner, denounced as "the Liberal Establishment" and its "backstage deals."

It just goes to show what a 1960s phenomenon Trudeau was. It was a deceptive decade, in which what was overtly a children's crusade of dissent and rebellion on the campuses was in fact aided immeasurably by the sympathetic reception it received from adult authorities – university administrators, press and politicians who covertly assented to its criticisms of society and the Vietnam War.

Nevertheless, Trudeau himself had real personal and political assets that were invaluable in the Canadian context. To begin with, he was an almost surreal specimen of the future *Homo Canadiensis,* what Christina McCall-Newman called "a racial hermaphrodite, the unmatchable bicultural man," the ideal to which sufficient eons of evolution and Liberal government would presumably refine the lumpen Canadian masses. He was a rich, bilingual Francophone intellectual, a part-time law professor and writer educated at the Université de Montréal, Harvard, the London School of Economics and the Sorbonne, whose middle name proclaimed for all to see the Scottish and United Empire Loyalist heritage of his mother. It was left to later observers to realize, when Trudeau's insensitivity to English Canada could no longer be denied, that Grace Elliott's family was among those unusual Quebec Anglophones who had assimilated into Francophone society, and that she herself, a devout Catholic, was essentially French.

Additionally, as a member of Montreal's progressive intelligentsia Trudeau had long-established links with the Canadian socialist movement. He had campaigned for the CCF; had founded with others in 1950 a seminal magazine (linked with the left-wing Catholic review *Esprit* in Paris), called *Cité Libre* in telling contradistinction to the perceived rural idiocy of Quebec politics; and edited a book, published with the financial support of leading Anglophone socialists, celebrating the 1949 strike at Johns-Manville Company's mine in Asbestos, Quebec, a strike that had become a rallying point for Trudeau and a generation of Canadian radicals. This did him no harm at all with the influential Anglophone Liberal left.

Throughout Trudeau's political career, there were rumors that his links had extended much further to the left. These were almost certainly fed by leaks from dissident members of the RCMP Security Service. Among their numerous complaints was the frustration of their long-running investigation of possible security risks among the Canadian elite. By the late 1960s, according to John Sawatsky in his *For Services Rendered,* the RCMP apparently felt it had identified 262 suspected security risks in key positions in Canada – the celebrated "Featherbed File."

Trudeau's early activities must have attracted the RCMP's attention. He had spent a considerable amount of time in the Soviet bloc in his professional student mode after World War II, and he admitted during his leadership campaign in 1968 that Communist organizations had financed his travels there. He also said he believed he had been "blacklisted" by the U.S. immigration authorities in the 1950s for being interested in what he called "progressive things." At the height of the Cold War in 1952, when he was thirty-two and had already held a significant post in Ottawa, Trudeau attended an economic conference in Moscow arranged by the Soviet Union as part of a campaign to undermine the U.S. strategic embargo. The Canadian delegation was otherwise made up of Communists. This provoked a spectacular controversy in the French press in Quebec, where he was fiercely attacked by Catholic anti-Communists.

Nevertheless, regardless of what the RCMP thought about the question of security, by 1968 the Anglophone press was too impressed with the dangers of McCarthyism to touch the issue. So universal was this anti-anti-Communism that even the former Moscow correspondent of the conservative Toronto *Telegram*, Peter Worthington, found his paper refusing to publish a discussion of Trudeau's early career. In 1978, George Radwanski in his semi-authorized biography, *Trudeau*, based on exclusive interviews granted as part of the Liberals' preparation for the looming election, was able to slip over the Moscow conference in a bland phrase. In the same year David Somerville's *Trudeau Revealed*, an excellent discussion of Trudeau's left-wing background using Quebec sources, received almost no reviews in Canada's Establishment media, although nonetheless quietly selling some 27,000 copies.

The full history of the direct and indirect influence of Communism upon the bourgeois elites of the twentieth century will probably have to wait for some scholar of the twenty-first. The intense emotions aroused by the topic have deprived contemporary debate of language sophisticated enough to make the necessary distinctions. Anything short of cloaked conspirators meeting at midnight under Ottawa's Peace Tower is simply too subtle to be discussed.

Unsullied by his left-wing associations, Trudeau was able to exploit his ethnic androgyny to the full in the 1968 general election, which he called directly after becoming Liberal leader despite promises to the contrary. As a Francophone, he could speak directly to the Québécois. His answer to their militancy was that room would be made for them to participate more actively in Canadian Confederation. Besides soothing nationalist pride, this implied obvious direct personal benefits for Francophones in terms of jobs and influence – an important consideration in a political culture reduced by bosses like Duplessis to a condition Trudeau himself once succinctly described as "profound immorality."

But in a significant twist, Trudeau was also able to appeal to militant Anglophones. He told them that he was against all compromise with the separatists and any special status for Quebec. Everyone should be treated equally everywhere. This sounded just fine to Westerners, who were even then tired of Quebec's complaints and thought the province should be "put in its place." The Tories, who were toying with a *deux nations* policy that would have conceded Quebec to the Francophones as a sort of reservation within Confederation, found themselves outflanked both on the left and the right. On June 25, 1968, the Liberals won their biggest victory in fifteen years, restoring their position in Quebec and Ontario and even invading the West.

What Trudeau actually meant by equality between two groups of such dissimilar size, of course, would only emerge later.

Appropriately for a man educated in the rationalistic tradition of France as opposed to the almost mindless Anglo-Saxon empiricism native to the majority of the people he was to govern, Trudeau's basic policies can be described as "the four isms": bilingualism, socialism, centralism and nationalism.

Bilingualism was not Trudeau's invention – the Royal Commission on Bilingualism and Biculturalism had published an elaborate rationale for it in 1965 and 1967 – but under him it was to be imposed with a doctrinaire attention to detail that no Anglophone prime minister would have mustered. Bilingualism was the child of his heart, the product of his formative experiences as a Québécois, and all other policies were subordinated to it. Because very few Anglophones can speak French and Canada is not remotely a bicultural society, most commentators treat bilingualism as a harmless decorative detail and have given little thought to its implications. For example, only two references are noted in the index of *The Canadians,* the 1985 bestseller by *New York Times'* correspondent Andrew H. Malcolm: that the Federal government is "officially bilingual," and that both national anthems are sung at baseball games. In fact, however, bilingualism is central to the functioning of the modern Canadian polity. It merits separate discussion in the next chapter.

The Canada Trudeau inherited had a fairly free-market economy, and confederal institutions that were all bent out of shape, partly by Anglophone sectionalism but mostly by the need to accommodate a mutinous Quebec. Trudeau's actions in both these areas were usually fairly cautious. As he had written in his pre-Liberal incarnation, in an anthology of socialist essays edited by a future NDP president, "in terms of political tactics, the only real question democratic socialists must answer is: how much reform can the majority of the people be brought to desire at the present time?" Additionally, bilingualism came first. But at various moments he let his true feelings show – as in the celebrated year-end CTV interview in 1975, when he caused a national furor by casually remarking that wage and price controls had been introduced because "we haven't been able to make it work, the free-market system" and that what was needed was a "New Society" in which the government would "take a larger role in running institutions." Even before his 1980 re-election and the subsequent energy policy and constitutional initiatives, the statist and centralizing instincts Trudeau shared with his socialist former colleagues were unmistakeable.

The fourth "ism" is Nationalism. This, of course, refers specifically to the protectionist and frequently anti-American movement that was already developing in English Canada when Trudeau entered federal politics. His attitude to it was complicated by his divergent intellectual and cultural background, and his other priorities. Basically, however, the Liberals under Trudeau gave the Nationalist movement what it wanted. And, particularly since 1980, they gradually assumed its leadership, attempting thereby to co-opt sorely needed Anglophone support.

Naturally, it would be comforting to think that Trudeau's policy prescription was the product of a superior intellect, just as it would be nice to believe that Confederation was designed on some more lasting principle than expediency. Assessing the quality of any politician's mind is much more difficult than is often realized by those unfamiliar with the political species and its treacherous natural habitat. But where Pierre Trudeau was concerned, nothing excited Canada's pundits to more confident superlatives. George Radwanski: "Trudeau has an intellect unrivalled among Canadian politicians and quite possibly among his foreign counterparts as well. . . ." Christina McCall-Newman: ". . . Trudeau's intellect was unmatchable in Canadian politics, an instrument as sharp and pitiless as a sword . . ." Richard Gwyn: "In sheer power and range, Trudeau's mind is the finest of all our Prime Ministers . . . by his mind alone, Trudeau dominates almost everyone who meets him."

This belief was crucial to Trudeau's public reputation. Even Canadians who were otherwise quite resistant to Establishment media opinion generally accepted what they were told to think on the subject. They often prefaced criticisms of their controversial prime minister with some version of "he's brilliant, of course, but . . . ." A corollary was George Radwanski's assertion that the election of Trudeau "was, in a limited sense, an experiment with the Platonic concept of a philosopher-king, a leader chosen exclusively for the quality of his thought."

In reality, there was surprisingly little evidence to support this enthusiasm. Trudeau was highly articulate, an inveterate dropper of intellectual names and maker of literary allusions. During the 1980 election campaign, he engaged in a running "poetry war" with reporters in his entourage, identifying stanzas they quoted from memory. But as wordsmiths, journalists are professionally inclined to over-value verbal facility, and to confuse the intelligentsia with the intelligent.

Canadian journalists historically have had a greater tendency than their U.S. counterparts to abase themselves before cliques in the governing party. This can be attributed to cabin fever induced by Ottawa's subarctic wastes, but, more practically, it reflects the fact that Canada is a small society pervaded by government activity and has been for many years effectively a one-party state. Paths cross frequently. Back-scratching is better for your health than treading on toes. Such circumstances guarantee that Canada's "collected conventional wisdom" remains distinctly unquestioned, let alone fermented.

Trudeau was usually portrayed as a born scholar, but there was even some dispute over this. His sister reported that he hated his law courses at the Université de Montréal, and at least one observer at Harvard felt that he was there to enjoy himself; no degree seems to have resulted from his time in London and Paris. The one indisputable consequence of Trudeau's college career is that it served to insulate him even more than most Quebeckers from English Canada's formative World War II experience, which began when war was declared on Germany in 1939. By entering law school in 1940, Trudeau was able to claim student exemption from regular military service. His two-year M.A. course at Harvard began in 1944, while the Liberals were finally being forced to send conscripts overseas.

In his subtly self-promoting way, Trudeau himself once implied that his much-admired political and economic studies were not altogether serious: "I have probably read more of Dostoevsky, Stendhal and Tolstoy than the average statesman, and less of Keynes, Mill and Marx." This was a particularly interesting admission for one who was hired, presumably on the basis of his education, as a "junior economist" on the staff of Canada's Privy Council office in 1949.

A little learning may be a dangerous thing, but in Canada it can also be an effective thing, at least for Pierre Trudeau. A significant episode occurred in 1976. The country was still reverberating from the imposition of wage and price controls and Trudeau's subsequent musings about capitalism's failures and the need for "new societies." But in the course of an irritable interview with *Fortune* magazine's Herb Meyer, Trudeau denounced the prevalent view that he had become a disciple of John Kenneth Galbraith, who was born in Canada and whose abiding faith in the efficacy of state intervention in the modern economy has always found an audience in his native land. He was actually much more influenced, said Trudeau, by Wassily Leontief and by Joseph Schumpeter, under whom he had studied at Harvard.

Who they? editors scrawled on reporters' accounts of the incident in newsrooms all over Canada. Nobody had much idea, but Trudeau's reputation as an intellectual was reinforced, and it was generally agreed that he could not be crudely classified as a socialist, as the business community had been insisting, and his aides denying, since his CTV interview. At this distance, however, it is fairly obvious that Trudeau knew little more than the media did. Otherwise he would hardly have taken the risk of someone discovering that Leontief was at least as much of an interventionist as Galbraith, and that Schumpeter had prophesied the rise of the socialistic New Class in terms so applicable to Canada as to be embarrassing. Trudeau's motive appears to have been no more complicated than sheer snobbery, since he realized many academic economists dismiss Galbraith as a popularizer.

The truth was that Trudeau was basically ignorant about economics. He seemed to like it that way. As late as 1979, he was still giving interviewers the essentially superstitious line that inflation was all caused by Canadians' greed, although for over three years the Bank of Canada had been paying public homage to the monetarist contention that inflation was the product of government mismanagement of the money supply.

Actually, Galbraith's ideas had indeed been the subject of one of the periodic fads that marked Trudeau's public career. He had read Galbraith's *Economics and the Public Purpose* while vacationing in Jamaica, the year before the CTV interview, and his interest in Galbraith was aided and abetted by his Privy Council Office economics advisor, Ian Stewart, later to emerge as a key civil servant in the implementation of the highly statist National Energy Program. These intellectual fads blurred Trudeau's ideological profile. In 1978, he was even briefly converted to the cause of cutting government expenditure by a talk during the Bonn Summit with West German Chancellor Helmut Schmidt, and on his return announced a program of reductions without consulting Finance Minister Jean Chrétien. But they do not suggest much of what Radwanski calls a "philosophical framework," or a particularly discriminating mind. Another such fad was "participation" in government, which was internationally in vogue around the time Trudeau became leader. Unfortunately, it turned out that those participating often wanted policies, such as capital punishment, that Trudeau opposed. Accordingly he evolved a distinction between "participation" (you) and "decision-making" (him) that, as he rightly observed in 1970, "isn't always understood."

But it should be noted that in a sense Trudeau really did believe in participation. The distinction he was to draw later apparently just hadn't occurred to him before. When he first became party leader he spent some considerable time perplexing the simple pols in the Liberal machine by attempting to use it to mobilize and consensus-build among the great Canadian public, which of course had other plans for its weekends. His attempt at a perpetual heart-to-heart with Canada was naive, impractical and ultimately foolish.

And this seems to be true of Trudeau-think in general. Like his much-vaunted administrative reforms with their endless proliferating committees, it bore the fatal mark of academia – and of the intellectual dilettante. According to Richard Gwyn, for example, at the height of the uproar of bureaucratic planning and studying in Ottawa that followed Trudeau's 1968 election victory and that echoed similar enthusiasms in Lyndon Johnson's Washington and Harold Wilson's Whitehall, Trudeau kept rejecting drafts of External Affairs' foreign policy review as "unscientific," and

> an inspired departmental officer sat down with a bottle of scotch, the entire back file of *Cité Libre* and several texts on scientific management and redrafted the report to cast its main recommendations in the form of a hexagon and then stuffed into the text, like raisins in a rice pudding, every buzzword he could think of, from "conceptual framework" to "coherent" and "co-ordinated." Approved instantly, the review was published as a set of multi-colored booklets in a nifty-looking box. Critics promptly pointed out that it said nothing at all about the only aspect of foreign relations that really mattered: U.S.-Canadian relations. Trudeau explained that this subject was still being studied.

Pierre Trudeau's 1971 marriage to Margaret Sinclair, when she was twenty-two and he was fifty-one, perhaps reveals most of all about his intellect. Margaret was then in her flower-child phase, similar to but less expensive than her later Warhol/Halston/Studio 54 phase, and Trudeau bought the whole thing. "She convinced the country's best critical mind to take seriously what a close friend of Margaret describes as 'her revolution bullshit,' " reported Richard Gwyn, manfully reconciling the irreconcilable. "Insatiably curious intellectually, and quite without a sense of the ridiculous, Trudeau questioned her intently and intensely about troubled youth, Consciousness Three, peace, love, freedom, identity, organic baking, and everything else in the Whole Earth Catalogue." She even convinced him that the entire cabinet should take up transcendental meditation. Marriages do not occur entirely by accident. Perhaps part of the explanation for this improbable, doomed alliance was that like was calling to like. Beneath the trappings of education and temperament, both partners may have had unexpectedly similar minds – fashionable, conventional and banal.

Trudeau was probably the most prominent example internationally of what might be called the Sow's Ear syndrome – as in, "you can't make a silk purse out of a." Except that with human beings, you can get at least polyester. Expensive education and social advantage can be substituted for native intellectual power with sufficient results as to satisfy all but the most demanding. Or as one Trudeau-watcher quoted by Gwyn concluded: "A sharp mind but not a deep one. He has trained it as he has trained his body, he stretches it to the limit."

When considering Trudeau's radical prescription for Canada, two other aspects of his way of thinking should also be noted. First, he operated from a base of preconceptions that he would not readily give up. Some were a matter of heritage. Margaret, who by her own account seems to have hooked and reeled in this most confirmed of bachelors with supreme skill, judged it a necessary step to convert to Roman Catholicism before her marriage, although her conversion was no longer required by the church. It wasn't practically necessary or politically wise since obviously neither of them was leading a life of faith, and it could hardly delight English Canadian Protestants. But more important were the preconceptions dating from his membership in Montreal's left-wing Francophone intelligentsia in the late 1940s and early 1950s: the parochial obsession with the language issue, the skepticism about the Cold War, the determination that Mao's China be recognized, the romantic sympathy for Russia, the inclination to the literary and legal rather than the technical and commercial. These remained the best guide to Trudeau's likely responses in any given situation, from his disruptive last-minute insistence that Taiwan be excluded from the 1976 Montreal Olympics to his exculpatory comments about the 1981 imposition of martial law in Poland and the 1983 shooting-down of the jetliner KAL 007. Events that did not fit into this framework did not engage his attention. "Where's Biafra?" he quipped when asked about the Nigerian blockade of the Ibo secessionists (although of course in this case the Soviet Union was supporting the Nigerian side).

The second conclusion must be that Trudeau was never greatly impressed by facts, as opposed to theory, or dogma. He travelled all round the world in his youth, yet "does not recognize differences either of color, or of race, or of culture ... No one who knows Trudeau can recall him ever indulging in even the mildest of cultural stereotyping. ...." Richard Gwyn felt this was evidence of an open mind, but it might equally suggest a closed, even inert or empty one. Of course, for men of the left like Trudeau, issues of race and nationality have always been unfathomable atavisms. Unfortunately, he was to become prime minister of a country whose politics were essentially those of cultural difference.

Canada today cannot be understood without reference to these charcteristics of Pierre Trudeau. They explain the equanimity with which he was able to view the chaos caused by policies, like the National Energy Program, of whose rationale he had become convinced. And they explain the stark fact that, notwithstanding the approval of "the country's best critical mind," and the mobilization of every major political party, an entire national elite and all the King's (or Governor-General's) horses and men/women, the bilingual solution that is being applied to the fundamental problem of Canada's divergent "founding nations" is absurd on its face. Trudeau's prescription for Canada amply confirmed the acuity of the famous question Sweden's Count Oxenstierna is supposed to have asked his son: "Do you not know with how little wisdom the world is governed?"

Heart rather than head was the secret of Trudeau's political greatness, even though when first in political life he talked endlessly about "rationality" and hung prominently in the stairwell of the Prime Minister's official residence at 24 Sussex Drive in Ottawa a quilt embroidered with his self-deluding personal motto: *La Raison avant La Passion*. In the 1970 FLQ kidnapping crisis, he provided the authoritarian leadership the panicking country craved, refusing all concessions, declaring martial law and telling a CBC-TV interviewer, in words no American president would have dared utter in public, that "there are a lot of bleeding hearts around who just don't like to see men with helmets and guns. All I can say is, go on and bleed. ...." In 1976, after the Parti Québécois was elected in Quebec, Trudeau's performance was in many ways even more remarkable. The Canadian elite was stunned by the bilingualism strategy's utter failure to appease separatism. Trudeau unwaveringly ignored the inconvenient development, and in the course of time everyone else has come to ignore it too.

Simultaneously, Trudeau by sheer force of character succeeded in arresting the normal metabolism of the federal Liberal Party. As early as 1975, many Liberals assumed that he would be prepared to step down so that the leadership could be rotated to the other "founding race" and the party could perform its decennial self-renewing ritual in time for the next election. But he declined, precipitating the resignation of John Turner, then Finance Minister and heir apparent, although Turner as a cautious *apparatchik* did not reveal his bitterness publicly. "Bruce Hutchison, the newspaperman, protegé of John Dafoe, biographer of Mackenzie King, and the old Liberalism's most lyrical voice, told Turner that by this act Trudeau showed he didn't understand the Canadian duality," wrote Christina McCall-Newman. "The truth was of course, that Trudeau understood the nature of the duality very well and had set out to alter it radically ten years before."

Trudeau proved equally resistant to party pressure after the fading of Anglophone Canada's reflexive national-unity spasm that boosted his popularity in the wake of the Parti Québécois' 1976 victory, and again in the early 1980s after the National Energy Program and the constitutional struggle. Many observers, including Brian Mulroney, began to suspect that he might even fight his sixth election as Liberal leader. But in the end he did resign, although too late for the Liberals' normal rejuvenation processes to work.

The visceral origins of Trudeau's effectiveness as a public figure can be traced to the nature of his personality. A small man who needed a lot of sleep, when awake he seemed to be compulsively athletic, a great skier, canoer and dancer at official receptions. A similar restlessness apparently pervaded his much-discussed but certainly active social life as a bachelor and single parent. He brought this intensity to debate, intimidating challengers by the ferocity of his response. A favorite Trudeau technique of handling interviewers – interrupting to ask questions that many never recovered from answering – probably owed at least as much to sheer aggressiveness as to the Jesuit education that usually got the blame.

This vehemence was combined with a romantic and drama-loving streak. Normally impassive, Trudeau cried at funerals; a notorious miser, he dressed with a flamboyance verging on narcissism. And it sometimes found expression in a physical courage which was clearly spontaneous. The nationally televised image of Trudeau facing down a bottle-throwing separatist mob at the 1968 St. Jean Baptiste Day parade in Montreal while the rest of the platform party fled was the crowning touch to that year's election campaign. But no such considerations required him to flout safety regulations on a prime ministerial helicopter flight over water (on return from a visit to the islands of St. Pierre and Miquelon when the back-up machine was grounded), or to offer to kill a threatening peasant in a bar in Nova Scotia during the Clark interregnum in 1979 when he was sixty years old. (The peasant retreated.) A similar fearlessness marked his public career, and in an era of especially pusillanimous politicians – intimidated in part by shibboleths created by Trudeau himself – added greatly to his allure. No one else would have replied, when asked by Francophone reporters what he would tell critics who complained that both his official constitutional advisors were Anglophones, "I would tell them *merde*." Few would have reacted with his coolness in the midst of the Watergate pandemonium when transcripts revealed that Richard Nixon habitually referred to him as an "asshole." ("I've been called worse things by worse men.") "The troops will need nerves of steel," he told Liberal officials as they entered the gruelling period of trench warfare before the 1979 election. "He means nerves like his," one of them remarked afterwards.

So much of what has been written on Trudeau slips into bathos because of this emotive dimension that is difficult to define. There was a somber drama about this slight, solitary figure, aloof even from his cabinet colleagues, living alone with his children like an aging king in Frazer's *The Golden Bough*, prowling his Sacred Grove sword in hand, defying his challengers to show themselves and refusing to be sacrificed to appease the Fates, whether political or personal.

The practical consequence of this dimension, however, is a truism that is worth examining. Trudeau was a genuinely charismatic leader. When he was popular, he bound Canada together. When unpopular, he was a convenient scapegoat for problems that are actually fundamental to the Canadian Confederation. Thus, for example, many Canadian Liberals sincerely believed their failure on the Prairies could be blamed on Trudeau clunkers, such as when he asked worried farmers in Winnipeg in 1969 why he should sell their wheat for them, or when he dismissed the Western swing to the Tories in the general election of 1972 as evidence of anti-French "bigotry." In reality, however, Canada's size, heterogeneity and internal contradictions make the reconciliation of all sections almost impossible. The country is rather like one of the artificial new states of Africa, occupying territory arbitrarily carved out by the colonial powers, where a cult of the ruler's personality can play a vital unifying role. But a leader who lacks Trudeau's unusual background, temperament and personal gifts will be that much less able to distract attention from the irrepressible conflict within Confederation.

This conclusion is one that the observer of Canada must approach with care. It may appear to echo too closely Goldwin Smith's comment on Sir John A. Macdonald:

> When this man is gone who will take his place? Who else could make Orangemen vote for Papists, or induce half the members of Ontario to help in levying on their own province the necessary blackmail for Quebec? Yet this is the work which will have to be done if a general breakup is to be avoided. Things will not hold together on their own.

But Smith was right at least as far as the Tories were concerned: for them, Macdonald was irreplaceable, and most of their few subsequent moments in power were under leaders who basically (if unwillingly and by default, in the case of Joe Clark) followed the very different strategy of attempting to weld English Canada into a governing majority, rather than to find allies in Quebec.

The federal Liberal party was the first to experience the difficulty of life after Trudeau. In their long years of power, the Liberals succeeded in organizing Canada's Confederation so that they were its natural government. Their entrenchment of bilingualism and their institutionalization of the appeasement of Quebec put a premium on their monopoly of Francophone support. Their various schemes of economic intervention had developed vocal client constituencies in the electorate, and adopting the mantle of Canadian Nationalism made these incursions politically difficult to disentangle, as the Tories discovered during the brief government of Joe Clark when they attempted to implement their campaign promise and dissolve state-owned Petro-Canada.

But it would be equally true to say that Pierre Trudeau had succeeded in organizing the Liberal Party so that its natural leader was himself – or someone so like him as to be his clone. Quebec was more than ever essential to the Liberal federal electoral strategy. However, the loyalty of Francophone voters to the party was always significantly diminished by the presence of an Anglophone leader – the last mass desertion had occurred during Lester Pearson's tenure – and now the Liberals faced challenges not only from Brian Mulroney, who could pass as a Francophone in a pinch, but also from the Parti Québécois, which had vowed to make its influence felt in the federal election.

Under these circumstances, the logical choice to succeed Trudeau would have been Finance Minister Jean Chrétien. But here the Liberals made the mistake of believing their own propaganda: they felt obliged to honor the convention that the leadership had to alternate between the "founding races." Ironically, the Anglophone leader they chose, John Turner, had no appeal even to the one group in English Canada that was attracted to Trudeau's version of Liberalism: the Anglophone left. The Liberal Party workers were demoralized in the 1984 general election campaign, and the fortunes of the NDP revived dramatically.

This is not to say, of course, that the Liberals without Trudeau can never win a federal election – or, more accurately, that the Tories under Brian Mulroney cannot lose one. Somebody has to win, as Joe Clark proved. But it will be more difficult for the Liberals to rebuild a durable electoral coalition and re-establish themselves as the party of government. On the other hand, Mulroney is not attempting to create an entirely new electoral coalition, as Sir Wilfrid Laurier had done after Macdonald's death, but instead is trying to steal Trudeau's formula and govern Canada from a Quebec base in alliance with the Anglophone centre-left. And this, of course, is seriously impeded by the fact that he is not Trudeau and the Tories are not the Liberals. In the end, life without Trudeau will prove difficult not just for his party but for his country.

"All political lives, unless they are cut off in midstream at a happy juncture, end in failure," Enoch Powell has written, "because that is the nature of politics and human affairs." Pierre Trudeau gave his party a series of the most brilliant victories, most recently in circumstances so adverse that all but he had despaired; but in the last analysis they were pyrrhic. He was not able to stave off the Liberals' ultimate defeat, nor even to prevent the Liberal leadership from passing, against his express wishes, to John Turner, a break in the apostolic succession of Liberal leaders stretching back to Mackenzie King. He could not prevent a *deux nations* situation in Canada.

Trudeau sought to create a Canadian policy that required the frustration of elemental forces: nationalism in Francophone Canada, in an age when self-determination was triumphant everywhere in the world; the unilingual character of Anglophone Canada, when it was being drawn ever deeper into North America; the inexorably developing divergence between the two Canadian "founding races"; even the much-maligned forces of the free market itself, whose intransigence in the face of state action was once again being recognized in most capitals of the Western world (except Ottawa) by the early 1980s. His efforts were heroic and met with remarkable success. But a state that must be led by heroes is not secure, particularly when the forces working against it are, if anything, all the more formidable for their interlude of frustration.

When Professor McNaught equated Trudeau's political fate with that of Canada, he was expressing the general Establishment belief that all that was needed for Canada's survival was for the Anglophones to become sufficiently enlightened to choose such a splendid leader. Events have refuted that belief, and McNaught may prove to be correct in a very different sense than he expected.

6

Bilingualism: The Essence of Trudeauism

The best thing would be for the people to give up the French language (except as a cultural courtesy) . . . that they also give up English (except as a cultural courtesy); they would then practise telepathy.

– T. Lobsang Rampa, author of numerous books on "the third eye," and a Canadian immigrant

An apparently innocent waspishness is not the least of the charms of the two volumes of autobiography extracted from Margaret Trudeau (née Sinclair) by Caroline Moorehead, her English ghost writer. And Pierre Trudeau's Ottawa offers an irresistible target for satire:

> When the night of the dinner came around, I had made a special effort to look pretty. The first question that Wendy put to me was: "Do you speak French?" Pierre didn't give me a chance to reply. Unwittingly, for we had never discussed my languages, he said: "With a good old French name like 'St. Claire,' what do you expect?" *"Ah bon,"* said Wendy. And, despite the fact that both she and her husband were English-speaking, and that the other guests spoke it perfectly, the whole dinner was conducted in French. The terrible thing was that I didn't understand a word – I couldn't speak French at all. The moment at which I should have told them passed by. Then the laughter and the jokes were such that all I could decently do was plaster a grin on my own face and pretend to be following them. No one spoke to me. They were only interested in Pierre and in their own lives.
>
> At 10.30 Pierre had to go back to Parliament. Rudely brushing aside all offers of dessert I fled from the house after him, wailing at him in the car that I had never felt so insulted, so betrayed, in my life. Pierre looked helpless, but it was then that we made a firm

resolution: no more social experiments. Which was why, when we were married eighteen months later, the event came as such a total shock to the world.

The social intercourse of politicians and their courtiers is inevitably politic, if not always courteous. But an interesting additional subcurrent of cultural truckling is discernible in this mid-1969 dinner party put on for the Prime Minister by one of his closest personal staffers, Tim Porteous, who was later parachuted into the federal civil service where his wife, Wendy referred to in the quote above, had already become prominent. For Ottawa Anglophones, what they now obediently view as the arrogance of the Mackenzie King-St. Laurent era has been replaced by what is in fact obsequiousness, however high-minded the motives that inspire it.

Also significant is Pierre Trudeau's assumption that his Vancouver-bred mistress would be able to speak French. Despite her bubble-head image, Margaret was actually relatively highly educated – she was about to begin graduate work in psychology at the University of Ottawa when marriage intervened. Yet to expect that this meant that she would be bilingual was exactly as unrealistic as expecting it from her counterparts in Seattle or San Francisco. Languages are simply not central to the education of English-speaking North Americans, on either side of the border. Discovering this probably did not improve Trudeau's private opinion of them. Independent observers like Christina McCall-Newman and Richard Gwyn both noted that he continued to converse in French at dinner parties, despite his wife's incomprehension. "He despised me at heart," Margaret has said she concluded in 1974, "as an uncultured, unsophisticated Western Canadian."

Trudeau's firm resolution to abandon "social experiments" applied only to those affecting his personal convenience. He never intended to abandon the greatest social experiment of all: official bilingualism. In Ottawa's rarefied little world, the almost complete absence of Canadian demographic reality behind this policy is easy to forget. It stands precariously on a remarkably narrow social base among Canadians as a whole. Only 15.3%, about 3.7 million, reported to the 1981 census takers that they could "conduct a conversation" in both official languages. And this almost certainly exaggerates the number who are sufficiently bilingual to function professionally in either language, a much more difficult achievement than being able to order dinner and exchange a few good-will *bonjours*.

The practical effects of a generation of unanimous and overwhelming Establishment enthusiasm for bilingualism must be judged marginal at best. After basically being stable for many years, the proportion of Canadians claiming to speak both languages has indeed increased, but with painful slowness. As far back as 1931, it was 12.7%, sinking slightly to 12.2% in 1961 before rising in 1971 to 13.4%, or about 2.8 million. Moreover, interpreting statistics of this sort is notoriously tricky. For example, some demographers have hypothesized that the uptrend since 1961 is merely the result of Canada's falling birth-rate; the number of young children in the population has decreased, and children are less likely than adults to be bilingual.

It cannot even be said with confidence that an uptrend in the number of bilinguals will continue. Any increased propensity of Anglophones to learn French will probably be counterbalanced by the decreased need for Francophones to learn English in order to function in their Quebec stronghold, where provincial government policy discourages instruction in the subject. In fact, the proportion of Quebec students in second-language instruction actually fell between 1970 and 1985. Indeed, notwithstanding ceaseless moaning from both separatists and federalists about the plight of French, the proportion of unilingual Francophones in Canada's over-nineteen population rose from 11.6% in 1931 to 14.7% in 1981. One overall conclusion, however, is inescapable: Canadians are light-years from the fluency in each other's languages common to most other multilingual democracies. Even in such a troubled case as Belgium, where about 60% speak Flemish and 40% French, around half the population is bilingual. And there is no serious prospect of change in Canada in the foreseeable future.

This inadequate social base for official bilingualism is further weakened by the unequal distribution of Canadians claiming to be bilingual. Almost all of them are located in or near the province of Quebec. In 1981, 56.1% lived in Quebec itself, down slightly from 57.4% in 1971 and 63.7% in 1931. This small decline is probably due in part to the relative growth of the bilingual presence in the federal capital of Ottawa, just across Quebec's western border in Ontario, a province that in 1981 reported a further 25.1% of bilingual Canadians. New Brunswick, on Quebec's eastern flank, had 5%.

Moreover, substantially over half the bilingual group reported French as their mother-tongue: some 2.2 million in 1981, compared to 1.1 million who reported English. (The balance was mostly either immigrants or native peoples, and they are known in Ottawaspeak as "allophones.") That still meant that for every Francophone who could speak English, nearly two could speak only French. But for every bilingual Anglophone, there were nearly fifteen who could speak only English. None of them can aspire to the highest office in the land, according to the principle laid down by Establishment commentators at the time of the 1983 Tory leadership race: that any successful candidate must be fluent in French. They constitute an improbably large bloc, however, to be permanently reduced to the status of second-class citizens.

Unilingualism is not in any way surprising, perverse or unnatural. Outside of Quebec, most Canadians never hear a word of French spoken from one year's end to another, unless they accidentally tune in to the federally subsidized coast-to-coast French-language TV and radio network. In the vast area of Canada west of Ontario there are a mere 86,665 individuals using French in their homes, according to the 1981 census. And although it is less often noted, inside Quebec the situation is almost a mirror image. Many of the perhaps 70% of the Quebec population who are unilingual Francophones live outside of Montreal and have no contact with the Anglophone minority in that city. The latter in any case are concentrated in ghettos whose isolation has become a well-established Canadian cliché.

This Canadian bipolarity, which is growing sharper every year, is an even more devastating rejection of the bilingualism experiment than the obstinate non-materialization of significant quantities of bilingual Canadians. The numbers of Anglophones and Francophones respectively inside and outside of Quebec is diminishing, not merely in relative but in absolute terms. There were 890,000 Quebeckers who spoke English at home in 1971; in 1981, there were only 809,000. There were 675,000 Canadians outside of Quebec who spoke French at home in 1971; ten years later, there were only 666,000. Whatever their government may say about the efficacy of the policy in enabling the two communities to live together, the people of Canada have been quietly voting against it with their U-Haul trucks.

Numbers alone cannot convey the difficulties confronting official bilingualism in Canada. Pierre Trudeau dealt with another in characteristic fashion when he asserted in 1976, at a banquet given in honor of the Queen's visit that, "the French and English cultures are so influenced by each other, that there is really no discontinuity between them. They can be seen as a single entity." This statement is absolutely untrue. Even given the peculiar social ambience in which Trudeau moved, it can only be regarded as willful blindness to the stark reality. The division between French and English Canada is profound. Essentially, the two Canadian cultures do not interact at all.

They are indeed "two solitudes," in the famous phrase of the novelist Hugh MacLennan. The Francophones might appear North Americanized to a certain extent, if only by virtue of sharing the same flora, fauna, climate and automobiles as their neighbors. But the Anglophones in their day-to-day lives give no more indication of French influence than their kith and kin south of the border or across the Atlantic. Canada's two "founding races" do not read the same literature, endure the same journalism, see the same films, watch the same television, or share any of the experiences that would make them a common people.

This is what the American-born Toronto urbanologist Jane Jacobs meant when she observed in her brilliant 1980 Massey Lectures, later published as *The Question of Separatism: Quebec and the Struggle over Sovereignty,* that ". . . on some level of sheer feeling, not of reason, Quebec seems to me already separate and different from what I understand as my national community." And it is a gulf that Berlitz cannot bridge. Many of the English Canadians today who can speak French are no more bicultural, let alone necessarily sympathetic to or even interested in the aspirations of Quebec, than their unilingual compatriots. They have merely learned a foreign language. If they are thereby inclined to look to a foreign society, it is to that of Paris rather than to that of Montreal or Quebec City.

In this context should be viewed the curious Canadian fashion of the "total immersion" of Anglophone children in schools where they are taught entirely in French. The total immersion vogue is often cited by those Central Canadian pundits who wish to believe that the country has really, finally, accepted bilingualism, just as Trudeau had been proclaiming in his doctrinaire way all along. As is usually the case with Canadian language questions, this is an illusion based on ignorance or statistics. Total immersion programs can show rapid percentage growth because the absolute numbers involved are derisory: only some 150,000 students enrolled out of an eligible 4.3 million in 1984-85. Total immersion programs are also heavily subsidized, and their popularity may well be in part merely another desperate lunge by middle-class parents trapped by the deteriorating schools common to all North America, and mindful of the element of coercion introduced by the federal government's bilingual hiring preferences.

Total immersion is reserved almost uniquely for Anglophones. It is against Quebec government regulations to immerse the province's French-speaking children. Francophones elsewhere have often insisted on separate schools to preserve their children from the dangers of assimilation/contamination, and their efforts to do so, as in the much-publicized local struggles in Penetanguishene, Ontario, and Bathurst, New Brunswick, promptly become progressive *causes célèbres*.

That the children of the majority should be required to bear the brunt of acculturation, particularly when their language is that of the entire continent, is a measure of the extent to which the minority has the moral initiative in Canada. In the U.S., by contrast, the negative consequences of educating a child in other than its native tongue, such as the dreaded "damaged self-concept," formed part of the rationale for the 1968 Bilingual Education Act, which broke a long American tradition and began public school instruction in foreign languages.

Surprisingly, the efficiency of immersion as a method of inculcating bilingualism seems to be less than total. In Quebec, where the Anglophones were the first to embrace it as a supposed escape from their historical plight, studies have indicated that significant proportions of the graduates from immersion schools cannot function in French at college level. A further difficulty that limits the political efficacy of the program is obvious even in an approving 1983 *New York Times* report of a school in an "upper-middle-class neighborhood" in Ottawa:

> "I can speak French much better than my parents," said Sarah in fluent and Parisian-accented French. "And I can speak French much better than my parents and better than my sister," said David, also in French. Sarah scowled the scowl of elder sisters in every language. Ever since kindergarten the children have attended schools where French is the language of instruction and they will continue to do so through high school.
>
> "We never speak French at home or on the street," Sarah said, "and we hardly ever speak English in school." Under questioning, David conceded that he sometimes passed notes to his classmates in English, sometimes became angry in English and when playing dodge ball, or *chasse-ballon,* yelled in English to his classmates and in French to his teacher.

These children are not being taught *joual,* the French-Canadian dialect whose name derives from its corruption of the French *cheval,* horse, and in which many Québécois have taken an angry pride. The issue of accent is another dark Quebec mystery that outsiders have difficulty comprehending, but it is obviously important – Brian Mulroney's Quebec idiom, it is universally agreed, gave him a significant advantage over John Turner, whose technically adequate French apparently smacked of the Sorbonne. Additionally, as H.H. Stern (a language specialist at the Ontario Institute for Studies in Education) has concluded – to quote a *New York Times* paraphrase – ". . . even with fluency in French, the children still lacked social contact with French Canadians . . . the program has not narrowed the gap between the two solitudes."

Or, to make the same point another way, the Queen herself, as a card-carrying members of the European monarchs' union, can speak French. But nobody has mistaken her for a French Canadian.

Notwithstanding any of this, the form of bilingualism that has been imposed upon Canada is more demanding than in societies where it actually has some cultural reality. In Belgium, only Brussels is officially bilingual. Nine out of ten Belgians live in unilingual regions where either one or the other language is used exclusively for government and education. And this is in a country with less than one-third of one percent of Canada's land area, and half its population (united moreover, in the most part, by the Roman Catholic religion, not that it seems to do much good). Yet in Canada, in defiance of all the facts and any pretense of administrative practicality, established policy essentially makes the assumption that Francophones and Anglophones are absolutely coextensive and coterminous throughout the Canadian state, and it undertakes to offer them federal services in both languages everywhere. At the same time, every pressure is brought upon the provincial governments to do the same, particularly in education. Thus every sign and every announcement in airports across Canada is duplicated in French, although no one in the teeming crowds understands it, just like the bowls of milk left by Irish peasants on their doorsteps to propitiate the phantom nation of Little People with whom they believed they shared their land.

However, some of the implications of this version of bilingualism are worldly in the extreme. Ensuring "equality" between two language groups so dissimilar in size and character requires constant political intervention to correct the unsatisfactory results that would otherwise be produced by the normal workings of democracy and a free society. Few people realized this immediately, essentially because of the disingenuous way in which the policy was generally presented. "Bilingualism, in truth, was nothing less than a social revolution," wrote Richard Gwyn, who reported the process as Ottawa correspondent of the *Toronto Star*. "Like the introduction of the post-war welfare state, like the counter-cultural revolution of the 1960s, it was a development that effected fundamental changes in the character of the country. But in contrast to those transformational phenomena, no one in authority in Ottawa in the late 1960s and early 1970s let on that massive change was about to happen."

It is an interesting exercise to compare Gwyn's analysis of bilingualism in his biography of Trudeau, published in 1981 when Trudeau's Liberals were enjoying a Roman triumph over Tories, separatists and oil industry executives, with that of another Establishment supporter of the policy, George Radwanski, later editor of Gwyn's paper, the *Toronto Star*. Radwanski's biography of Trudeau appeared in 1978, when he was the Ottawa correspondent of the Montreal-based *Financial Times*. He wasn't letting on, either.

The 1968 Official Languages Act, according to Radwanski in 1978,

> provides simply that where there is reasonable demand, every citizen has the right to deal with the federal government, its agencies and Crown corporations in either English or French. This enshrinement of both languages as official and equal in all matters under federal jurisdiction in no way diminishes the rights of any private citizen – on the contrary, it only adds new rights – but this has never been adequately understood in many parts of Canada. . . . These misconceptions have been caused partly by Trudeau's failure to persevere in explaining what he was doing, partly because of the failure of the news media to dispel confusion about the legislation, and partly by the refusal of many people to listen to reason.
>
> Anyone who takes the trouble to verify the record, however, will see that Trudeau has clearly and consistently stressed the limited scope of the Official Languages Act from the outset. "Bilingualism is not an imposition on the citizens," he told a meeting of the American Society of Newspaper Editors in 1966. "The citizens can go on speaking one language or six languages or no languages if they choose. Bilingualism is an imposition on the state and not the citizens." Eight years and many repetitions later, in 1974 he was still speaking in identical terms, telling a panel of Parisian journalists in an interview: "I never expect that the average Quebecker in Sainte-Tite-des-Caps will become perfectly bilingual, nor that the anglophone in Calgary or Moose Jaw must know French. . . ."
>
> The only instance where the Official Languages Act imposes anything on individuals is in the case of a limited number of federal civil servants. . . .

In 1981, by contrast, Gwyn was prepared to admit that the policy meant that unilingual Canadians "would be disadvantaged in life, through no fault of their own. . . . The central inescapable fact of bilingualism was becoming clear: it meant loss of power for unilingual English Canadians." The reason for this was that

> . . . bilingualism, in the end, had to mean, well, *two equal languages;* being a little bit bilingual being as impossible to achieve as being a little bit pregnant. On the day after the Official Languages Act was passed, the *Calgary Herald* came right to the point: "For the more rewarding jobs, bilingualism is being made a practical necessity." Initially, these "rewarding" jobs meant just the top ones at Ottawa; inevitably, though, it would soon mean all the middle-rank jobs that fed the top; then jobs in the "para-government," all the way from the Canadian Manufacturers' Association to the Canadian Labor Congress, on down the line to jobs in all companies which had dealings with Francophones, and to some provincial government positions. Eventually, unilingualism could mean a life sentence to job immobility.
>
> Trudeau knew this all along. He fibbed about it as a necessary means to an end. As late as April 1977, for instance, he said in Winnipeg that bilingualism did not mean "that a lot more Canadians will have to be bilingual" nor even "most civil servants". . . .

Gwyn maintained that "white lies like this are the acceptable tools of every politician's trade." He did not comment, perhaps understandably, on their function in the profession of journalism. In order that this particular lie might go unchallenged, and the lives of thousands could be disrupted without hope of relief, honorable men were savagely calumniated and even driven out of Canadian public life for the crime of speaking the truth. The precise hue of a deception on this scale is surely open to question.

The scope of Trudeau's version of bilingualism first became evident in the federal bureaucracy. The federal government is the single-largest employer in Canada. Some 220,000 Canadians work in the civil service proper, and about 236,000 in Crown corporations. This is a strategic segment of the country's job market in which unilinguals are at a decisive disadvantage in making a career. Some 27.7% of positions in the civil service have now been deemed to require bilingual proficiency, as opposed to Trudeau's original estimate of 10%. The original unilingual occupants of these positions were generously allowed to convert themselves at taxpayers' expense. The result, in Gwyn's words, was "a gigantic boondoggle. . . ."

From 1974 on, more than 2,000 civil servants each day trooped off to five different language schools in Ottawa and across the river in Hull. There, they were chattered at by 600 language teachers, sometimes to be reduced to tears by petites *Québécoises* who were either separatists or feminists or both, and who delighted in their chance for revenge. Assistant deputy ministers, solidly into their fifties, blinked and gulped their way through *Dialogue Canada,* a "structuro-global" audio-visual course featuring the bilingual adventures of a portly little cartoon character called Angus Mac-Gregor, a retired Cunard captain from Vancouver, given to expressions like "Holy Sufferin' Catfish." At the end, provided they kept their heads down and avoided nervous breakdowns, they passed their LKE (Language Knowledge Examination), a licence, as the cynical put it, "never again to have to utter a word of French."

By 1976, even the Commissioner of Official Languages, who is empowered to monitor the progress of bilingualism, had concluded that the expenditure on these maneuverings far outweighed any resulting benefits. Making the telling point that only 11% of the Anglophone graduates of civil service language schools attained full fluency, he recommended in his annual report that the money be spent on teaching French in the schools, which was exactly what Moncton's Leonard Jones had been condemned for saying in 1974. Shortly afterwards the PQ election victory in Quebec rendered all public doubts about bilingualism once again taboo. But Trudeau had already rejected this "schools option," ostensibly because "we can't tell Quebec, 'Cool it fellows, in forty years we'll be able to talk to you'. . . . We might save some money . . . but we wouldn't save the country." Such a change of policy, of course, would have sharply reduced his government's powers and patronage.

As the U.S. experience with affirmative action/racial quotas has shown, an enterprising bureaucracy equipped with an excuse like official bilingualism can intervene surprisingly far into a society's life. In Canada, one such example was reported in the *Financial Post* on May 7, 1983. The article dealt with the effect of stricter Transport Canada language regulations at Fredericton airport.

Velma Abbott, owner of Fredericton's Airport Restaurant, was given notice in mid-April that Transport Canada would require bilingual service by September. None of her seven waitresses is bilingual.

"I'll just have to hire new staff," she says.

None of the eight women who staff car-rental booths at the airport speaks French. To satisfy the new policy, all must either learn or be replaced.

"I think it's stupid," says an angry Judy Martinson.

She claims that in 12 years staffing the airport's Avis booth, she has never had problems with a customer because of language. . . .

And the regulations were not confined to officially bilingual New Brunswick's major airport but would affect minor regional airports in places like Yarmouth, Nova Scotia, and Wabush, Newfoundland.

New Brunswick is Canada's only official bilingual province because its provincial government chose to have this specified in the "patriated" constitution, hoping to win points with the third of New Brunswick's population that is Francophone. Quebec's provincial government, of course, has taken the other tack, legislating to suppress the use of English in public and commercial life. Ironically, the same issue of the *Financial Post* carried, right below this report on airport bilingualism, a story from Montreal on the Quebec government's surprise announcement that it was considering extending its regulations compelling the use of French in business to firms with more than fifteen employees, instead of the previous fifty.

The essentially symbolic nature of Transport Canada's reform is also important to note. Since most Francophone New Brunswickers live in the north and east of the province, Francophones arriving in the south-central city of Fredericton must brace themselves anyway to face a largely Anglophone population, unless they propose to spend their entire visit in the airport. And, indeed, the Commissioner of Official Languages has complained that French-speaking New Brunswickers do not always appear to care about being served in French. In 1982, he noted that nearly half the federal income tax returns from the north-eastern county of Gloucester were completed in English, although the inhabitants are 80% Francophone. (". . .the habit of using English, even when the alternative is readily available, seems hard to break. . . .")

Another interesting, if minor, development on the airport front is the federal government's insistence on bilingual services in Wabush, which is not in the island of Newfoundland proper, but in Labrador, the huge strip of subarctic mainland coast administered from Newfoundland and claimed by Quebec. Both provincial governments are keenly if discreetly aware of the explosive potential of this old-fashioned European-style border dispute. To the extent that it strengthens the Francophone presence in Labrador, Ottawa's intervention is helping Quebec.

The extreme ambitions, or dreams, of bilingualism's promoters are usually only revealed in moments of expansiveness, and even then often by implication. For example, they clearly have their eyes on the business community. In 1978, the Sun Life Insurance Company was honest enough to announce publicly that it was sick of the attempts of successive Quebec governments to force it to work in French and that it proposed to shift its head office from Montreal to Toronto. Chartered banks and others had been smuggling their headquarters out of Montreal by degrees for years, but in the orgy of national breast-beating that followed the Parti Québécois' election victory in 1976, Sun Life was denounced by "everyone." At the Sun Life policy-holders' meeting, the Establishment case was put, appropriately, by R.B. Bryce, an elderly, bald man who looked and sounded just like a former Clerk of the Privy Council and head of Canada's civil service should.

Bryce's speech received the imprimatur of full reproduction on the editorial page of the *Toronto Star*. He said that in his view "and in the view of many of my friends ... Sun Life, as one of our national institutions, should be so managed in future as to be an organization in which able French-speaking Canadians, including those educated in Quebec universities, will feel they can work effectively and into which they will come and be welcomed up to the highest levels their abilities justify. Only if this is true of most of our institutions, both in the public and the private sector, can we expect the country to hold together in the long run."

This pious hope, of course, conceals a lethal vagueness on practical details, the flaw that reaches to the heart of the bilingualism concept. The issue facing Sun Life was not whether the company would employ French Canadians or sell insurance to them. As one pro-management Francophone pointed out at the meeting, the company had dealt with its Quebec customers in French since the last century. In recent years, Francophones had entered Sun Life's top management, only to be hired away by the Quebec civil service. The issue was: what language was the company to work in? The Parti Québécois insisted it should be French. This was obviously anomalous for a worldwide operation whose business was overwhelming in English. It would also necessitate radical surgery on the serfs actually doing the work at Sun Life, who were mostly unilingual Anglophones.

Bryce, however, had a model in mind for Sun Life. Not surprisingly, it was the federal government.

> In the public service in Ottawa, thousands of my former colleagues have gone to a great deal of trouble to make it possible for French-speaking Canadians to work more effectively and comfortably in the service. Their efforts have succeeded to a considerable degree, as is evident to anyone who sees the inner workings of departments now and compares them with ten years ago. Indeed, it is evident in the streets, in the restaurants, in many public places, that young Francophones find Ottawa now a much more congenial place in which to live and work.

This peculiar interest in young, as opposed to middle-aged or even elderly, Francophones can presumably be dismissed as fashionable fatuity. But Bryce was also saying something quite specific. Stripped of euphemisms ("effectively," "comfortably") he meant that for its key positions the Canadian civil service now officially required fluency in both official languages, with several departments ordered to work wholly in French – and that Canadian corporations, even those headquartered outside Quebec, should do likewise. Their officers should be bilingual and whole sections converted to working in French, whether or not this was required by the market. No other interpretation is possible if his words were not just benevolent noise.

Bryce's argument was all the more remarkable because federal bilingualism was not designed to multiply Francophones in Ottawa restaurants, but to pre-empt separatism. And, as the PQ's election victory in 1976 made clear, it had failed. The PQ came to power and made Quebec an officially unilingual state, the political expression of the Francophone nation, a fact that no one seems prepared to challenge. Yet here was the same rationale still being used to justify further claims by politicians on private citizens, and the arbitrary commandeering of private property to subsidize politically favoured groups. This is what Sun Life's agreement to spend its policyholders' resources on "francization" would have entailed. The ultimate implication of the bilingual policy is a Canadian society with politics in command. It is now encroaching and will in the future encroach further, however gradually and unobtrusively, upon the traditional liberal freedoms of English Canada.

With a predominantly Anglophone government in power in Ottawa, there may well be relatively less effort to expand official bilingualism in the immediate future – although the issue offers the Liberal Party infinite potential to embarrass Mulroney in Quebec.

With this in mind, one of Pierre Trudeau's last acts as prime minister was to use the federal government's power to impose bilingualism on the overwhelmingly Anglophone Yukon and Northwest Territories. However, preparations for the next major campaign – the extension of official bilingualism from the federal government to the business world, the last redoubt of *anglophonie* – were already visible. One line of attack that has already been developed is through the Crown corporations, which are directly subject to the Official Languages Act. Thus, as Peter Foster noted in *The Sorcerer's Apprentices,* the planting of the state oil company Petro-Canada in resolutely Anglophone Alberta in 1976 meant the arrival of a garrison of bilingual civil servants, including French Canadians "who seldom failed to point out the differences between Montreal and Calgary" – and the introduction of the approved Ottawa switchboard style: "Good morning, Petro-Canada – *bonjour.*"

The bilingual policy has its own momentum. The federal judiciary is quite capable of facilitating new forms of bilingual incursion through creative interpretation of the "patriated" constitution. And the straightforward zealotry of bilingualism's enforcers in the federal bureacracy should not be underestimated. Even in the spring of 1983, with the Liberals in their low-profile mode, the staff of the (Francophone Liberal) speaker of the House of Commons caused a minor scandal by entering the office of the acting leader of the opposition and removing, without his knowledge, wood panelling carved with mottoes in English so as to replace them with bilingual versions; and by attempting, for the same reason, to disfigure the unilingual Books of Remembrance that commemorate Canada's war dead, a particularly insensitive move given the notoriously low proportion of Francophones in that category. In these prominent cases, bilingualism was stayed, at least temporarily. But humbler victims, like Fredericton's airport waitresses, rarely get such reprieves.

The one part of the country where bilingualism is not promoted with the full weight of federal authority is, paradoxically, Quebec. Trudeau's Liberals reacted with extreme caution to the disconcerting spectacle of Quebec, the jewel in bilingualism's crown, the only part of Canadian society even superficially bicultural, being turned to dross. In 1977, Trudeau declined to mount a court challenge to the Parti Québécois legislation. This legislation would make French the only official language of Quebec and severely restrict English-language schooling in the province. Trudeau demurred on the grounds that "I don't want to give Mr. Lévesque the choice of timing and issues." The federal government has conspicuously avoided involvement in such litigation when it has been stimulated by Quebec Anglophones, although it invariably supports Francophones in similar cases in the rest of Canada. This paradox is presumably the result of brutal political reality: dispossessing the Anglophones was too popular with the Quebec Francophones to be interrupted. At times, Ottawa has even appeared to be acquiescing tacitly in the creation of a unilingual French-speaking enclave in Quebec – or, as Gwyn naturally puts it, "English Canadians no longer questioned Quebec's right to be 'as French as Ontario is English.' " But nevertheless, the PQ's continuing unilingual course was seemingly a *prima facie* breach of the new Canadian constitution and the Charter of Rights proclaimed in 1982. Legal action designed to explore this possibility is now slowly working its way through the courts and some of Quebec's language laws are being struck down as a result. Parti Québécois constitutional advisor Claude Morin has accurately described the situation as "a political time bomb."

Meanwhile, back in Ontario, the bilingual experiments have gone right ahead setting up their lab equipment, as if René Lévesque had never been born. Progressive Conservative Premier William Davis and his Liberal successor David Peterson have in fact raised the question, just how English is the province to which Quebec compares itself, in wishing to be equally French? The comparison was always specious, because Ontarians who speak French in their homes are, at 3.9%, a much smaller minority than the 12.7% of Quebeckers who speak English; they do not remotely approach the same central economic or historical role; and four-fifths of them can speak English anyway. But at precisely the moment when the Quebec government was imposing French as the province's only official language, the Ontario government was stealthily moving towards bilingualism – "trying to implement bilingual conditions without fanfare," as Establishment pundits Sheppard and Valpy have noted approvingly, "so as not to alienate the 'hoary Tory' vote in their political heartland. . . . Agreeing to institutional bilingualism would be little more than a symbolic step for Ontario, which already provide[s] most of these services. . . ."

Official bilingualism, it's worth repeating, is not simply a matter of showing goodwill to the minority: it actually inflicts tangible costs on the majority. But a certain type of professional politician finds it natural to reward enemies and punish friends, and the nominally Tory government of Premier William Davis developed this strategy to a fine art. Subsequently, Peterson's Liberals have been even more overt about their intentions.

Davis' enlightenment, and their own province's retrogression, did not prevent a group of Quebec Liberal MPs from demanding during the constitutional struggle that Trudeau compel Ontario to proclaim official bilingualism. Nor did it prevent the Ontario Tories, in the noble tradition of bilingualism's advocates, from attempting to make political capital by accusing their provincial Liberal opponents, during a provincial by-election at the height of the constitutional crisis, of favoring official bilingualism. However, the case of Ontario's Tories does serve to illustrate the extent to which bilingualism has become an end in itself for the Canadian political elite, a ritual commitment to goodthink quite unrelated to any practical value and unaffected by increasing evidence of asymmetry in its application. As Keith Spicer, the former Commissioner of Official Languages, commented during the 1983 Tory leadership race, the media consensus that the new leader must be bilingual was, ironically, generated by "a mainly unilingual English press corps." Twenty years after the Quiet Revolution, confirmed the *Toronto Sun*'s Douglas Fisher, "Canada's national press corps remains, with few exceptions, unilingual."

Bilingualism is expensive. The Commissioner of Official Languages estimated in 1982 that spending on official language programs inside and outside the federal public service would reach $453.2 million in 1982-83. This is a small but distinct 0.6% of total federal expenditures, approximately the percentage the U.S. spends on the National Aeronautics and Space Administration or the Environmental Protection Agency. The estimate, moreover, is certainly low. There are genuine questions of accounting methodology involved in such a survey, and it would be reasonable to assume that some part of the outlay is buried in departmental budgets, even if Ottawa did not have every motive to do so. For example, the Official Languages Commissioner's estimate does not deal with the cost of replacing federal employees undergoing language training, nor of course with costs incurred by the provincial governments. George Radwanski, a passionate supporter of the program, admitted that the "total cost" of bilingualism was estimated to be $500 million back in 1976, or 1.3% of that year's federal expenditures.

The Official Languages Commissioner's figures still warrant closer investigation, however. Intriguing line items are the $62.5 million spent on bilingualism in the armed forces, which, relative to the numbers involved, is a quite disproportionate share of the $242.9 million expended within the government apparatus as a whole; and the $21 million granted to "official-language minority groups," local lobbies set up to press for more services in their own language. The usual asymmetry applies here also: in 1981, for example, 94% of such funds was going to Francophones outside Quebec, and only 6% to Quebec Anglophones, although it was the latter's position that was under legislative attack.

The Commissioner's report, of course, did not attempt to grapple with the true economic cost of bilingualism. Nor have there been any independent academic studies of the issue, a disgraceful instance of self-censorship by Canada's publicly funded universities.

In general, the economic cost of government regulation is not simply the administrative expenses of the regulatory agency, but also the cost of compliance borne by those regulated, and ultimately the intangible burden on the economy of the disruption in efficient allocation of resources, for example, various types of opportunity costs. The multiplier involved is startling.

American research suggests as a rule of thumb that the private sector's compliance costs alone are at least twenty times the budget of the regulating agency. In the case of Canada's bilingual policy, much of the compliance cost is at present falling upon the federal government itself, since Establishment designs upon the private sector have not yet been fulfilled. But some impact is already felt: those bilingual cornflakes boxes have to be paid for, to say nothing of private language lessons for the ambitious. And even in the federal bureaucracy, there is presumably a price associated with the diversion of top officials' energies and the abrogation of what a bilingualism supporter in the House of Commons, David Orlikow (NDP-Winnipeg North) once denounced as "old concepts about merit" in the hiring and promotion of Francophones. This must be reflected in the quality of the service received by the public.

"Hardly extravagant for a program essential to Canada's survival as a nation," said Radwanski in 1978 of his own estimate of bilingualism's cost. "Francophone rights cannot be bought, sold, subtracted, divided or multiplied in terms of dollars and cents in the budgets of a troubled economy, and that will apply, I promise you, for as long as I am Secretary of State of Canada," Serge Joyal told one of those federally funded French-language pressure groups in Nova Scotia in 1982.

Wielding these emotional arguments, the Canadian elite has bludgeoned into silence most public opposition to the bilingual policy. The Liberals have succeeded in institutionalizing what Christina McCall-Newman calls their "major shibboleth." To call a Canadian politician anti-French or a "bigot" is the direct equivalent of accusing an American politician of being anti-black or "racist," and has the same magical panic-inducing properties. The moral hegemony of bilingualism has been greatly strengthened, of course, by the acquiescence of successive Tory leaders, the putative defenders of English Canada.

Nevertheless, there can be no doubt that English Canada's resentment of official bilingualism, although amorphous, is profound. It has certainly been a silent but important factor in the astonishing disintegration of the federal Liberal party's position west of Ontario. And sometimes it has crystallized dramatically. In 1983-84, the Manitoba NDP government's attempt to adopt a measure of bilingualism on the provincial level provoked extraordinary public wrath. In a moment of misguided populism unusual in Canada (and not likely to be repeated), Manitoba liberals had earlier made possible a form of plebiscite in the province similar to local initiative provisions in the U.S. The plebiscite held on bilingualism resulted in a negative vote of a lopsidedness normally found only in the Soviet Union. Official bilingualism lost even in the Francophone districts, a devastating indication of its irrelevance to the practical concerns of the minority. Eventually the provincial Tories, to the horror of their federal counterparts, paralyzed the legislature with obstructive tactics, and the NDP measure was withdrawn.

Equally dramatically, opposition to bilingualism on the national level crystallized in 1976, around the issue of forcing bilingualism on Canada's air traffic controllers. The victims of bilingualism are usually too scattered and unorganized to gain the attention of the Anglophone majority, upon whom the policy impinges only indirectly. But the air traffic controllers and their supporters were adroit and ruthless enough to close down the country with a national strike, amid an astonishing outpouring of popular support. In a revealing comment, Trudeau described this confrontation as "the worst crisis to national unity since the conscription crisis [of World War I]." His government was forced to seek shelter under a royal commission. Bilingualism, however, was saved by the bell. The Parti Québécois victory later that year was interpreted, illogically, as placing the policy beyond criticism. Deprived of the limelight, the air traffic controllers had no protection when the Clark government implemented the royal commission's 1979 recommendation in favor of French as part of its vain attempt to curry favor in Quebec. But for the Liberals, the episode remained a chilling presentiment of what lurks out there in the black lagoon of English Canada.

In a lighter vein, another hint of Anglophone resistance was the remarkable underground success of the book *Bilingual Today, French*

Tomorrow. This attack on bilingualism by Jock Andrew, a former lieutenant commander in the Canadian Navy, was published in 1977 by BMG Publishing Ltd., a small independent house that was one of the few Canadian parallels to the American conservative movement's extensive development of alternative institutions in the years before President Reagan's election. (Another of its titles was David Somerville's *Trudeau Revealed.*) Andrew's polemic was completely ignored by the Canadian Establishment media, and was placed in bookstores only with great difficulty. Nevertheless, without benefit of any reviews, it sold some 130,000 copies, over ten times the normal print run of a Canadian best-seller, and is still being ordered regularly. *Bilingual Today, French Tomorrow* put itself beyond the pale by propounding the incredible thesis that bilingualism was simply the first step in a process which will end with the compulsory conversion of Canada into a unilingual French state. In fairness to Commander Andrews, it must be said that there have been instances of Francophone intellectuals fantasizing linguistic reconquest of even New England areas, and the recent history of Quebec provides at least as much empirical evidence for his contention as for wishful claims like that of Richard Gwyn in *The Northern Magus* that the attitudes of Quebec Anglophones "have changed from condescension, through disbelief and resentment, to a sense of excitement at living out a gigantic social experiment." For that matter, the Establishment consensus that Francophones have been the victims of systematic discrimination in Canada's first hundred years is not without a dash of demagogic simplification.

An ironic footnote came five years later. Secretary of State Serge Joyal, in the speech cited above, actually told his sympathetic audience ("we're among family, let's talk among ourselves") that "everything we undertake and everything we are doing to make Canada a French state is part of a venture I have shared for many years with a number of people. . . . The idea, the challenge, of making Canada a French country both inside and outside Quebec – an idea some people consider a bit crazy – is something a little beyond the ordinary imagination. . . ." Joyal was no doubt referring awkwardly to the Trudeauvian fancy of a co-extensive French nation in Canada, rather than to any direct subjugation of Anglophones. But given that he promised his audience federal subsidies to Francophone communities, and federal support in the struggle "to make Canada a country that reflects us, our ideals," English Canadians might be forgiven for wondering what the difference in practice is exactly. Paranoids, in short, have enemies after all.

Canada's bilingual experiment has been, above everything else, a supreme exercise in social engineering. It is essential to note that its immediate effects have been highly regressive. As Gwyn said frankly, "There was no getting away from it: during the late 1960s and early 1970s, most *bilingues* belonged to the same distinctive breed, upper middle-class Francophones and those upper middle-class Anglophones, most from Montreal, who by the happenstance of their parents or their career patterns, had a chance while young to learn French." These are precisely the groups from whom power in Canadian society has been slipping: the Francophones, because their relative proportion of Canada's population is falling; the Montreal Anglophones, because their city is being eclipsed by Toronto and the West; even the established upper-middle-classes of both groups, because of the new wealth of the oil fields and the industrial estates. Gwyn, writing in the optative mood characteristic of Canadian Nationalists, claimed that by 1980 bilingualism's "geographic base" had widened, but he admitted that the phenomenon's socio-economic base remained the same. For the first time in its history, Canada was developing a social elite of young, upper-middle-class, bilingual graduates.

This means that Ottawa is committed to a course that will increasingly collide with the norms of North American society, norms currently shared by English if not by French Canada: minimal class distinctions, high social mobility, and the determination of status by private and commercial activity rather than by political and governmental prescription.

Free people do not generally learn new languages at the request of their governments. The Irish, for example, have utterly failed to revert to Gaelic, although at the time of independence at least the ideal of doing so was viewed with general public good will. It may be that Canada's Anglophones will simply cede the federal civil service and much of political life to the Francophones, as has already happened in Quebec and in the similar case of English South Africa. But the disparity in size between the two Canadian language groups will make even this compromise difficult to achieve. Conversely, just a small increase in the number of bilingual Anglophones will make it impossible for the bilingual program to operate as a de facto policy of preference for Francophones, as it does now. Ottawa has already shown that it will not scruple to interpret bilingualism as a mandate for an ethnic quota – for example, in the armed forces, according to Gerald Porter in his distressing study *In Retreat: The Canadian Forces in the Trudeau Years*. To do so explicitly, however, will further raise the program's political cost in English Canada. Yet to refrain would reduce its value in French Canada. In short, success, even supposing it to be attainable, could well spoil bilingualism.

As long as the federal government continues to be dependent on Quebec, the fatal weaknesses of the official bilingual policy will be hidden or ignored. But at some point they will inevitably be exposed. The divergent ethnic composition of the two major parties guarantees it, regardless of the Tory leadership's best intentions. Douglas Fisher pinpointed this danger in June 1983, when opinion polls seemed to show the Liberals certain to lose if they called a general election:

> Of the 36 members of the cabinet, 15 are French-language-in-the-home types; of 27 parliamentary secretaries, 13 are French; of the 21 chairmanships of House committees, nine are held by French; of the 145-odd Liberal MPs, some 95 are French-language types but 90 of these are bilingual. Of the 100-odd Tory MPs, only two are French and only about six of the rest are bilingual. Of the 30-some NDP MPs, none is French and only two are near being officially bilingual. . . .
>
> Next election, unless Mulroney leads back a dozen-or-more Quebec MPs and a few from New Brunswick and the franco strip along the Ottawa river and into Northern Ontario, we'll have the reverse of the present situation in Parliament. Its consequences may be bitter. . . . [The Tory leader] is unlikely to be able to place French-language people in posts in anything near their proportion of numbers in the population or in the House.

Fisher concluded that "the brutality in the numbers and origins of MPs has been a grand advantage to French-language MPs. Don't cry prejudice when the advantage has to go the other way." Mulroney's 1984 sweep of Quebec circumvented the danger – for now.

And Fisher's admonition will almost certainly be in vain. Waving the bloody shirt of Tory atrocity is too well established a Liberal reflex when campaigning in French Canada. *"Ils mangent les Canadiens francais,"* André Ouellet used to tell rural Quebec Liberal associations in the 1970s. The Liberal attitude was illustrated by the fact that when facing defeat in 1979, they deliberately filled most of Quebec's quota of vacant Senate seats to prevent any incoming Tory government from compensating for its lack of electoral success in Quebec by appointing Francophone supporters to the Senate and cabinet. This was as close a parallel as democratic politics can offer to the practice of poisoning wells in desert warfare.

Pierre Trudeau never showed the slightest sign of compromising on official bilingualism. Indeed, "entrenching" it was probably his principal motive in precipitating the constitutional struggle after 1980; certainly he gained little else. But his marriage to Margaret presumably taught him, at the very least, a little more about the difficulties the policy must contend with in English Canada. Few Anglophones could have had a better opportunity or more incentive to become bilingual than Margaret. Yet Richard Gwyn reports that in late 1979, after the couple's separation and during Trudeau's brief experience of opposition, when he was allegedly planning to retire and move with their children to Montreal, Margaret let it be known that she proposed to follow and "her friends wondered how on earth she could survive there without French."

7

U.S.-Canadian Diplomacy: or, the Longest Undefended Special Relationship in the World

The Americans are our best friends, whether we like it or not.

- Robert Thompson, leader of the Social Credit Party

If the myth of bilingualism and biculturalism is what binds Canada's two cultures into one apparent whole, then a misconceived view of the U.S.-Canadian relationship is the myth that permits Canadians to pretend that they really live in a distinct and separate country. All roads lead to Rome, and all the vital organs Canada has developed outside its skeletal structure are trained on the United States. "Good relations, superb relations" with the U.S. were one of the many benefits Brian Mulroney claimed would follow from his election as prime minister in 1984. Actually, his Liberal predecessors had been emphasizing the same thing for a couple of years. The Central Canadian Establishment's attitude to the U.S. follows a cyclical pattern, reaching peaks of arrogance in direct proportion to the strength of the economy and inverse proportion to the proximity of an election. The most recent cycle has been particularly violent, however, and the obfuscation surrounding this most fundamental issue is even denser than usual.

In the spring of 1982, a group of Washingtonians gathered in the auditorium of Johns Hopkins School of Advanced International Studies to hear the Canadian ambassador, Allan Gotlieb, give a lecture on Canada-U.S. relations. Following Pierre Trudeau's re-election, the National Energy Program and the other alarms of 1980-81, Gotlieb

99

had achieved a prominence on the American scene unusual for a Canadian ambassador. He was aided by an outspoken novelist wife, and the services of Prime Minister Trudeau's former press secretary, now attached to Canada's embassy in Washington. There were even rumors that Gotlieb's own rapid rise through the civil service was due to his friendship with Trudeau, plus "sharp elbows." But his progress was actually all "on the basis of merit," Gotlieb assured Toronto writer Elaine Dewar, who was mordently recording the scene for *City Woman* magazine. He did admit, however, to being "intellectually tough."

Appropriately, there occurred a minor illustration of that difference between the national temperaments that means so much to Canada's Nationalists. A speaker told a joke. He pointed out that there had been a fire at the Canadian Embassy that morning, caused by the burning of confidential documents. The last time that had happened was at the Japanese Embassy just before they declared war. Was Gotlieb going to do that today?

> The audience roars. Gotlieb does not smile. He does not even blink. Instead, after he is introduced, he rises slowly and begins to speak. Canada, he explains, has embarked on a course of nation-building of which the operations of FIRA and the NEP are but a part. Then he spells out the way things were between the U.S. and Canada, and the way things are going to be.
>
> The old relationship was guided by what he calls the Ten Commandments. These rules included: no shared institutions with any real power; no linkage between issues; no intermediaries in disputes; no press leaks; no central bureaucracies in either country in charge of the relationship as a whole; no formal foreign policies; as little involvement as possible by politicians; no reliance on summit meetings to resolve matters; and above all, no public criticism of each other's policies on other nations. Most of these rules, he says, have been broken and swept away.
>
> Then he delivers the zinger: "The Canadian side," says Gotlieb, "has recognized the very real need to address the state of public opinion in the United States vis-à-vis developments in Canada and some of the conflict areas. . . . Diplomacy is now very public – this speech is an example and it's not going to change."
>
> Gotlieb *has* declared war, a war for the hearts and minds of the American voter and the American legislator. From now on, Canada will behave officially in America as the Americans do, wading in the streams of the special interests, attempting to direct the flow of American politics our way.

A year later, with the Liberals swinging into their well-practiced, hatch-battening-down pre-election drill, "it" had of course "changed." Canadian officials were passing the word to their friends in the press that, as the Montreal *Gazette* headlined in March 1983, *Relations with U.S. Aren't as Bad as They Look* ("breezes of bickering are blowing, but hardly winds of war"). And *three* years later, after the election of Brian Mulroney with his talk of "superb relations" with the U.S., the change was almost total – except for the continued starring role of Ambassador Gotlieb. His diplomacy was still very public, but by July of 1985 he was earnestly assuring the *Wall Street Journal* that he recognized American problems: "Your deindustrialization is our deindustrialization. We share the auto industry. We don't believe protectionism is the answer, and we don't believe we should be hitting each other."

Nevertheless, the "old relationship" Gotlieb described did once exist, albeit subject to human errors and omissions. And he was expressing (or perhaps exploiting) a rejection so deeply felt by some members of the Canadian elite that it will eventually resurface. In which case Gotlieb will no doubt be prepared to articulate it once more.

The response of Gotlieb's American listeners to the news that a foreign power intended to interfere in their domestic affairs was also noteworthy: they did not react at all. But they asked plenty of questions about "the NEP, FIRA and where Canada stands on the idea of a nuclear freeze."

While Pierre Trudeau was Prime Minister, there were no fewer than five different presidents in the U.S. But the contrast in continuity was even greater, because there is simply no equivalent in Canada to the political appointments within the civil service that a U.S. president can make – and unmake. Americans sometimes portray their bureaucracy as the "permanent government." But in Al Jolson's words, they ain't seen nothing yet – not compared to the real permanent government that exists in Ottawa. Canadian civil servants are so absorbed in their own aura of Olympian impartiality that Michael Pitfield, Clerk of the Privy Council, Canada's highest-ranking civil servant and effectively the Prime Minister's chief of staff apparently hoped to survive the Tory victory of 1979 and – according to Jeffrey Simpson in his *Discipline of Power* – broke down when the time came for him to go. Firing a civil servant of Pitfield's eminence turned out to be prohibitively expensive for Canadian taxpayers because of the compensation arrangements thoughtfully designed for itself by the bureaucracy. Almost no others were dismissed. And within a year, Trudeau was re-elected and Pitfield returned.

The Department of External Affairs, which is chiefly responsible for official relations with the U.S., has historically set the tone for the entire civil service. The Department's first head, O.D. Skelton, a professor of political science from Queen's University was also one of the earliest professional-level civil service appointments after the spoils system was abolished at the end of World War I. Not coincidentally, he was also a committed Liberal, chosen by the architect of the Canadian Liberal one-party state, Mackenzie King, who was Prime Minister of Canada, off and on, for twenty-seven years. Skelton brought allies to Ottawa, and took a close interest in the annual examinations for graduate recruits. A remarkably homogeneous group of able "mandarins" rapidly emerged, who were to dominate Canadian policy from the Depression until the 1960s. During this period, External was, in Christina McCall-Newman's words, "the seed bed for the civil service. For thirty years it had sent the best and the brightest of its officers out into the other departments. . . ." As late as the early 1970s, one out of every three deputy ministers – the officials heading each cabinet department – was an ex-diplomat. From 1963 to 1968, even Canada's prime minister – Liberal, naturally – was an ex-diplomat, in the blandly charming form of Lester Pearson.

From the point of view of this powerful institution, U.S. relations were basically a problem of bureaucracy. *Everything* was a problem of bureaucracy. Hence the characteristic interest in secrecy; the elimination of public conflict; the stern control of elected officials and the minimization of opportunities, like summit conferences and overall strategy-shaping, for them to get their paws on matters of substance; the emphasis on negotiations; the determination to substitute detail for drama.

This tendency was greatly reinforced when the American representatives in the 1930s were discovered to be an identical type, liberal internationalists backed by a firmly established progressive government. As John Holmes put it, echoing the title of the memoirs of former U.S. Secretary of State Dean Acheson, Canadian diplomats were "Also Present at the Creation."

> We were all at the end of the Second World War conscious of creating a new and improved world, a system of united nations into which could be fitted in due course bodies such as NATO, the Commonwealth, the Arab League, or the Pan American Sanitary

Organization to perform specific functions within the whole. The American contribution to this creation was unique and critical . . . [but] the universe is, I think, better ordered because of our useful hints.

. . . U.S. views were not uniform. There were wide gaps between the State Department and Congress, and often we were supporting the internationalists in the State Department against the "primitives" in the Senate, as Dean Acheson called them.

This somewhat idealistic view of world politics might not have impressed Machiavelli. But his absence (in any immediately recognizable form) from the Canadian or American teams negotiating to set up the United Nations Organization was a further proof of their essential commonality. As is the fact that, after nearly thirty unencouraging years for the United Nations' ideal, Holmes could still look upon their handiwork and pronounce it to be good, or even important.

Like all professional diplomats, the Ottawa mandarins regarded outsiders' sweeping simplicities about foreign affairs with distaste. But in fact their own approach to the Canadian-American relationship was underpinned by a few rather grand assumptions. Military force was now unthinkable, although in 1857 Ottawa had been chosen as Canada's federal capital partly because it offered greater protection against an invasion from the south, and as late as 1891, twenty years after the Treaty of Washington had inaugurated the undefended border, Goldwin Smith had felt obliged to ridicule, in *Canada and the Canadian Question,* his fellow-countrymen's contemporary talk of war. Basic agreement existed between the U.S. and Canada about the global situation, the threat from Nazi Germany and then from the Soviet Union, and indeed went beyond that to fundamental values that both shared. Consequently, outstanding issues as they arose could be settled safely by continuous consultation at every level of the respective bureaucracies. More than thirty separate U.S. agencies currently deal directly with their Canadian counterparts every day. Issues that could be reduced to antiseptic technical questions were referred to the International Joint Commission, which was founded in 1909 and by the early 1980s had divided along national lines only three times. Top off with a dollop of personal warmth between president and prime minister, which perhaps was most notable between Roosevelt and Mackenzie King, and you had the much-discussed "special relationship," complex, intimate and familial, an exception to de Gaulle's dictum that sovereign states in their interaction could only be "cold-hearted monsters."

Today, the original mandarins are long gone from Ottawa. Their civil service now bears the stamp of Pierre Trudeau, and their key diplomatic formulation has been publicly condemned by Ambassador Gotlieb, the acknowledged leader of a younger External Affairs' generation. Nevertheless, the mandarins' view still remains the best basic description of the official Canadian-American relationship.

The changes imposed upon the civil service during the Trudeau era apparently caused much individual distress. But to an outsider there seems to be some considerable political continuity. Mandarin doctrine, on close examination, always had a statist tinge. Under Trudeau, Ottawa's use of state power simply became cruder and more ambitious, in the area of U.S. relations as elsewhere. In the familiar pattern of the 1960s, liberal parents had produced radical children.

Dissenters from the traditional Ottawa consensus on U.S. relations usually begin by tripping over the commandment abjuring "linkage." Linkage is diplomats' jargon for the procedure by which issues are not resolved on their merits, but instead are treated as bargaining chips to be traded in complex deals with the other side. Apart from the injustices this necessarily engenders on individual issues, it also requires the sort of continuous coordination between governments that democracies find difficult to organize. It can easily degenerate into crude retaliation, leading in the end to the question of who has the most chips, a question which Ottawa in particular has not in the past been eager to address. But linkage instantly presents itself as the obvious policy to those who do not share diplomats' professional preference for the unrocked boat, especially if they dispute the assumptions underlying the adoption of a case-by-case approach. Thus, in the United States the concept recently figured in a spirited debate on the U.S.-Soviet relationship. American conservatives, including President Reagan, have generally advocated linkage in dealing with the Russians, partly because they do not accept the accommodation implied by detente, and partly because they don't believe the Russians accept it either. Similarly, Canadians who advocate linkage in dealing with the U.S. often have unfriendly designs upon the assumption that there exists a continental accord.

Still, the conventional opinion among professional diplomats, academics and other members of the foreign policy community on both sides of the border probably remains that summarized in 1982 by Annette Baker Fox, Director of Columbia University's Canadian Studies program: "What is clear is that unrelated issues between Canada and the United States should never consciously be linked, a practice which officials of both countries shun anyway, despite some unsophisticated pressure to do so." These naifs, however, included

Ambassador Gotlieb. "When you've got a lot of disputes, you've got to get your act together," he was arguing at the same time.

> For years there was no linkage between the issues between us. Well, the issues are becoming linked now. Congress is linking them. Linkage is the whole thesis behind reciprocity. So, the relationship must be managed as a whole. That means getting a hold on what the provinces are doing, what's going on on the Hill, in state legislatures, and everything going on in Ottawa. The need to be on top of the whole thing is *overwhelming*.

Some U.S. congressmen had indeed been huffing and puffing about reciprocity, the idea that Canada should be done by as it was doing, stimulated by constituent complaints about Canada's peculiar combination of nationalism at home and corporate takeover abroad. But, in the end, they had not blown anything down. Nor, to anyone with even a toe-hold on Washington, did it ever seem likely that they would. Gotlieb's words, however, should not be judged as those of an impartial scientist. Top civil servants face conflicting and volatile pressures and incentives, including obscure territorial imperatives difficult to assess from without. When Gotlieb, discussing linkage, cites the agreement on radio frequencies between Canada and the U.S. Federal Communications Commission – "It was made at the middle management level and not even brought to the *attention* of the senior level" – it is hard to miss a certain senior-level pique.

And the mood to which Gotlieb was responding did exist among the Canadian elite. There was always an incipient contradiction between unconfined functionalism in the U.S.-Canadian relationship and Ottawa's centralizing ("nation-building") ambitions, one of which was to gain foreign recognition. As John Holmes said, "On our side greater attention by Ottawa to national strategies – communications, cultural and industrial – and the increasing number of our international commitments have required closer surveillance also of our free-wheeling officials."

Moreover, after the resurrection of the Liberals in 1980 and the defeat of the Parti Québécois' referendum, Ottawa and its allies were euphoric. The concept of the government's "management" role was brandished everywhere. It was of course to be applied to the U.S.-Canadian relationship, as Gotlieb suggested. "Talking to Gotlieb, I had almost begun to think of the relationship as strictly a government-to-government matter," Elaine Dewar mused. ". . . [he] purveyed the perspective, so rampant in Ottawa, that *government* is the main actor in both societies, that government will write the future for both nations."

Canada itself was also to be managed. In February 1982, *Saturday Night* magazine sported a striking cover featuring a menacing metallic eagle. This illustrated an article in which, under such headings as "America is Angry" and "The Unfriendly Giant," York University historian Viv Nelles offered a Nationalist rationalization for the National Energy Program in which "management" served as a euphemism for the great North American bogey of socialism. "Canadian business, labor and political elites came to the conclusion that the proposed energy-related mega-projects ought to be managed in such a way as to assist in the restructuring of Canadian industry. The long-awaited reorganization of the Canadian economy had begun." America was not so much angry as asleep, of course, and the National Energy Program was actually more of a raid by Ottawa on the oil-rich provinces. But Canadian Nationalist polemics are habitually conducted in what Marxists call "the optative mood." Ordinary people use cruder names.

Who, exactly, had long been awaiting this reorganization of the Canadian economy? The answer to this, of course, explains much of the pressure building in Canada against Gotlieb's "old relationship" between the two countries. The Reversal of Beliefs discussed in Chapter Four meant that, in Canada as in the rest of the English-speaking world, Liberals have abandoned classical liberalism. One symptom of this was that Liberals now favor state intervention and tariffs where once they advocated free markets and free trade. Thus the automatic and decentralizing tendency of the "old relationship" is in conflict, not merely with specific ambitions of the Canadian elite, but with some of its deepest beliefs about how societies should be run.

To the extent that the U.S. appears to be the last best hope of classical economics, this clash has an added bitterness. "Here in Canada," said Pierre Trudeau pointedly after a visiting President Reagan had favored the Canadian Parliament with a description of his economic program in March 1981, "our own realities have sometimes made it necessary for government to intervene to further enterprise. Those realities, and that necessity, are still with us." U.S. Congressional Democrats, needless to say, would have applauded this defense of government (and did, when Reagan said something like it in his second State of the Union address.)

Like most ideologies, naturally enough, Canadian liberalism can only partly be understood in intellectual terms. The variety that has flourished in the Ottawa mandarinate in particular has always contained a strong emotional undertow of alienation – "alienism." Before World War II, according to Christina McCall-Newman, "the mandarins had a shared passion: they disliked British condescension intensely and they wanted out from under the Empire." This was despite, or perhaps because of, the fact that they were largely British-educated. The Oxford men at External especially remained a proud clique for the rest of their lives, much to the irritation of their fellows, who felt looked down upon, probably with justice.

The mandarins' passion had the further psychologically interesting trait of being covert. It had to be. In Canada at that time, as their historian, J.L. Granatstein, has written in *The Ottawa Men,* "The Empire-minded, those who believed that Canada's place was "at Britain's side, whate'er betide" were the majority, certainly among English-speaking opinion-makers." When in 1938 Skelton and his aides realized that Canadian public opinion would simply not allow a policy of neutrality in the event of a war between Britain and Nazi Germany, "this pleased them not at all."

There can be no doubt that the U.S. is now the beneficiary of a similarly repressed and ultimately unappeasable resentment on the part of elements in the Canadian elite, festering all the more because they are surrounded by an undubitably North American populace. For instance, Ottawa chose the height of the 1962 Cuban missile crisis to take umbrage at the technical issue of whether it should have been consulted under the NORAD agreement. ("Yet one must ask what we could possibly have said or done . . ." sighed John Holmes.) "If we go along with the Americans now, we will be their vassals forever," External Affairs Minister Howard Green excitedly told Prime Minister John Diefenbaker's cabinet as it debated putting Canada's forces on alert.

Alone among the allied leaders, Diefenbaker publicly questioned the American stand. He had Opposition support, but this was not unique to Canada. There was whimpering among opposition parties throughout western Europe, but no other government felt free to join in; only France's Charles de Gaulle, despite his irreproachable nationalism, cut through to the bipolar strategic reality by backing the U.S. without bothering to look at the profferred photographic evidence of Soviet missile emplacements. Significantly, Diefenbaker's main advisor during the crisis was Norman Robertson, Skelton's successor as head of External and one of the last of the mandarin generation.

Equally significantly, the Canadian armed forces ignored their own government. Canadian NORAD units went on alert two days before receiving cabinet permission, and although not even covered in the NORAD treaty the Canadian Army and the Royal Canadian Navy mobilized as well, the latter under the subterfuge of an exercise and initially without even the connivance of the Defense minister. The Navy subsequently put to sea, enabling the U.S. Navy to move south into the Cuban blockade zone and making Canada the only U.S. ally to provide armed assistance during the crisis.

Even by his appalling standards, Diefenbaker's relationship with President John F. Kennedy was bad. Alleging interference in Canada's affairs, he in effect ran against Kennedy in the 1963 general election. He lost. As Lawrence Martin's nationalistic account *The Presidents and the Prime Ministers* concluded mournfully, Kennedy had succeeded in "galvanizing the political world and reaching out to Diefenbaker's own countrymen, displacing him in their affections." During the next sixteen years in office, however, the Liberals and their supporters were to complete their ideological revolution – and also the reorientation of their resentments.

As a first priority, Canadian Nationalists advocating the new U.S. relationship proclaimed by Gotlieb at Johns Hopkins wanted Canada to act more forcefully in the American arena. This might have appeared to be a form of getting tough, but it could (as usual) be blamed on the Americans. After New England senators and Reagan Administration conservatives dry-gulched in quick succession the East Coast fishery treaty and the Law of the Sea treaty (both negotiated by the Carter Administration) Professor Stephen Clarkson seized the opportunity to reiterate "the notion, so hard for the Canadian diplomats to accept, that Canada cannot afford not to intervene directly in the American political process." If the U.S. Senate was going to sabotage signed and sealed agreements like this, "Americans can hardly complain" – he continued, somewhat optimistically – if Canada got involved not just with Congress but with "interest-group politics" and "media management" as well.

Clarkson felt so strongly about Canada's need for an "American strategy" and a "managed relationship" that he concluded his exhaustive study for the Canadian Institute for Economic Policy, darkly entitled *Canada and the Reagan Challenge: Crisis in the Canadian-American Relationship,* with the remarkable recommendation that Canada's ambassador to Washington be

> a senior politician holding Cabinet rank in the Canadian government. ... A Flora MacDonald or a Donald Macdonald, a John Turner or a John Crosbie would be able to carry out Canada's American strategy, presenting Ottawa's position loud and clear to

the White House, to Congress and to the American media. Participating in the weekly cabinet meeting in Ottawa, he or she would bring to the Priorities and Planning Committee [the crucial decision-making body in the Trudeau system] immediate connection with the Washington scene that no External Affairs memorandum could equal. On returning to Washington, he or she would be able to bring the view of the Canadian government directly to whatever trouble spot had to be confronted, short-circuiting the diplomatic channels whose delays and hesitations can account for a good deal of the misunderstanding of Canadian actions that spreads so quickly around the corridors of the Capitol.

Foreign governments, like U.S. presidents, unquestionably do find the U.S. Senate's power over international treaties, and the general unpredictability of U.S. political life, very annoying. "This acclaimed system of government may be beautiful as democratic theory," said the normally restrained John Holmes, "but for a country with which other countries have to live, it is self-indulgent." The fact is, however, that no democracy operates very efficiently in its foreign relations – a problem Canada has avoided largely by forgoing a conventional concomitant of democracy: changing governments.

Clarkson's idea of stationing a "strong" Canadian cabinet minister permanently in Washington – the politicians he mentions have all been viewed as potential Liberal or Conservative leaders – is intriguing. The U.S. and Canada might or might not have a "special" relationship, but appointing a species of reverse proconsul like this would certainly make it unique. A key member of the Canadian government, commuting weekly between capitals – with the access and authority to speak for Canada "loud and clear" in the White House and on Capitol Hill – going "directly" to trouble spots in the relationship – "short-circuiting" the regular channels of diplomacy between sovereign states – surely this is revolutionary, unprecedented? Well, not quite.

At the beginning of the 1980 U.S. presidential election campaign, such diverse candidates as Edward Kennedy, John Connolly, Jerry Brown and Ronald Reagan all went on record as favoring some sort of "North American Accord" involving Canada and perhaps Mexico. The most dramatic proposal came from Reagan. He made the idea a major theme in his nationally televised official announcement of his candidacy on November 13, 1979. He even said that "if I am elected President, I would be willing to invite each of our neighbors to send a special representative to our government to sit in on high-level planning sessions with us. . . ."

Political commentators responded with their usual petulance when confronted with an unauthorized idea, and this strange moment was quickly forgotten. It couldn't be forgotten too quickly for official Ottawa. After Reagan's election, when he asked for pre-inauguration meetings with the leaders of Mexico and Canada, Pierre Trudeau said he was too busy with a state junket to Africa. Reagan had to be content with Mexico's Lopez Portillo, who presented him with a white stallion.

Eerily, Clarkson's proposal unconsciously echoed that of Reagan over two years before. Clarkson and Reagan have totally opposed goals, but depending on circumstances the differences between their plans in practice would probably be nugatory.

This illustrates once again the curious tendency of Canadian Nationalism, in the act of achieving its purest expressions, to discredit its animating thesis of a Canada that is and should be distinct. What is bred in the bone comes out in the flesh. Common culture counts. Sending a cabinet minister to Washington is an entirely natural response to the fundamental importance of the U.S. to Canada, both materially and morally, regardless of what the various Canadian factions would have the ambassador say. Canadians would not so gaily contemplate "intervening" in American political life, as Ambassador Gotlieb wanted, if it were not something that they instinctively recognize, feel an affinity for and in essence share. This can't be said of, say, Mexico, or the Soviet Union. But by "wading in the streams of the special interests," Gotlieb is tacitly conceding that Canada is just another special interest, running down to an American sea. It is marvellously easy for Canadians to form alliances within the U.S., for example with the Northeastern states on the issue of acid rain, which Ottawa claims is caused by sulphur dioxide effluvia from the coal-burning industries in the Midwest. Naturally, the Midwest strikes back, alleging that Canada just wants to corner the market for its hydro-electric power, and anyway, what about Inco's smokestack in Sudbury, Ontario, the single greatest source of sulphur dioxide pollution in the world? It's all part of the game. And Canada is the player wearing the Maple Leaf charm.

Thus the reason Gotlieb's audience at Johns Hopkins did not protest Canada's intention to meddle in U.S. affairs was not solely masochism, or the phlegm of an imperial people resigned to the yowling of lesser breeds. They positively expected Canadians to meddle in American affairs, *because they thought of them as Americans.* Gotlieb's assertion of independence was merely confirming the integration of the two polities.

In April 1972, President Richard Nixon visited Ottawa and made a speech to the House of Commons that, according to Lawrence Martin, "read as though it had been written in Canada, designed to appease the economic nationalists, designed to give the Liberal government freedom to carve out the direction it chose." It was widely greeted as signalling the end of the special relationship. Speeches on such occasions, said Nixon:

> . . . have often centered on the decades of unbroken friendship we have enjoyed and our four thousand miles of unfortified frontier. In focusing on our peaceful borders and our peaceful history, they have tended to gloss over the fact that there are real problems between us. They have tended to create the false impression that our countries are essentially alike. It is time for Canadians and Americans to move beyond the sentimental rhetoric of the past. It is time for us to recognize that we have very separate identities; that we have significant differences; and that nobody's interests are furthered when these realities are obscured.

Nixon then went on to what might be described as the sentimental rhetoric of the present: unity-in-diversity, cohesion-without-coercion, growing-closer-without-growing-alike, and so on.

It will come as no surprise that Nixon's speech had indeed been written at least partially in Canada, by Ivan Head, Prime Minister Trudeau's foreign affairs advisor. Inevitably, Head was often compared by the Canadian media to Henry Kissinger, then Nixon's colorful Assistant for National Security Affairs, and with whom he was supposed to liaise. There had been unusually close consultations about Nixon's speech, and the willingness of the White House to say exactly what the Prime Minister's Office wanted certainly bore the Kissinger diplomatic stamp. This non-special relationship was clearly rather special.

The Nixon speech is proof that some truths are forgotten because they are so obvious that mentioning them becomes a bore. This is particularly the case where journalists and diplomats, both inhabiting insulated and fashion-conscious little worlds, are involved. Before Eisenhower's 1953 visit to Canada, the head of the State Department's Canada section noted on a draft of an address to be given by the President that "the speech still contains a reference to the 'undefended frontier.' Frankly, this was considered a 'corny' topic for after-dinner speeches when I went to Ottawa twenty-three years ago. I still think it is a mistake for the President to mention it." Eisenhower took the precaution when he spoke of calling the theme "shopworn," but President Johnson was not so subtle ten years later, with the result that he found himself derided for using what the Toledo *Blade* said was "a threadbare and irritating cliché that ought to be banned by law. . . . The famous unguarded border fogs our thinking about Canada."

Another catch-phrase with a corniness problem is "special relationship" itself. It is a mark of the collapse of communication between Britain and Canada since World War II that frequent bulletins have been issued in Canada on the demise of the special relationship with the U.S., with no realization that exactly the same bulletins were being issued in Britain, which also believed it had a special relationship with the U.S. This was not because the U.S. was a secret bigamist. It simply reflected the reality that the Western Alliance had what de Gaulle called an "Anglo-Saxon core."

The truth is that the relationship between the two countries *is* special. The longest undefended frontier in the world *is* extraordinary. Only a shared North American parochialism and innocence of world history permits Americans and Canadians to think otherwise. Above all else, the relationship is one between peoples. In the early 1980s, there were 40 million crossings of the Canadian border by U.S. residents each year, and an astounding 34 million crossings, or 1.4 per head, by Canadians returning from the U.S. Canadians were left out when the New York City Museum of Immigration opened in 1972 – the telling official explanation was that they were not considered to be foreigners – but they are estimated to be the third-largest immigrant group in the U.S. In California alone, according to the 1980 U.S. census, there are nearly half a million inhabitants who are Canadians (or have Canadian parents), some 2% of the population. Conversely, 470,991 U.S. residents are reported to have immigrated to Canada between 1946 and 1980. Immigration is currently thought to be in balance at about 20,000 each way a year, and despite the 1960s immigration reforms of both countries, Canadian and American families still overlap the border along its entire length. Canadians follow sports, read American magazines, watch American television. Official and commercial intercourse, as already documented, is literally beyond count.

The two societies are in what Goldwin Smith called "practical fusion." Much of Ottawa's policy has simply been an attempt to interpose itself between consenting partners. "Continentalism, as it has been called, was more like a force of nature," said John Holmes, reviewing the mandarin era. "The efforts of governments, in agreements reached with the United States, was to control and discipline that force rather than to encourage it."

And in the context of history, even the relationship between the Canadian and American polities can only be described as idyllic. The border clashes in the early years of U.S. independence have recently inspired best-sellers in Canada, but the fighting was not joined with great enthusiasm on either side or in Britain, it did not interrupt the exchange of peoples, and it does not remotely compare with the slaughter in Europe caused by the contemporaneous Napoleonic wars.

Lawrence Martin subtitled his study of U.S.-Canadian relations, "The Myth of Bilateral Bliss." He revealed such atrocities as the fact that Lyndon Johnson once swore at Lester Pearson, and that a Philadelphia radio station once wrote to Prime Minister Louis St. Laurent asking him how to pronounce his name. This is definitely blissful by comparison with Poland and its neighbors. Nor, despite President Nixon/Kissinger/Head, can it reasonably be concluded that the U.S. and Canada are countries that are essentially unalike and have real problems, in a world that contains Israel and Syria, Greece and Turkey, or, for that matter, the U.S. and Mexico.

Robert Thompson spoke no more than the truth in the comments in the House of Commons that provided this chapter's epigraph. And however much individuals in Ottawa and Toronto may regret the decision made by history, culture and their own compatriots, as Canadians they are confronted with the reality that Thompson pointed out to a fellow MP in the same memorable debate: "You've buttered your bread, now you have to lie on it."

Part Two

The Two Solitudes

8

From Failing Hands: The Eclipse of English Canada

That England, that was wont to conquer others,
Hath made a shameful conquest of itself.

   – William Shakespeare, *Richard II*

In April 1915, the Germans opened the second battle of Ypres with the heaviest artillery barrage yet seen in World War I, followed by the first-ever use of poison gas. Some French colonial units broke and fled, leaving the Canadian Expeditionary Force on their right threatened with encirclement.

The Canadians elected to hold the line. Among other preparations, they sent back to his unit a visitor they had been entertaining from the British Royal Flying Corps. He was Sir Oswald Mosley, later to be a minister in one of the first Labour governments in Britain and, later still, leader of the British Union of Fascists, but at that time innocently engaged in becoming a war hero. More than fifty years after the battle, Mosley wrote:

> From a small rise in the ground in the first stage of my return journey, I looked back to see what was happening. As dusk descended there appeared to our left the blue-grey masses of the Germans advancing steadily behind their lifting curtain of fire, as steadily as if they had been on the parade ground at Potsdam. At that point it appeared there was nothing to stop them.

Only Soviet film directors like Eisenstein in his *Alexander Nevsky*, Mosley commented, seem able to recreate a drama like the attack of the Prussian Guard, with its officers out in front drawing on their white gloves. Turning, Mosley saw the Guard's antithesis:

It was the Canadian reserves moving up to occupy the empty section of the line. They were an astonishing spectacle for a regular soldier, for they were advancing apparently without any discipline at all under a fire so intense that by our standards any advance would be impossible except by the finest troops under the most rigorous discipline. They were laughing and talking and walking along in any formation, while the heavy shells we called Jack Johnsons – after the Negro boxing champion: they were 5.9s and capable of wiping out a whole platoon with one explosion – were crashing among them in the most severe concentration of artillery fire men had yet known. Very soon after I passed through them – as we afterwards learned – they went right into the advancing Germans and that event very rare in war occurred, a bayonet fight in which both sides stood firm. Three days later the R.F.C. were engaged in trying to delineate the still indeterminate line after the changes brought about by the failed attack. I reported that the line went through a place called St. Julien where heavy fighting was taking place in what had been the little town. It turned out to be considerably behind the actual line. Some two hundred of the Canadians had forced their way right through and when surrounded, fought to the last rather than surrender.

The Canadians at Ypres, all volunteers and overwhelmingly Anglophone, did not share their descendants' chronic worries about national identity. To them, Canada was a distinct but integral part of the wider Imperial nation. To quote Sir John A. Macdonald: "A British subject I was born – a British subject I will die." He said it last in his final address to the House of Commons on February 7, 1891.

And Canadians did die in defense of the British Crown. A Canadian rode in the Charge of the Light Brigade at the Battle of Balaclava in 1854, winning the Victoria Cross, Britain's highest award for valor; Canadians took part in the attempt to rescue General Gordon at Khartoum in 1884 and fought in South Africa during the Boer War. The scale of Canada's losses in World War I, when, out of a population of some eight million, it put 625,000 men into uniform and lost 61,000 dead, can perhaps be gauged by a comparison with the U.S., which with a population of about 100 million lost just over 53,000 killed in World War I; a casualty rate equivalent to Canada's would have meant some 760,000 dead. This toll was not approached even by the approximately 290,000 U.S. dead in World War II, much less by the Vietnam War, when the U.S., with over 200 million population, lost just 47,000.

While the Ypres battle was still raging, in the early morning of May 3, 1915, the best-known poem to emerge from World War I was composed by a Canadian, Major John McCrae, First Brigade surgeon with the Canadian Field Artillery. In succeeding generations, it would be quoted throughout the British world on November 11, the anniversary of the Armistice ending the War to End Wars, when artificial poppies were everywhere worn to commemorate the dead.

> In Flanders fields, the poppies blow,
> Between the crosses, row on row,
> That mark our place; and in the sky
> The larks, still bravely singing, fly
> Scarce heard amid the guns below.
>
> We are the Dead. Short days ago
> We lived, felt dawn, saw sunset glow,
> Loved and were loved, and now we lie
> In Flanders fields.

McCrae, who was himself to die later in the war, was writing out of the shock of the death of a comrade. But his conclusion was marked by none of the pacifism that the twentieth century has come to expect of its war poets, particularly from World War I. Instead it expressed an unflinching patriotism more typical of the nineteenth century:

> Take up our quarrel with the foe:
> To you from failing hands we throw
> The torch; be yours to hold it high.
> If ye break faith with us who die
> We shall not sleep, tho' poppies grow
> In Flanders fields.

In Canada today such sentiments seem almost impossibly remote. In 1982, McClelland & Stewart, the leading Nationalist publishing house whose imprint is modestly subtitled "The Canadian Publishers," put out a bilingual coffee-table book "to mark the Patriation of the Constitution of Canada and to mark Canada's 115th Birthday." *Canada With Love/Canada Avec Amour* was full of pictures of Canadian landscapes. It featured an introduction by Prime Minister Pierre Trudeau and an essay by his friend Harold Town, a fashionable Toronto artist who had illustrated the Trudeau brochure distributed at the 1968 leadership convention. Both are worth reading as indications of what has happened to Major McCrae's Canada since World War I.

"This book is about Canada," wrote Trudeau. "Indeed, it is Canada, because a country is more than a national anthem, or a flag fluttering in the breeze. It is the breeze itself, and the sunset, and all these are captured in this book.

"And especially a country is the land and the mark that it carves on the souls of its people, and the claim it makes on their hearts."

Expanding on this theme, Town added:

As a people we are chained to the mystery of our endless sky, to the flooding rush of spring, the fat buzz of summer, and the ruthless death of winter through which in every crack of ice we see the green promise of a mystical tomorrow. We are wanderers in the largest uninhabited country in the world [sic], refusing to weld ourselves into a specific people who bear a banner of race or mission.

. . . Refusing to squeeze our lovely land into one substantive racial symbol, we stand on the threshold of identity, scuffling our feet on the world's longest undefended border.

. . . Canadians give themselves completely to the seasons; our seasons surround and encapsulate a historical vacuum. In this we are eccentric, for without plan or reason we have avoided civil war and mad international excursions.

Canadian Nationalists have a curious predilection for baroque prose, possibly once again as a polemical technique similar to their periodic cries of betrayal noted in Chapter One. But more significant is this semi-official volume's bland rewriting of history. Even if Town had momentarily forgotten about World War I, he was born in 1924 and lived as a non-combatant through World War II, during which other Canadians distinguished themselves in actions such as the Battle of the Atlantic, the Dieppe Raid and the 3rd Canadian Division's capture of Juno Beach on D-Day, and 42,000 of them fell – proportionately worse losses, again, than those of the U.S. More recently, 27,000 Canadians fought in Korea, sustaining 1,600 casualties, and Canada is to this day an important member of NATO, with forces stationed in West Germany facing Warsaw Pact units across the Iron Curtain. Even in the Vietnam War, although Canada, like Britain and unlike Australia and New Zealand, did not participate formally, Canadian government officials on the International Control Commission routinely informed the U.S. of its supposedly confidential deliberations, and many individual Canadians served in the American forces there. Canada in fact has had a quite remarkable record of "international excursions," mad or otherwise.

Furthermore, there can be few more "substantive" racial or ethnic symbols than the Crown, or for that matter the French version of *O Canada*. And, notwithstanding the mutual coolth of the "founding races," there are few polities ethnically more homogeneous or "specific" than Canada, since the Francophones, unlike America's Hispanic minority, are northern European in origin. Prime Minister Trudeau is quite right that "a country is more than a national anthem" – particularly in the case of *O Canada,* as was discussed in Chapter Four. But it is also more than a real estate package, powerful in the extreme though Canada's landscape can be. To argue that Canada is a scenic "historical vacuum" is simply absurd. But it is highly convenient.

The stark necessity of denying English Canada's history underlies this Orwellian compulsion in official Canadian ideology. It was never more cruelly apparent than in the document issued by the federal Liberal government in support of its constitutional reform proposals in 1978. This was a period when Ottawa was still stunned by the Parti Québécois victory in the Quebec provincial election two years earlier. The document – called, typically, "A Time for Action" – suffered from all the problems of committee-issued clarion calls. For example, it allowed as how Canadians "believe in the dynamics of individual enterprise, in the effective use of government institutions to serve our collective development, and in the sharing of the country's wealth and income among individuals and regions." Apart from its bold stand against the ineffective use of government institutions, this is the kind of statement which in combination with fifty Canadian cents ($0.35 U.S.) will purchase a cup of coffee – while leaving an opening for a resurgent Ottawa at a later date. But the document's fundamental problems were deeper. Once again, even at this moment of supreme national crisis, it could become passionate only about real estate: "Can there be a Canadian, for example, whose outlook has not been deeply marked by the stretches of seemingly infinite space – the high seas of our Maritime regions, the boundless horizons of our Prairies, the endless unfolding of the St. Lawrence valley, the limitless reaches of our Great Lakes?" And urgent, this time explicitly, only in its rejection of history: "Let us forget once and for all about the Plains of Abraham."

This is the direct equivalent of attempting to rally Americans with the cry "Forget the Alamo!" Canada's languages, laws and liberties all stem from that victory by Wolfe over Montcalm in 1759. This is true even for French Canada. After the Conquest, which removed the stifling attentions of France's colonial *intendants,* the 60,000 Francophones increased their birth rate and multiplied a remarkable one hundred times in the next two hundred years, while shielded by British diplomacy from the aggressive, assimilationist republic to the south. This was actually considerably faster than the growth rate of France itself, and contrasts completely with the fate of the rather similar number of Francophones Napoleon abandoned when he sold the Louisiana territories to the U.S. in 1803. Quebec spokesmen used to acknowledge as much themselves. "Be satisfied we will never forget our allegiance," Etienne-Paschal Taché, one of the last of the 1837 rebels to surrender, told the Quebec Assembly during the debate on the militia bill in 1846, "till the last cannon which is shot on this continent in defense of Great Britain will be fired by the hand of a French Canadian." But for the Anglophones, the battle on the Heights of Abraham was fundamental. Without it, English Canada would not exist.

"People will not look forward to posterity, who never look backward to their ancestors," said Edmund Burke in his book *Reflections on the Revolution in France.* Yet not looking back is exactly what Canadian Establishment ideology must require of English Canadians. The story of Canada essentially consists of the subjugation, brushing aside, ignoring, co-optation, bribing and/or appeasement of Francophones by Anglophones intent on building a state *A mari usque ad mare* – From sea even unto sea, in the biblical phrase they chose as a motto for their Dominion's coat of arms, prepared (of course) by the College of Heralds in London. But any reference to these ancestral activities could offend the Francophone component in the Liberal electoral coalition. It might even expose the extent to which the imposition of the Liberal Interpretation of Canada's history has in fact amounted to a slow-motion cultural revolution for English Canada, directly aimed at its values and loyalties.

Because the Liberals' Canada is artificial, a deracinated "hybrid, bicultural monstrosity" in René Lévesque's phrase, it cannot draw upon the common experience and beliefs that form the life blood of a healthy nation. Hence the continuous desperate efforts to substitute geography for history. This matters less to the Francophones, safely entrenched in their linguistic fortress and acutely conscious of their history, than it does to the Anglophones. English Canadians are being effectively dispossessed of their highest political expression, the Canadian state, and subjected to what amounts to a frontal lobotomy, the surgical excision of inconvenient aspects of their historical consciousness. Symbolically, Quebec automobile license plates carry the old Francophone nationalist slogan *Je me souviens* – "I remember." Ontario can only permit itself a feeble ecological "Keep it beautiful."

Thus it is English Canadians, not the Francophones, who display the psychological traits of a colonized nation. It is the Anglophones whose emblems and rituals have been removed or transformed, and who are being consciously manipulated in an effort to ensure their development along studiously inoffensive paths, with any atavistic outbreaks, such as the right-wing Prairie separatism of the early 1980s, anxiously monitored and violently condemned. Like the West German enthusiasts for "European Unity" in the decades following World War II (*their* automobiles bore "EU" plates) English Canadians can express their patriotism respectably only through an artificial construct – a bicultural Canada – whose relationship to their historic concerns is little more than nominal.

In order to participate in Canada as the Liberal establishment has defined it, ordinary English-speaking Canadians must engage in a collective act of self-censorship. All across Canada, a careful search will reveal disregarded memorials in incongruous places – on a wall in the modern post office of the petrochemicals town of Sarnia, Ontario; amid the thundering traffic of Toronto's University Avenue – to Canadian volunteers who fought in Imperial wars now rarely mentioned. It suggests the pleasing if eerie fancy that the locals are dwelling, like Andean peasants, amid the ruins of a civilization of which they have lost all memory. This is a token of how profound has been the cultural change inflicted upon English Canada since the beginning of the century. Casual conversation with Canadians reinforces the impression. A young woman observes in the course of a discussion that her country "has never been engaged in a major war." An English immigrant, one of the many "war brides" who met their Canadian husbands when the latter were posted overseas during World War II, remarks wonderingly that children are never taught anything about Britain in school any more.

English Canada's self-censorship is so effective that no dreams disturb this sleep. It seems quite natural for the liquor company Seagrams Limited to distribute in 1980 a promotional history of Canada, *The Canadian Journey,* whose only mention of World War I is in the context of French-language schooling and the firing of enemy aliens on the Prairies. This suppression has achieved impressive levels of refinement. For example, Louis Riel, the nineteenth-century leader of two minor Prairie rebellions against Canadian authority by French-Indian halfbreeds ("Métis"), has been turned into an official Canadian hero in the twentieth century. This is partly out of the pervasive North American guilt about aboriginals, partly a matter of the romantic sympathy of progressives for any revolution, and partly because he was always a hero to French Canada, whose alliance with Sir John A. Macdonald's Conservatives is conventionally supposed to have been terminated by Riel's execution for treason. Macdonald could hardly risk a pardon, because Riel himself had ordered the shooting of an Ontario Orangeman, Thomas Scott, who refused to accept the authority of the Métis "provisional government." Scott's only crime was remaining loyal to Canada. But recent Canadian historians, whether popular or academic, have regularly paused in their narratives to cast aspersions on his character: "arrogant and recalcitrant" – Kenneth McNaught, *The Pelican History of Canada;* "pugnacious" – Pierre Berton, *Why We Act Like Canadians;* "a violent man" – June Callwood, *Portrait of Canada;* "an obstreperous youth" – Donald Creighton (!), *John A. Macdonald: The Old Chieftain.*

None of these Anglophone authorities, however, seems to have found space to explain – and accordingly modern English Canadians are generally unaware – precisely why their forebears were so outraged by Scott's death. Eyewitnesses believed that, although horribly wounded, he had survived the firing squad. Hours later, he was reported to be semi-conscious and in agony inside his coffin. There was even a widespread apprehension that he was still alive when finally buried in a secret grave near the Red River on March 4, 1870.

Education, of course, has been rallied to the cause of selective amnesia. The war bride quoted above was quite right. In 1977, for example, the provincial government of Ontario promulgated guidelines for high school history that made it possible for students to graduate ignorant of the world wars and the British parliamentary system that has shaped Canada's own constitutional development. Instead, they were to traverse "core content areas" such as "Original Peoples," and "Social Reform." Louis Riel and the 1837 Rebellions survived, however. In explanatory notes, the government's education specialists observed that the revised curriculum would "develop an understanding of the Canadian identity and societal goals," just as the year spent on Canada's multicultural heritage would "develop increasing empathy and positive attitudes towards members of cultural groups other than one's own." By 1982, the Ontario Ministry of Education required high schools to seek special permission to teach credit courses in British history, and it was planning to revoke this permission in the only two cases it had allowed. The Grade Ten option the Ministry instructed the schools to offer in place of British history was "Canada's Multicultural Heritage." A woman protesting this policy commented:

> ... Credits are allowed in Hungarian, Lithuanian, Punjabi, Chinese (Cantonese and Mandarin), modern Greek, German, Italian and Portuguese. In these courses they study the language, culture and history of these countries. These courses need no special permission – only British History needs it.
>
> Isn't this ridiculous, when our laws, our language and our parliament come from Britain?

Restoring the British and Imperial dimension to Canadian history would put a number of official Canadian heroes in a different perspective. For example, the celebrated humorist and McGill University political science professor, Stephen Leacock, turns out to have been a leading advocate of a formal political federation of the British Empire, with an Imperial legislature in London made up of representatives from Canada and the other British nations. This idea was seriously considered around the turn of the century, incredible as it may now sound. It continued to echo, ever more faintly, for over fifty years. In 1903, the British Colonial Secretary Joseph Chamberlain actually resigned from the cabinet to begin a populist "Tariff Reform" campaign, aiming to underpin Imperial unity with preferential tariffs, and this policy, in attenuated form, did eventually become his party's orthodoxy. In 1907, Leacock spent a year as an "Imperial missionary," lecturing on the subject throughout the Empire, and financed by the Cecil Rhodes Trust. Leacock's Canadianism was unimpeachable. He believed, however, that "... Imperialism means but the realization of a Greater Canada, the recognition of a wider citizenship." And he was not shy about what he meant by Greater. In London, he riled up the natives with a newspaper article blaming the lack of progress towards Imperial unity on British inertia, and describing "John Bull" as an aging farmer whose sons – the Dominions – would have to take the management of his Imperial properties in hand. ("Offensive twaddle" – Winston S. Churchill.)

Another ardent supporter of Imperial federation was Colonel John Maclean, founder of the powerful Maclean-Hunter publishing complex and the magazine that bears his name — later to become synonymous with reflexive Canadian Nationalism. For Maclean, the idea's Canadian credentials were just a matter of apostolic succession: Sir John A. Macdonald, the founder of Canadian Confederation, had endorsed it in a long interview with him published in 1890.

Imperial federation, Macdonald had said, was not only desirable but at least as practical as the "political connection between Canadian settlements on the Atlantic and Canadian settlements on the distant Pacific, in advance of all railway and even telegraphic connections."

To emphasize the fundamental integrity of the Canadian Imperialists' position is not, of course, to argue that it could have continued unaltered. It was in essence an expression of Canadian patriotism, and might well have been diluted as Canada assimilated the large numbers of non-British immigrants who had arrived directly before World War I. This is by no means axiomatic, however: there is some evidence that the British link was simply accepted by the new arrivals as one of the various peculiarities of their new nationality. The loyalty of eastern European Prairie voters to the Progressive Conservative Party was apparently sealed definitively during the leadership of John Diefenbaker, an unbending monarchist and proponent of the British connection, who was himself of German descent. But the twentieth century was to bring harsher ordeals. As early as 1921, Leacock admitted that "the events of the war have entirely changed the outlook. All proposals for a formal federation and for a supreme parliament and for pan-imperial taxes are drifting into the background of academic discussion."

The subsequent development of Canada is variously presented. The Authorized Version sees it as the result of a heroic struggle to liberate a young nation from colonial chains. Other Canadians describe it as the machinations of the Liberal ruling clique which for its own partisan purposes, "erased our past, as a dark period of serfdom under an imperial yoke; and . . . denied the historical tradition in which our life as a people is rooted," as the Canadian writer John Farthing charged in the 1950s.

To a considerable extent, what happened was not made-in-Canada at all. In Britain after World War I, the Imperial idea was continuously on the defensive. Although there was some legislation and more lip service in the cause of Greater Britain and its world role, the British elite was not committed. This became clear after World War II, when the British Empire imploded with astonishing speed. Like a bankrupt company, it had fallen into the hands of liquidators without sentiment about or, arguably, understanding of its business. For Canada, this had radical implications. Charles de Gaulle brutally underlined them in his conversations with Britain's Prime Minister Harold Macmillan in the 1960s during the latter's attempt to join the European Economic Community. "Believe me," de Gaulle says Macmillan assured him, "we are no longer the England of Queen Victoria, of Kipling, of the British Empire of 'splendid isolation.' " This much must have been obvious, but de Gaulle still wondered whether Britain was

> ... prepared to submit to the constraints inseparable from such an association, one so alien to her historic nature and to what was still the basis of her existence? ... "From the economic point of view," I said to the Prime Minister, "could you British, who depend mainly on extensive trade with the United States and a system of preferential imports and exports with the Commonwealth, really agree to enclose yourselves with the Continentals behind a tariff wall which would gravely impede your American trade and exclude your former dominions and colonies? You who live cheaply on Canadian wheat ... could you ever consider feeding yourselves on Continental agricultural produce, in particular French, which would be necessarily more costly?"

Britain could, Macmillan apparently claimed. He also "protested, no doubt very sincerely, his desire to draw the necessary consequences as far as the United States was concerned." This new British policy was diametrically opposed to Canadian interests and in particular to those of John Diefenbaker. His new government was trying to reorient Canadian trade and politics towards Britain, and he felt betrayed by Macmillan's newfound obsession with "entering Europe." But he was pushed, squawking bitterly, out of the nest – and Canada with him.

English Canada has been left beached and disoriented by the ebbing of the Imperial tide. In the twenty years since Diefenbaker's government, Britain has continued to recede in the Canadian consciousness so rapidly that even those members of the intelligentsia aware of its passing lost the ability to grapple with its meaning. A year after the installation of the Maple Leaf flag, the eminent Manitoba historian W.L. Morton gave an address in which he pointed out that, contrary to official insinuation, "our Britishness, then, was not Englishness, but a local brew of our own which we called Canadian," and mourned "the world I lost last spring." In 1980, when Charles Taylor asked him about it,

> ... Morton was nonplussed and said he couldn't recall exactly what he had meant. "It was probably the flag," he finally ventured. "I was angry about that ... leaving out all tradition ..." Then his voice trailed off and he failed to elaborate .... When I asked

> Morton about his striking assertion [in 1964] about Canada's
> "moral purpose," he seemed anxious to avoid any inflationary
> misconception: "I guess I meant the rule of law . . . not much more
> than that. These things *do* have a moral purpose . . . decency in
> politics and that sort of thing . . ." Again his voice trailed off.

Such pitiful intellectual flotsam is all that remains to the conventional
Canadian Anglophone, once he gets beyond official congratulations
on his "tolerance." His heritage is reduced to the point where it
consists only of procedural or negative statements.

Worse fates, no doubt, have befallen nations. But English Canada
does pay an intangible price for its deprivation, a price that can be
detected in subtle ways. For example, its cultural crippling has had
undiagnosed, although much-lamented, consequences for its artistic
voice. The Australian film industry has produced incomparably more
successful films than Canada's although both operate under a comparable regime of government subsidy and tax breaks. The reason for
this is the strength of the Australian scripts. Most deal with recent
Australian history. Canadians also fought in the Boer War, the setting
for Bruce Beresford's *Breaker Morant*. The Newfoundland Regiment
was raised amid a colorful enthusiasm identical to the one Australian
Light Horse units portrayed in Peter Weir's *Gallipoli* and it met, in ten
minutes on the Somme, an equally terrible fate. But these subjects are
essentially prohibited under the Anglophones' self-denying ordi-
nance, the rare exceptions being either debunking or conventionally
pacifist. There have, however, been an opera and a CBC film about
Louis Riel. (And Francophones have made films about Quebec
history, with as much impact on English Canadians as any other
foreign art film.)

A side-effect of English-speaking Canada's post-Imperial trauma is
its pervasive and continuing disorientation and its deeply neurotic
public attitude towards the United States. This attitude was not as a
rule characteristic of the Canadian Imperialists, despite their more
robust sense of self. Indeed, they generally viewed the U.S. with a
friendly if competitive eye. During World War II, Leacock wrote that
the "two fixed points, two steady beams of light" for Canada were its
links with Britain and "our firm union of friendship in mind and
purpose with the United States." Colonel Maclean, whose wife was
from Boston, even envisaged a free trade bloc incorporating the
United States and the British Empire, and claimed that in conversations in 1925 his conjectures had been approved by President
Coolidge and his Secretary of Commerce, Herbert Hoover.

What disarmed yesterday's Canadian Imperialists was exactly what disturbs today's Canadian Nationalists: the phenomenon of a shared cultural heritage, something that Nationalists find threatening in the extreme. An explanation for the shrillness and xenophobia of contemporary Nationalism is provided by Richard Gwyn when he applauds the 1980 National Energy Program's attack upon American and other foreign interests: "The truth is that unless Ottawa espouses nationalism, there is not a lot left for it to espouse: bilingualism, as a rallying point for a pan-Canadian consciousness, just isn't enough." Ironically, in recoiling from the U.S. as a new manifestation of the wider English-speaking world, Canadian Nationalists even have begun to seize with glad cries upon residual aspects of British influence, such as state-sponsored enterprise, still strong albeit now anonymous. The theory is that if it isn't identifiably American, it must be uniquely Canadian. This theme will be taken up again later.

That English Canada in its Imperial period was simultaneously a self-confident nation and part of a wider identity is a paradox to its descendants, who are neither. It is easily misrepresented by those to whom its implications are disturbing. "It would be a great mistake to exaggerate the strength of the British connexion in Canada," says the Canadian literary mandarin Northrop Frye, in a typical sleight of hand amid an essay full of the usual platitudes about landscape's influence on the Canadian psyche. "There was a great deal of superficial loyalty, or at least a good many expressions of it, but there was also much resentment, and a feeling that colonials would have been treated with more respect in London if, like Americans, they had represented an independent nation." So much for Ypres.

Probably a fairer assessment of the attitudes of English Canada was given by the Canadian novelist Sara Jeanette Duncan, in a perceptive and remarkably prescient passage in her 1904 novel *The Imperialist*. Duncan, a successful Toronto journalist until her marriage in 1891 drew her into the Greater Britain of India and England, was herself a convinced Imperialist. But her young Canadian protagonist, Lorne Murchison, dazzled by meetings in London with a fictionalized Chamberlain, advocates the cause so idealistically while running in a federal by-election that the solid burghers of Elgin (probably Brantford), Ontario become disturbed, and he is deprived of the nomination by officers of his own party (Liberal, an interesting indication of its now-vanished sensitivity to Anglophone enthusiasms). He even loses the woman he loves to an upper-class English immigrant, who – a delicate touch – swiftly adopts the local conventional wisdom:

"I shall make a good Canadian, I trust. And as good an imperialist," he added, "as is consistent with the claims of my adopted country. That seems to be the popular view."

But Duncan did not confuse Elgin's pragmatism with lack of patriotism, although she saw clearly the problems it would pose for the Imperial Federation cause in which she believed. News of the Empire, she wrote, was brought to Elgin by American news services:

> . . . it was therefore, not devoid of bias; but if this was perceived it was by no means thought a matter for protesting measures, especially as they would be bound to involve expense. The injury was too vague, too remote, to be more than sturdily discounted by a mental attitude. Belief in England was in the blood, it would not yield to the temporary distortion of facts in the newspapers – at all events, it would not yield with a rush. Whether there was any chance of insidious sapping was precisely what the country was too indifferent to discover. Indifferent, apathetic, self-centred – until whenever, down the wind, across the Atlantic, came the faint far music of the call to arms. Then the old dog of war that has his kennel in every man rose and shook himself, and presently there would be a baying! The sense of kinship, lying too deep for the touch of ordinary circumstances, quickened to that; and in a moment "we" were fighting, "we" had lost or won.

Nature abhors vacuums in politics and culture as much as anywhere else. As the British connection and its Tory defenders declined, and the Liberal Party established its electoral hegemony in Canada, unifying its Francophone base and dividing the Anglophones, substantial efforts have been made to rationalize the new order via ideological constructs like the "Authorized Version" of Canadian history. An entertaining feature of this activity has been the frequent announcements by Liberal publicists of the final emergence of a truly Canadian nation, unsullied by foreign or Imperial stain, a performance comparable to their equally regular bulletins on the demise of Francophone separatism. Roy MacLaren even managed to write it into his elegant book about the little-known role of Canadian volunteers in the British conquest of Egypt and the Sudan at the apogee of the Victorian Empire. (This notable feat certainly justified his subsequent elevation to the federal Liberal cabinet.) Others have dated Canada's epiphany to 1939, like Hugh MacLennan in *Two Solitudes,* or to 1945, like *Maclean's* editor Ralph Allen in his grandiloquently titled 1961 history, *Ordeal by Fire: Canada, 1910-1945,* or, of course, to the 1967 Montreal Expo. And no particular event in the late 1950s inspired Bruce Hutchison to the following ripe piece of Nationalist baroque:

> Something strange, nameless, and profound moves in Canada today. It cannot be seen or labeled, but it can be heard and felt – a kind of whisper from far away, a rustle as of wind in prairie poplars, a distant river's voice, or the shuffle of footsteps in a midnight street. It is less a sound than a sense of motion.
>
> Something moves as it has never moved before in this land, moves dumbly in the deepest runnels of a collective mind, yet by sure direction toward a known goal. Sometimes by thought, more often by intuition, the Canadian people are making the final discovery. They are discovering themselves.

A case can also be made for 1970. In that year, at a lunch "which is now mythologized in some branches of the movement as The Beginning," according to an account written by Christina McCall-Newman in 1972, three men decided to found a pressure group for their version of Canadian Nationalism: the Committee for an Independent Canada. They were Walter Gordon, the former leader of the Liberal Party's left wing, who as Finance Minister under Lester Pearson had introduced a controversial nationalist budget in 1965; Peter C. Newman, then Editor-in-Chief of the nationalist *Toronto Star;* and Abraham Rotstein, an academic economist from the University of Toronto. Their creation was something of a nine-day-wonder in the small world of the English-Canadian intelligentsia. It attracted much joining, signing of petitions, attending of meetings and declarations of support. The Committee itself quickly became moribund, but it symbolized emotions that were coming to dominate Anglophone public debate, and it conveniently marks the moment when the Canadian Liberal elite finally acknowledged that it had reversed fronts and trained its guns on free market economics and on the U.S.A.

The weaknesses of Canadian Nationalism were already present at The Beginning. All three lunchers were Anglophones, all Torontonians, all prosperous members of the bourgeoisie. All, perhaps not coincidentally, represented professions that stood to benefit disproportionately from protectionism: Gordon as a scion of the pre-eminent Clarkson, Gordon and Company accounting firm, whose relationships with Canadian corporate clients were vulnerable to disruption from takeovers by U.S. firms equipped with their own auditors; Newman and Rotstein as examples of those "producers of Canadian culture" who, in the deadpan summary of a recent academic survey, "are more determined than consumers" to "keep Canadian cultural life Canadian." Early Nationalist campaigns were to aim at reserving Canadian university appointments for Canadians and promoting Canadian periodicals through punitive taxation of their American competitors. Two were members of Canada's small Jewish minority, a group normally cautious about nationalism, and one was not even a Canadian by birth but a central European refugee, anomalies which, although not without parallel in other nationalist movements, may help account for the peculiar artificiality of this Canadian variation. They were also all good political progressives and, at least in the case of Gordon and Rotstein, conscious advocates of government intervention in the economy.

This was significant because around this time it dawned on Canada's English-speaking socialists that espousing nationalism, albeit rather messy from the standpoint of a theory that condemned nation-states as antiquated and artificial divisions of the global proletariat, was very useful politically. A suitable slogan was developed to rationalize this ploy: "radicalism in Canada has to mean nationalism." "Radicalism in Canada has to mean nationalism in the sense that we must survive outside the American orbit economically if we're to escape the horrors of American imperialism," said another University of Toronto economist, Mel Watkins, who became deeply involved in the left-wing "Waffle" faction of the New Democratic Party, and later worked as an advisor to native groups agitating in Canada's North. After 1970, Canadian Nationalism would become increasingly socialist in content.

Nevertheless, Quebec socialists like Pierre Trudeau were initially suspicious. Coming from the utterly different Francophone milieu and as men of the left, they equated nationalism with xenophobic clerical-fascism in general and Maurice Duplessis in particular. They feared that any Anglophone manifestation must entail a backlash against bilingualism and thus provoke yet more intense Quebec Nationalism. But in fact questioning the Liberals' language policy was the last thing the Committee for an Independent Canada had in mind. Their "nationalism" was highly selective, and their concerns not at all closely related to any practical interests of the broad mass of English Canadians.

A significant description of the brave new Canada that Canadian Nationalists hope and claim to have discerned has been conveniently provided by Pierre Berton in his book *Why We Act Like Canadians: A*

Personal Account of Our National Character. This deeply revealing essay on the Canadian national character and its fundamental differences from the American norm was one of the best-sellers of the 1982-83 season and has influenced several subsequent journalistic commentaries. Berton – who is of Empire Loyalist stock, his cognomen celebrating earlier Huguenot ancestors – is one of the most able Nationalist publicists. Even the inevitable landscape rhapsodies in *Why We Act Like Canadians* were quite bearable. By writing his book in the form of open letters to a long-suffering American friend, he imbued it with the unmistakeably patronizing accents of a complacent elite – but under the circumstances, this was perfectly appropriate.

Why We Act Like Canadians was unkindly attacked on the grounds of factual inaccuracy by academics, the "remote and ineffectual dons" who constitute journalists' natural enemies today just as they did when Hilaire Belloc defended G.K. Chesterton against them in the early years of this century. Such criticisms are in a sense beside the point. The book was actually an attempt at a myth-making, wish-fulfilling work of art. For example, Berton called Louis Riel "a good Catholic." This was literally absurd, because Riel's heretical and megalomaniacal tendencies were well documented. But Riel's deviance was ignored by Francophone politicians eager to make an ethnic symbol out of him. And the necessities of French Canada continue to be "the major shibboleth" for modern Canadian Nationalists as for the federal Liberals ... where the two can be distinguished.

Berton's piety towards the Francophones – he claimed that their non-assimilation had been "an immeasurable gain" for Canada, whereas a fairer statement would be that it has caused endless problems – was typical of the lunching Beginners. And in fact he was one of the 200 original "sponsors" of the Committee for an Independent Canada. But what most clearly marked him as an appropriate spokesman for them is that this ritual homage actually concealed an Anglocentric ignorance of French Canada and an unthinking insensitivity towards its historical plight. Most of the time in *Why We Act Like Canadians,* Berton really was generalizing about English Canadian traits, basically forgetting that the Francophones existed. Thus he made the argument that Canadians were a cool, undemonstrative, "northern" nation in contrast to Americans (the taciturn Yankee seems to be extinct) and those hot-blooded Mediterranean types from "Italy, Spain, Greece and" – whoops! – "*southern* France ..." (Emphasis added.) The adjective was obviously a last-minute attempt to adjust for Canada's highly demonstrative Latin fact, some of which, however, traces its origins to Normandy.

This Francophone flaw is not new in Canadian Nationalism, but it appears to be irreparable. Goldwin Smith's comment about the Canada First group of the 1870s, which in some ways anticipated today's nationalists, is still definitive: "Enthusiasm was blind to the difficulty presented to the devotees of Canadian nationality by the separate nationality of Quebec, or if it was not blind, succeeded in cajoling itself by poetic talk about the value of French gifts and graces as ingredients for combination, without asking whether fusion was not the thing the French most abhorred."

Another key trait Berton shared with the CIC founders – and with Canada First – is an unconscious Central Canadian Torontocentrism. His version of the landscape ploy inadvertently provided a peculiarly gross manifestation. Referring to the Canadian Shield, which is what geologists call the low, rolling, glaciated granite upland that centers on Hudson Bay, Berton insisted: "We are a Shield people, Sam, a wilderness people. Every city-dweller from St. John's to Victoria is within a few hours' drive of lake, mountains or Precambrian rock. The Shield unites us . . . ridge after ridge of rumpled granite stretching for thousands of miles from the Great Lakes to the Arctic, imprisoning unnumbered serpentine lakes."

The Canadian Shield does cover over half of Canada's land area, although it is not uniquely Canadian, as Berton seemed to think – New York State's Adirondack Mountains are its southern extension. But at least a third of Canada's people and most of its habitable land, in British Columbia, the Prairie provinces and the Maritimes, are dominated by quite different geologies: the northward extensions into Canada of, respectively, the Western Cordilleras, the Great Plains and the sea coast of what geologists have named the "Appalachian Region." St. John's, Newfoundland, and Victoria, British Columbia, are hundreds if not thousands of miles from the Canadian Shield. But Toronto, Ottawa and Montreal are close to it; civil servants and journalists have summer cottages there. Somehow, that looms larger.

All propaganda is a judicious mixture of truth, half-truth and fantasy, especially when the writer is convincing himself. But the blend has to be pretty raw to accomplish the essential pre-requisites for the Canadian Nationalist world-view: obliterating the memory of the British connection, and conjuring up a pink elephant like an alleged fundamental difference between the English-speaking peoples of North America. These objectives are intimately linked. Eliminating the British dimension, and much of Canada's history with it, makes Canadian characteristics, frequently inherited from Britain, appear stark and unique in the context of North America. The Nationalists deny Canada's British past to detract from its American present – and future. Thus Berton argued that a difference in national temperament has made Canadian history significantly less violent than American history: "It is fashionable to poke fun at this Canadian caution. We have no Boston Tea Parties, no Valley Forges, no Bull Runs to celebrate in song and story; but then we have fewer graves to tend."

So much for Ypres – again. Conforming to Nationalist practice, Berton essentially ignored Canada's "international excursions" throughout his book. And he disposed of the Battle of the Plains of Abraham, which actually *is* celebrated in song (for example in the poignant *Brave Wolfe*, which is among the oldest of North American ballads and was once known all over the Maritimes and New England) by announcing that "the Conquest" is "a word expunged from our dictionary of Canadianisms."

The British connection itself poses a trickier problem. Berton did echo conventional wisdom in attributing Canada's lawfulness and greater deference to authority to British influence. But the cause of emphasizing Canadian independence requires that the vital and continuing nature of this relationship be minimized. Berton's solution was a sort of sleight-of-hand. He argued that the contrast between the uproarious gold rush in Alaska and the simultaneous closely regulated Canadian affair across the border in the Yukon indicates a distinctively Canadian attitude to law and order: ". . . a man could lay down his pack, or even a sack of gold, in the middle of the trail and return for it in a week, knowing no one would touch it . . . The Klondike stampede was the only *organized* gold rush in history." Only a careful reader will note that the Mounties were wearing "the *Queen's* scarlet" and that the legendary Superintendent Sam Steele in his capacity as censor purged from Dawson City theatres "any remark that he considered disrespectful of *sovereign,* country or *empire.*" (Italics added.) For even at this late date, Canada was a true daughter of the Empire. Far from being unique, her civilized gold rush was remarkably like comparable developments in Australia, South Africa and the other frontiers of the British world.

Actually, Berton may also have been wrong about American uproariousness. Recent research – for example, Professor Roger McGrath's *Violence on the Frontier* – suggests that the West's fabled wildness was largely confined to specific groups, notably young men duelling over points of honour. According to McGrath's work, the overall incidence of robberies and burglaries was considerably less than 10% of that of modern New York City, which as a result of immigration should really be viewed as an extension of the Third World. And Count Sienkiewicz, a Polish observer of the 1849 California Gold Rush, noted exactly the same respect among miners for one another's packs and gold.

For that matter, Berton himself is a sufficiently good reporter that he quite often could not resist recording colorful facts that utterly contradict his contentions. Thus, after holding forth about the quintessentially Canadian nature of the Yukon gold rush, he suddenly added, "Let me remind you that in those days Dawson was really an American town. Its population was at least three-quarters foreign . . . . Western gunfighters like Buckskin Frank Leslie rubbed shoulders with western gun molls like Calamity Jane. These old frontiersmen sometimes talked big but in practice acted as tamely as any Canadian." Later, he remarked that before World War I, more than 600,000 American immigrants settled in the Canadian West. Of all the 'ethnic' groups to arrive, they were the largest, the most powerful, the wealthiest and *the most easily assimilated.* (Emphasis added.) Why did these Americans act so tamely and assimilate so easily? There can be only one answer: because they shared with their Canadian hosts a fundamentally common culture. Berton's entire book, of course, is supposed to be proving the contrary.

The same maneuver of deleting Britain and distorting America is observable in Berton's exposition of the claim, dear to the hearts of the contemporary Nationalists, that Canadians have somehow naturally developed into devout social democrats, unlike their capitalistic cousins to the south. Berton began with the conventional point that the 1867 British North America Act speaks of "peace, order and good government." "Life, liberty and the pursuit of happiness are lesser-Canadian ideals . . . . The other side of order and security is authority. We've always accepted more government control over our lives than you have. . . ."

Nevertheless, from this dubious base, Berton proceeded to argue that deference to authority led straight to the modern Canadian welfare state. And he concluded that this Canadian predilection for state intervention extends into economic policy, partly as a consequence of the desire to be independent of the U.S.: "From the days of the Rideau Canal to the year of Petro-Canada, we have been a public-enterprise country . . . [Public enterprises] form the bricks and mortar in the national bulwark we were forced to construct to protect ourselves from you . . . . Nobody in this country calls this socialism . . . ."

This is the common Nationalist misinterpretation of Canada's economic culture. It is a caricature, ignoring, among other things, the American "public enterprise" tradition that produced the Tennessee Valley Authority, the notoriously powerful New York State Parks Commissioner Robert Moses, and – predating the Bank of Canada – the Federal Reserve system.

The real point, however, is that the *étatisme* that Berton was presenting as typically and uniquely Canadian is in reality part of something Daniel Patrick Moynihan once diagnosed as "the British Revolution," the successor to the classical liberal American Revolution and the totalitarian Russian Revolution. While U.S. Ambassador to the United Nations, Moynihan wrote in a 1974 memorandum to the U.S. State Department that "British culture had been in the first half of the twentieth century incomparably the most influential in the world, and that culture was increasingly suffused with socialist ideas and attitudes." (As if anticipating slippery Canadian semanticists, Moynihan asked acidly "to be indulged the term 'socialist,' for there seemed to be none better.") After World War II, when the former colonies were relinquished, "It was not generally perceived that they were in a sense already spoken for – that they came to independence with a pre-existing, coherent, and surprisingly stable ideological base which, while related to both the earlier traditions, was distinct from both, [namely] the Welfare State of the British Revolution." Monyihan even identified two further characteristics of this British revolution: a suspicion of, almost a bias against economic development (British socialism " had emerged in the age of the Diamond Jubilee, and was fixed in its belief that there was plenty of wealth to go around if only it were fairly distributed") and pervasive anti-Americanism. "More anti-American, surely, than it was ever anti-Soviet. America was both capitalist *and* vulgar. British socialism was ever genteel."

Needless to say, all these themes are instantly recognizable to any student of Canada. The National Energy Program, which assumed indefinitely rising prices, delayed the exploitation of resources and extended Ottawa's role in the name of reducing foreign ownership, is only the best-known expression of them.

Nationalists in Canada justify such policies by arguing that they are "the Canadian Way," that a native Canadian tradition exists which legitimizes them so that they need not be defended on their own merits. They can hardly afford to admit that this tradition is not unique at all, but deeply derivative – and that it derives from Britain, whose influence in every other aspect is to be denounced as "colonial trappings," scrutinized critically and, as in the case of heraldic symbols or public service unilingualism, frequently eradicated.

Berton also exhibits an important Nationalist syndrome when he deals with the sacred cow of Canadian ethnicity. "I want to respond to your point that Americans and Canadians spring from the same Anglo-Saxon stock," he wrote his anonymous interlocutor. "That's not exactly true: our rulers have certainly been Anglo-Saxon; but here in Canada the ruled have come from a variety of backgrounds." This article of nationalist faith is so fervently held that visiting foreign journalists, applying for enlightenment to their local equivalents as is their professional wont when in any new society, can be cruelly misled. Thus the *Christian Science Monitor* in mid-1983, in an article datelined Toronto, described Canada's differences from the U.S. in terms that must have made its American subscribers think they were reading about Brazil:

> For one thing, despite the English heritage, culture and look to much of Canada, Canadians are not predominantly of British extractions – at least not any more. They are a polyglot people, a conglomeration of races and peoples, a rich, vibrant social milieu, a diverse melting pot – some say more so than the U.S.
>
> Canadians include descendants of English, French, German, Ukrainian, Chinese, Japanese, Yugloslav, Polish, Carribean blacks, Latin Americans – some 25 percent of whom are first-generation residents of Canada, who arrived after World War II when Canada opened its doors to a floodtide of immigrants.

Such statements are not merely untrue, they are the exact reverse of the truth, as the merest glance at census figures would have revealed. Canada is ethnically much more homogeneous and more British than the U.S., particularly when Anglophone Canada is considered apart from the Francophone community. Over 40% of all Canadians told the 1981 census-takers that they were of British origin, and nearly 6% more said that they were a mixture of British and other ethnic origins. Chinese, Japanese, Indochinese and a large "Indo-Pakistani" group constituted only about 2% of Canada's population, and Latin Americans 0.4%. About 1% were immigrants from Africa and the Caribbean Islands. By contrast, in the U.S. about 14% are of British stock – much less than in Canada, although still the single largest ethnic group. Another 8% are Irish, whom the Canadian census-takers regard as British. Perhaps 12% are black, 6% "Hispanic" – almost all Latin American – and 2% Asian, mostly Chinese, Indochinese and Japanese.

Canadian Nationalist ideology has not only effectively transposed the two countries' ethnic reality, but also obscured the strikingly similar nature of their core English-speaking populations: in both cases, their second-largest component is German, followed by Italian and eastern European. Whatever the explanation for this curious procedure, its effect once again is to exaggerate the differences between Canada and the U.S., and also to induce a form of false consciousness in English – particularly British – Canadians, so that they are literally unaware of their origins and the strength of their numbers.

Closely related to the myth that English Canada is not dominantly British is the Nationalist myth that Canada, unlike the U.S., has not attempted to assimilate its immigrants but instead has evolved spontaneously a unique policy of adjusting to them, allowing them to retain their "culture" and "identity." As Berton noted: "We don't talk about a melting pot here in Canada – never have. We boast, instead, about our 'Canadian mosaic,' another distinctive phrase that will be new to you." This assertion, of course has no historical basis, as Berton is compelled to admit: "I've been reading the western Canadian newspapers for those immigrant years after the turn of the century and it's quite clear that the Eastern Europeans' success or failure was measured not only in terms of economic prosperity but also in the speed with which they learned English and adopted Canadian customs." Nor is it true that ethnic Canadians are any less absorbed into the English-speaking mainstream today than their counterparts elsewhere in North America, as the *Christian Science Monitor*'s correspondent would surely have realized if he had continued to trust his eyes rather than believing what Nationalists were pouring into his ears.

Yet Berton expresses the Nationalist orthodoxy when he says that, "our ethnic minorities have managed to retain their identity and are now being praised for having done so," indeed, "an entire government department" – the cabinet-level Multiculturalism Canada of the Office of the Secretary of State – is now devoted to enhancing and subsidizing these differences. This development could only occur because English Canada is so essentially united that real cultural divergences are an unfamiliar phenomenon and their political drawbacks are quite unsuspected. (There are French Canadians, of course, but they are invisible in their Quebec ghetto, and the official "poetic talk" about the "immeasurable gain" of their presence cannot safely be challenged in public.)

The myth of the Canadian mosaic also requires willful blindness to the reality of the U.S. and the rest of the English-speaking world. For as usual the Nationalists have constructed a straw Uncle Sam against which to strike their uniquely Canadian poses. American scholars have been questioning the efficiency of the melting pot at least since Daniel Patrick Moynihan and Nathaniel Glazer published *Beyond the Melting Pot* in 1963. At exactly the time that the Canadian elite was developing the mosaic rationale, its American equivalent was moving in the same direction.

At the end of the nineteenth century, belief in the superiority of "Anglo-Saxon" values had been so much the social norm in every English-speaking country that it was nothing for a prominent American politician and future president, Theodore Roosevelt, to frame his history, *The Winning of The West*, in not just cultural but frankly racial terms, saying bluntly that, " . . . it is of incalculable importance that America, Australia, and Siberia should pass out of the hands of their red, black and yellow aboriginal owners, and become the heritage of the dominant world races." For WASP supremacists everywhere, however, the twentieth century has been a most distressing experience. Roosevelt's position is simply no longer respectable. In the U.S., as Columbia University's Diane Ravitch has observed,

> . . . in the late 1960s, the call to black power and black pride was soon followed by other assertions of group consciousness . . . descendants of immigrants from southern and eastern Europe proclaimed the arousal of a white ethnic movement and celebrated Italian power, Slavic power, Polish power, and Irish power, among others. Champions of "the new ethnicity," as it was widely called, declared that "the melting pot" had failed and that White-Anglo-Saxon-Protestants had foisted assimilation on immigrants in order to rob them of their cultural heritage and identity.

The impact on American education has been dramatic. In 1968, the U.S. Congress passed the Bilingual Education Act; in 1974, the Supreme Court in *Lau v. Nichols* ruled that school districts must create special programs for non-English-speaking children, which federal bureaucrats rapidly interpreted, via the so-called "Lau remedies," as a requirement for bilingual education. By 1977, the U.S. federal government was funding the teaching of 300,000 children in their native tongues and the preparation of teaching materials in sixty-eight languages; by 1980, thirteen states had mandated bilingual education. This was a purely political development. As Ravitch points out, there has never been any "research basis" for the claim that bilingual education helps non-English-speaking children adjust faster than the traditional total-immersion approach, and indeed its supporters do not really regard it as a transitional program but as a means of promoting "ethnic solidarity." As in Canada, the elite abruptly abandoned the policy of assimilation despite its record of success.

A still more remarkable parallel is found in Australia, whose ethnic homogeneity exceeds even that of Canada. Although Berton and his kind regard "multiculturalism" as one of those "distinctively Canadian words," it has put in an Antipodean appearance right on cue. Australian official policy towards immigrants in the 1960s has been described by one observer, Raymond Sestito, as one of "organized assimilation," but,

> ... by the mid-1970s, Italians and Greeks, along with other migrants, were enjoying considerable benefits not thought possible five years earlier. The ideas of ethnic rights and participation were now becoming prominent. Governments were telling everybody that Australia was a multicultural society. Today multiculturalism is accepted government policy. The Australian Institute of Multicultural Affairs, ethnic radio and television (in Sydney and Melbourne) and many other government services for Australian migrant communities are now in existence.
>
> The topic of multiculturalism is not only confined to government but has now become a topic of major concern throughout Australia's social and economic institutions. ...

Why this global mushrooming of multiculturalism? Part of the answer must be that multiculturalism is the policy consequence of the alienation from the majority culture that characterizes left-wing parties in the English-speaking world, as discussed in Chapter Four. If you are disaffected from your own culture, you will not approve of its imposition on other people. In the U.S., the movement has been quite explicitly linked with loss of faith in national institutions. "The surge of the new ethnocentrism," Diane Ravitch continues,

> coincided with the intensification of the Vietnam war and of the protest movement against it on the streets and campuses of Amer-

ica. Against this background of social dissension, social crisis, urban riots, and anti-war fervor, the American system came under harsh attack for its defects . . . .

[For example,] since the Bilingual Education Act was up for renewal during the crisis-ridden days in the summer of 1974, as pressure was building for President Richard Nixon to resign because of the Watergate scandal, his administration's opposition to the legislation merely strengthened its support in the Democratic Congress. The new version . . . sponsored principally by Senators Edward Kennedy and Alan Cranston of California, incorporated a version of bilingual education that satisfied ethnic militants.

In Canada, as in Australia, multiculturalism developed while the English-speaking majority was confused – and misled – about the collapse of its previous Greater British identity. And, of course, it provided a useful further rationale for the continued appeasement of the Francophones that was necessary to hold the Liberals' electoral coalition together.

A second reason for the multicultural phenomenon is systemic rather than ideological. Multiculturalism was invented by politicians, not by the people. In his study of the Australian version, Raymond Sestito discovered that opinion polls showed multiculturalism to be decidedly unpopular with the host community. The polls also indicated that the new immigrants themselves had not initially demanded it, being primarily concerned with earning a living. "Australia's political parties," Sestito concluded, "have been the initiators of multiculturalism, rather than responding to group pressure . . . . It would not be wrong to suggest that before the parties started promoting multiculturalism, few migrants had thought of it." Similarly, in the U.S., according to Diane Ravitch, "opinion polls consistently showed overwhelming majorities opposed to [bilingualism]." Yet in Australia, the U.S. and Canada such policies go marching on.

Sestito's explanation for this paradox draws on the "economic theory of politics," sometimes known as the "Public Choice" theory, which applies the axioms of classical economics – for example, that individuals tend to act rationally to maximize their self-interest – to political situations. Large groups like immigrants are slow to organize because, apart from anything else, the marginal benefit obtained by any one individual who works for the group is too small to attract his energy and time. But when political parties are in competition with each other, the politicians themselves will seek to segment the undifferentiated electorate. They will appeal to it on the basis of whatever salient characteristics they can identify, offering programs with benefits concentrated on the special interest group, and costs dispersed across all taxpayers.

The arrival on the scene of tax dollars, of course, instantly creates a lobby with a direct interest in demanding more of the same. An increasingly frantic auction develops between the political parties on the one hand and the ethnic groups with their newly subsidized professional leaders on the other. Sestito argues that the cohesion, harmony and common values of the community as a whole are what economists call "public goods'" like clean air, enjoyed by everyone regardless of their individual behaviour. Such goods invariably suffer as long as each individual has an incentive to abuse them to the full, and no incentive to moderation – that would merely leave more for his rivals. The classic example of this syndrome is the degradation of the public range in the U.S. As long as each grazier could hope to profit by adding cattle, he would do so regardless of the land's long-run carrying capacity. This is the famous "Tragedy of the Commons." A similar process is at work to bring disaster to the political ecologies of Canadian and Australian societies, reducing them to the equivalent of dust-bowls.

Sestito wonders "whether this policy of having the best of both worlds is sustainable . . . at some point parties must decide whether they will try to gain more votes from the migrants or lose votes from other sections of the community." Of course, exactly when this happens will depend upon the skill of politicians both in orchestrating their minority special interests and, especially, in silencing majority reaction. In Canada, much of what I call the Liberals' hegemonic ideology has precisely this narcotic effect on Anglophones. The Canadian political elite might well hope that the combination of reinforcement for their Francophone base and multicultural bridgeheads in English Canada represents a permanently viable electoral strategy. To borrow from Brecht: the government is dissolving the People and electing a new one.

This phenomenon of multiculturalism pierces the ersatz Nationalism currently being peddled in Canada to its hollow heart. The two are actually mutually exclusive ideas. On the one hand, at the Nationalists' behest, Ottawa has created an array of policies, regulations and subsidies, such as "Canadian content" requirements for broadcasters, the ostensible purpose of which is to preserve and protect "Canadian culture." On the other hand, with the Nationalists' approval, it has systematically encouraged the massive immigration of totally divergent ethnic groups and the retention of their language and customs, the only possible effect of which must be, in Berton's phrase, "[to change] this country out of all recognition." These two policies are diametrically opposed. Either Canada's culture is unique and must be defended, or it is wanting and should be transformed.

And if the Nationalists did not realize this contradiction, they need only have asked the Quebec provincial government. In 1977, exploiting otherwise-dormant rights under the BNA Act, it obtained *with Ottawa's agreement* an effective veto on immigrant entry into the province, explicitly in order to prevent further adulteration of the French-speaking community. Additionally, as Berton noted rather unhappily, in Quebec ". . . the babble of immigrant tongues is being officially stilled and a man can be jailed for putting up a sign in any language except French. If that sounds spooky to you it does to me, too. It, too, is part of the essence of Canadianism, but it's not easy to explain to an outsider." It is so difficult, in fact, that Berton offered no explanation at all, other than a shameless attempt to equate Quebec's language policies with "the national instinct to put security ahead of civil rights." In actuality, however, there are no parallels in the rest of Canada to Quebec's language legislation. They are more properly sought in Europe, along with the rigorous concept of nationalism that inspires them.

If radicalism in Canada has to mean nationalism, so Canadian Nationalism turns out to mean radicalism. It is essentially a cover for a hidden agenda of unlimited social engineering, concerned not with the past but with the future, not with patriotism but with power. When scratched, Canadian Nationalists turn out to be not true nationalists, but progressives of a familiar Anglo-American type. For them nationalism is ultimately an uncouth, reactionary and probably racist atavism, valuable only as a demolition tool. Thus the Winnipeg *Free Press's* John W. Dafoe, a leading Liberal anti-Imperialist publicist of the Mackenzie King era, began to remark, as his party established itself as Canada's permanent government, that, "Nationalism is simply a stop on the way to Internationalism." Anthony Westell finished his book, *The New Society* (published in broad support of Trudeau's 1975 musings about the need for more government intervention in the Canadian economy), by arguing that Canadian Nationalism, while not wrong, puts "the issue in out-of-date and therefore misleading terms . . . . The real choice for Canadians is what role to play in the new supranational society." He predicted a sort of world federalism. And official Ottawa is, of course, as ardent a supporter as the American and British liberal elites are of the United Nations, the

New International Economic Order, the Law of the Sea Conference and the other artifacts of modern progressive internationalism, all of which must inevitably detract from the sovereignty of the industrial democracies.

The Public Choice theory employed by Raymond Sestito to analyze the apparent contradictions of multiculturalism can be extended to Canadian Nationalism itself. Nationalism in Canada has never been purely idealistic. Over a hundred years ago, according to Goldwin Smith, some supporters of Canada First were "merely nativists who desired that all power and all places should be filled by born Canadians" as the original "generation of immigrants from England which had occupied many of the leading places in the professions and commerce was passing off the scene." More recently, Nationalism has provided a catchy tune for politicians to whistle as they go about their work of developing dependent client constituencies within the electorate as a whole.

The most familiar such constituency is probably the protected industry in Central Canada, such as textiles and shoe manufacturing. But in some ways a more significant one is communications and culture – "a sacred trust," as Brian Mulroney felt compelled to describe it at the merest hint of free trade negotiations with the U.S. The presence of the Canadian state in the cultural area increased rapidly during the Trudeau years. Disbursements from the main federal cultural agency, the Canada Council, rose from less than $10 million in 1969-70 to over $42 million ten years later. "Just 20 years ago the Canada Council was funding 13 theater companies and festivals. At last count there were more than 220 professional theater companies in Canada and 160 of them received funds from the Council," reported the *Canada Year Book* in 1981. Various government agencies provided 40% of performing arts organizations' revenues by 1978. In 1957, Ottawa began making grants to publishers. By 1980, a total of 110 of the 164 publishers surveyed by Statistics Canada reported receiving grants. The Federal Cultural Policy Review Committee (informally known as the Applebaum – Hébert Commission) admitted that "the degree of government involvement in supporting writing and publishing is considerably greater in Canada than in other nations that share our cultural heritage," and it noted that even well-established commercial authors are increasingly applying for state aid. (For example, Christina McCall-Newman's long-awaited *Grits,* although virtually certain to be a landmark in Canadian publishing history, was partly financed with grants from the Canada Council and the Ontario Arts Council.) The federal government even controls the most important literary prize, the Governor-General's Award. Other aspects of direct state involvement in culture and communications include the monolithic Canadian Broadcasting Corporation, the National Film Board and some ambitious provincial government subsidy schemes. Additionally, in the name of Nationalism, the Canadian state has greatly expanded its indirect authority over the media, through discriminatory taxation, licensing, regulation, Canadian-content rules and restrictions on foreign ownership. This policy "delivered the smaller publishers into the hands of . . . the two Canadian giants [Maclean-Hunter Limited and Southam Incorporated]" by denying them access to American capital, expertise and possible takeover offers," according to one of its victims, W.W. Seccombe, a principal in Seccombe House 1971 swallowed by Southam in 1971.

Roland Huntford argued in his unsympathetic study of Sweden, *The New Totalitarians,* that by subsidizing Swedish culture the ruling Social Democratic Party was able to turn it into an instrument of indoctrination for the socialist point of view. The situation in Canada is more subtle. The state is not as omnipresent as in Sweden, and controlling culture is not as easy in a country that speaks a world language like English – which is perhaps why Nationalists such as publisher Peter Martin in his 1971 brief to the Ontario Royal Commission on Book Publishing, can occasionally be heard regretting that inconvenient fact. "Canadian governments have not sought to use their programs of support as levers of censorship or propaganda," insisted the 'Applebert' Commission.

This contention can be debated: the Royal Commission itself went on to endorse ideas about federal government action being required to foster "a balance of voices," whatever that means. And for some reason the voices currently balanced in Canadian debate seem to say little that would disturb the Canadian or even the Swedish government. Nevertheless, what cannot be disputed is that a large and growing proportion of Canada's intelligentsia is on the government payroll. Human nature being what it is, they can be relied upon, at the very least, to resent arguments that threaten to remove them.

Perhaps the Public Choice concept most applicable to Canadian Nationalism is that of "rent-seeking." Rent-seeking, as described by its inventor, the economist Gordon Tullock, is the process by which individuals and groups attempt to get society at large to pay them a subvention. Tullock argues that most societies in history have been organized in this way. Government officials and their clients extract income in the form of salaries, bribes and the proceeds of government-sponsored concessions and monopolies. Everyone else invests time and money in evading them – "rent avoidance." An obvious form of rent-avoidance in Canada is crossing the border to avoid high supermarket prices or Air Canada fares; most Nationalist restrictions, however, are aimed at corporations and fall only indirectly on the public. Because the Canadian political elite is interested in rent rather than radical reform, they have made little real effort to reconstruct the Canadian life-style, with its American television and its Florida vacations, or the Canadian economy, which remains resource-based and U.S-oriented. They just want to grab more of its fruits for themselves. Only a minority of Nationalists advocate, or even seem to have thought out, the logical end point of their policies: exchange control, wholesale expropriation of foreign assets, a siege economy.

This is not to say that these things could not happen, or that the effect of Canadian Nationalism has been minor – both in what it has done and even more in what it has undone. There can be little doubt that, like the bandages the mandarins in pre-Revolutionary China bound around their female babies' feet, Nationalism has seriously constrained the Canadian economy in developing as it could. But then Nationalism, like foot-binding, is after all an elite fashion, predicated on the assumption – as Moynihan noted – that Canada is so well provided for that, like the mandarins' daughters, it will never have to earn a living.

Canadian Nationalists are not on the whole a very likeable lot. Some of them may well be sincere, and they have exploited, as I discuss in the next chapter, a certain popular sentiment in Canada, although its depth is open to question. But too frequently their personal self-interest is distressingly obvious.

Friction among allies is inevitable, no matter how noble their common cause. The role of a small junior partner was (and is) emotionally testing. But the failure of Canada's Nationalists to reconcile themselves to reality is so persistent as to invite psychological explanation. It is hard to share the surprise H.S. Ferns, one of Mackenzie King's wartime aides, expressed in his autobiography that the publication of King's diary revealed "a foolish and childish immaturity of private personality."

In addition, it is salutary to recall that the world has not stood still during the years that the Nationalists have dominated Canadian debate. Among other things, the era saw the Vietnam War, the crushing of dissent throughout the Soviet bloc, the loss of U.S. strategic superiority, the invasion of Afghanistan, the holocaust in Cambodia. Dante reports that a special section of hell is reserved for those who are unable to make up their minds on the great issues of the day. But what about those who prattle incessantly about Canadian content?

Canadian Nationalism is one of the toadstools of history. It flourished amid English-Canadian confusion after the Imperial tradition was cut down. But it has no roots. It can never provide a nourishing cultural diet because it is based on negatives and deception, and it does not address – indeed, it is compelled to deny – English Canada's historical experience. With time and English Canada's recovery, healthy new growth will replace it.

Three hours north of Paris, the great Canadian war memorial stands on Vimy Ridge, looking out over the plains of northern France towards Belgium. The skies are often grey, but sunbeams pick out in the distance the heaped waste from coal mines, mute testimony to the activities of generations of industrial ants. On Easter Monday, 1917, the skies were grey and it was snowing when the Canadian Corps broke the German Army's hold on the escarpment that had anchored its front line since the beginning of the war. The battle was the greatest single military victory in Canadian history, and on the monument that was erected there afterwards are inscribed sixty thousand names, those of every Canadian who died in the war. Reading them brings home the magnitude of the Canadian effort – and its overwhelmingly Anglophone nature.

All around the era are neat but lonely military cemeteries, obviously little visited. Their Remembrance Books tell an interesting story. It is normal to be impressed by the extreme youth of those who died in World War I. But far more evocative of the intense feeling in English Canada at the time is that small Ontario towns like Hamilton and Peterborough sent men in their late thirties, with wives and children to support, halfway across the world as volunteers, to fight for their King and their country. And here they lie. "If ye break faith with us who die," promised Major McCrae, "We shall not sleep." But as the chill spring rain comes sweeping across the turf, the graves seem quiet enough.

9

We Shall Not Sleep: English Canada Rediscovered

The beaver is a good national symbol for Canada. He's so busy chewing he can't see what's going on.

– Howard Cable

There is an animal called the Beaver, none more gentle, and his testicles make a capital medicine. For this reason, so Physiologus says, when he notices that he is being persued [sic] by the hunter, he removes his own testicles with a bite, and casts them before the sportsman, and thus escapes by flight. What is more, if he should again happen to be chased by a second hunter, he lifts himself up and shows his members to him. And the latter, when he perceives the testicles to be missing, leaves the beaver alone. . . . The creature is called a Beaver (Castor) because of the castration.

– The Bestiary: A Book of Beasts, Being a Translation from a Latin Bestiary of the Twelfth Century Made and Edited by T.H. White

The testicles of a beaver are internal and cannot be bitten off.

– Translator's note

What, then, is the true nature of English Canada? Every traveller knows that national character exists, but defining it is notoriously difficult. Fundamental to any consideration of Canadian character, of course, is the fact that the Canadian state actually contains two quite different nations, the Anglophones and the Francophones. These two nations are like ships passing in the night. For a moment, the casual observer on the shore might mistakenly assume that their masts, funnels and hulls constitute a single entity. But time makes it clear that they are distinct, and heading in different directions.

Furthermore, although the Anglophones constitute a substantial majority of the Canadian population, the Liberal and Nationalist ideology of Canada's official classes results in significant misrepresentation of English Canada as a whole. This is partly because of the elite's function of mediating between the two communities. Thus some aspects of the official Canadian character can plausibly be attributed to the Francophones' influence, although the final result certainly misrepresents them also.

English Canada is a part of the greater English-speaking nation of North America. This is not to say that it is in any way inferior or illegitimate. It is a distinct section, like the South or the Midwest, differing in nuance from the other sections but sharing a fundamentally common culture. That Canadian Nationalists have been able to raise doubts about such an obvious reality, when the interaction between Canada and the U.S. is so overwhelming is a classic case of ideological hegemony transcending objective material reality.

Canada's relationship with the North American nation was in some ways presaged by its relationship with the Imperial British nation, just as a woman's relationship with her husband is in some ways presaged by her relationship with her father, or the husband's with his mother. Indeed, compared to the rest of mankind, the English-speaking countries still retain a remarkably high degree of unconscious cultural unity. They are members one of another, to adapt St. Paul, welded together by the ineluctable force of language. The history of Canada has been its traverse between the British and American poles of the English-speaking world.

English Canada itself, of course, is developing sectional divisions, although these still answer to the name "Canadian" – mostly. But even this sectionalism is more easily understood in the context of North America as a whole. This is why, when Joel Garreau redrew the map of the continent for his ingenious best-selling study of contemporary sectionalism, *The Nine Nations of North America,* he ignored that undefended frontier altogether, except in one vital respect. Newfoundland was assigned to his "New England" bloc, and the rest of English Canada was merely the northern extension of either "Ecotopia" (the environmentalist Pacific Coast), "The Empty Quarter" (the resource-rich interior), "The Breadbasket" (the agricultural plains and prairies), or "The Foundry" (the industrial belt of the Great Lakes and Eastern seaboard). But Quebec, as always, stood alone. (Garreau's other categories were "Mexamerica," "Dixie" and the Caribbean "Islands.")

Just as a glass can be perceived as half full or half empty, depending on your perspective, so the sectional nature of North America often misleads observers, particularly those preoccupied with their own section or unmindful of international comparisons. One manifestation is the "great curb controversy." This involves one of the sophisticated professional techniques journalists have developed for gauging foreign societies (aside from talking to cab drivers). Here is one of several recent examples of its application to Canada, in the hands of the *New York Times'* Michael T. Kaufman:

> I was walking down an antiseptically tidy street in downtown Ottawa when I became aware of some 20 pedestrians waiting on the curb. The light was red, but there were no cars in sight. No policemen, either. It was a narrow little street. The rain was fairly heavy and unpleasant. But still the small crowd waited patiently – rather stupidly, I thought – until the light changed.
>
> I had arrived in Canada, my new home, just that day, and at first I assumed that there must be some kind of police campaign under way – perhaps plainclothes men employed in an anti-jaywalking detail. After almost a year of living north of the border, I have come to realize that, no, this is just the way things are in Canada. Authority, rules and proprieties are all hallowed and respected, and that includes traffic lights. Order is accepted as a higher virtue than freedom, security as a greater boon than liberty.
>
> Like most Americans, I had assumed that an all-embracing North American civilization radiated from New York to Toronto and on to Yellowknife and Hudson Bay, and the discovery of just how different Canadian values are from our own came as quite a surprise. . . .

Now it is true that Canadian pedestrians are indeed law-abiding, although not by comparison with the Japanese. And if you think North American civilization "radiates" from New York – one of the few cities in the world where automobiles are in danger of being run down by pedestrians – Canada will certainly appear alien to you. But so, notoriously, does much of the U.S. In the South, the natives appear suspiciously polite, in California, enragingly casual. And any morning on Capitol Hill in Washington, D.C., pedestrians can also *be seen waiting at traffic lights with no cars in sight!* You can even get a jaywalking ticket across town at the crowded intersection of Connecticut

Avenue and K Street, although if your identification turns out to be an Ontario driver's license, the cop may relent.

Other U.S. observers have instinctively understood Canada's sectional status. After studying a batch of Canadian literary magazines sent to him in 1959, the American critic Dwight Macdonald wrote: "Suppose that our Northwest were to secede, culturally, from the union and set up its own special Northwestern division of arts and letters; the result would not be unlike the present situation in Canada." This was a perceptive choice. The Pacific Northwest, the Midwest and Yankee New England are the U.S. sections that perhaps most closely resemble English Canada.

"Historically, a Canadian is an American who rejects the revolution," said Northrop Frye. This aphorism is much cited, but as an analysis of Canada, it is more melodious than meaningful. Frye himself has elsewhere argued, somewhat paradoxically, that Toryism, monarchism and the British connection didn't really mean that much to Canadians, which leaves little to distinguish the two North American communities. In contrast, Goldwin Smith belonged to the school of thought that holds that the American Revolution wasn't actually a revolution at all: the colonies, deeply divided, claimed only to want their rights as Englishmen, and were supported by the English Whigs. "Had the Americans been as wise and merciful after their first as they were after their second Civil War, and closed the strife as all civil strife ought to be closed – with an amnesty – British Canada would never have come into existence. It was founded by the Loyalists driven by revolutionary vengeance from their homes. . . ." And the fact is that in terms of the fundamental issues of constitutional government and the rule of law, Canada and the U.S. have – nuances notwithstanding, relative to the rest of the world – finished up in pretty much the same place.

Like a worm, English-speaking North America was cut in two by the American Revolution. But the Canadian Loyalist political tail promptly grew a Liberal head, and the Revolutionary U.S. head a Conservative tail. This was apparent as early as 1789, when leaders of both countries reacted with horror to the French Revolution. Political debate in both countries is still conducted in the same language, literally and metaphorically.

The Canadian Liberal elite themselves illustrate this point. As Marie-Josée Drouin and Barry Bruce-Briggs have written in *Canada Has a Future*:

> While most members of the Canadian New Class consider themselves "nationalist," the rise of the New Class is a threat to the

potential development of a distinctive Canadian nationality . . . . Of all the elements in Canada, it is the New Class that are most like their equivalents in the United States. Their "anti-Americanism" is in itself American, because the same elements in the United States are also anti-American. While Canadian anti-Americanism is ancient, its contemporary manifestations and style are themselves imports from the United States. . . . Most of the contemporary Canadian complaints about American materialism, racism, exploitation, vulgarity, *et al.* are the stock in trade of the Harvard faculty or the staff at the *Washington Post.* The *Toronto Star* is not as hard on Americans as is the *Boston Globe.*

"Indeed, it is hard to think what would engage the energies of Canadian activists if there were no American causes to copy!" Anthony Westell has said, less acerbically.

The relationship between both countries' liberal elites is intimate and symbiotic, to the point where Westell has commented that Ottawa only develops a foreign policy when the Democrats are not in the White House. A 1983 *Washington Post* story reported that the Reagan Justice Department was requiring that three Canadian films about nuclear war and acid rain indicate they were issued by a registered foreign agent – the National Film Board of Canada. The story sounded much more shocking because of the piercing cries of outrage emitted by Canada's Environment Minister. ("Something you would expect from the Soviet Union, not the United States.") The requirement was actually routine, but this did not become clear until a thoroughly good time had been had by all. The only difference was that what Canadian liberals denounced as American, American liberals denounced as Reaganite. Similarly in 1981, when opponents of Budget Director David Stockman's plan to cut the U.S. foreign aid program leaked the plan to the press, visiting Canadian External Affairs Minister Mark MacGuigan was on hand in Washington to add his eagerly quoted opinion that such a move would "work against American interests," previously not one of his more obvious concerns. He couldn't have said it better if he'd started life as a professor at the University of Detroit, instead of the University of Windsor.

Canadian Nationalism can no more escape its North American nature than it can its own shadow. Even at moments of supreme Nationalistic excitement, this looms mockingly. When Professor Stephen Clarkson (because of the imminent confrontation with the U.S. that was allegedly provoked by the unexpected materialization of President Reagan) offers a scheme for a cabinet-level Canadian plenipotentiary in Washington, it turns out to echo Reagan's own proposal during the 1980 presidential campaign. When the Canadian magazine publishers' long quest for protection from the competition of *Time* magazine is finally rewarded and Ottawa legislates to prevent advertisers in *Time* from deducting the cost as a business expense for tax purposes, the monthly *Maclean's* magazine is promptly converted into a sort of imitation *Time,* blindly forcing a genuine Canadian institution into the weekly newsmagazine mould. This characteristically American formula has by no means proven automatically successful in other countries. It failed outright, for example, in Britain. When in 1971 President Nixon mistakenly referred to Japan as the U.S.'s largest trading partner (although Canada-U.S. trade exceeds that of Japan and the U.S.'s next three trading partners combined) the editor of *Maclean's* writes:

> . . . four months later, we are still asking ourselves in bumpkin bewilderment – how could he not know it? And the answer that keeps coming back from the void is: Because he does not realize we exist.
> . . . the idea that to the American president we are a noncountry makes us bloody mad.

This implicitly concedes, of course, that "we" regard ourselves as part of the American political community. Otherwise why would "we" care what some American politician thought or said? Fittingly, this plaint originally appeared in the *New York Times.*

The rest of the *Time* saga, rarely told, provides a moral to point up this tale of repressed nationality. George Radwanski gave the conventional ending when he said in *Trudeau* that after 1974 "the government succeeded in driving *Time* magazine out of Canada." But it didn't. Time Incorporated simply fired the staff associated with the magazine's Canadian edition, slashed advertising rates to offset the loss of tax deductibility, and raised subscription prices to slough off uneconomic circulation. Weekly sales staggered down from about 550,000, but then stabilized. An astonishing 365,000 copies of *Time* are now sold in Canada every week, more profitably than ever – and what Canadians are buying in such numbers is a U.S. edition without any Canadian content at all. Thus, this Nationalist "success" was utterly self-refuting. It merely succeeded in demonstrating how completely American Canadians actually were. Meanwhile, despite state protection from American competition, *Maclean's,* with a circulation of 700,000, did not suddenly turn into the expected gold-mine. But it was able to offer work to refugees from *Time* Canadian, now eliminated as an employer of Canadian journalists. Under this new yoke, their labors were mysteriously discovered to be culturally acceptable after all.

No matter how hard Canadian governments try to legislate a distinct Canadian culture into being, they can't overcome the fact that English-speaking Canada is part of the North American social fabric. Even in 1891, it was obvious to Goldwin Smith that "the structure of society in British Canada is identical with its structure in the United States. . . . Canadian sentiment may be free from the revolutionary tinge and the tendency to indiscriminate sympathy with rebellion unhappily contracted by American sentiment in the contest with George III; but it is not less thoroughly democratic." Smith thought that not only Old World institutions, such as a peerage and a non-elected Upper Chamber modelled on the House of Lords, but also the "oligarchical" House of Commons itself would prove difficult to transplant to the New World, where the requisite class structure did not exist. And indeed, its transplanting has proven far from successful in Canada's case, as I shall argue shortly.

North America's relative lack of class rigidities has also meant an absence of class politics in the European sense. This phenomenon has even caused some observers to propose a local amendment to Marx's global prognostication of inexorable class conflict and revolution, a heresy known in the trade as "American exceptionalism" and associated with Jay Lovestone, whose espousal of it in the 1930s led to his expulsion from the American Communist Party. Canada, where politics focus not on class but on the higher plane of region, religion and race, must clearly be accounted as part of this American exception.

The Canadian elite is perfectly well aware of their flock's North American predilections. But just as real estate agents in American cities have developed an elaborate terminology to describe different neighborhoods without directly mentioning the crucial fact of race, so Canadian Nationalists have learned to discuss various schemes for regulation to remedy American influence without ever admitting, perhaps even to themselves, that they are talking about coercion. Thus John Meisel, former Chairman of the Canadian Radio-Television and Telecommunications Commission, has written, "it is inconceivable that market forces could address the central concern of Canadian broadcast regulation – the need to promote a Canadian presence on the airwaves." This disguises as a market failure the devastating fact that ordinary Canadians cannot be trusted to watch Canadian programming of their own free will.

Simultaneously, however, an undercurrent of anti-Americanism certainly does exist in Canada. It's not hard to understand. Voltaire once said that every man has two countries: his own and France. Now, in the twentieth century, everyone in the world is an American citizen. Politically, militarily, commercially, culturally, the U.S. has become the cynosure of mankind that France was two centuries earlier, evoking every emotion but indifference.

Nowhere is American influence more omnipresent than in Canada. Canadians are fascinated with the tumultuous spectacle south of the border. It pervades their consciousness and informs their actions to the point where they are no longer aware when they are imitating it. "As soon as our cousins south of the line decide to adopt Great-grandmothers' Day we will uncritically adopt it too," complained Archibald MacMechan back in 1920. Echoes of the U.S. are everywhere. In Toronto alone there is a Sutton Place, a Park Plaza; the police are routinely called "Toronto's Finest," just as in New York. In Ottawa, Parliament stands upon what poetic license terms a "Hill," just like the Capitol does. Journalists ape their Washington peers and periodically agitate about the insufficiency of prime ministerial press conferences, despite the weekly House of Commons institution of Question Period, which in other parliamentary democracies like Britain is judged to render regular prime ministerial press conferences inappropriate. ("It is not far off the mark to say that *most* Canadians expect their system to operate like the American, and are confused when it does not," commented Queen's University Professor C.E.S. Franks.) When the relatively unknown Joe Clark became Tory leader in 1976, the *Toronto Star* headed a story "Joe Who?" This rare specimen of a Canadian political joke was seized upon with such universal delight that no one remembered that the quip was an import, first popularized by the American media to express their incredulity at Richard Nixon's choice of Spiro Agnew as his running mate in 1968. For that matter, the "Trudeaumania" that greeted Pierre Trudeau's arrival on the political scene was a clear case of what George Radwanski accurately diagnosed as "Kennedy envy," just as the "Sixty Days of Decision" that began Lester Pearson's first term as prime minister in 1963 paralleled the first "Hundred Days" of the older generation's hero, Franklin D. Roosevelt. And Trudeau's farewell speech to the Liberal convention in 1984 closed with the same inspiring assertion about The Dream Never Dying that Senator Edward Kennedy had used at the Democratic convention in winding up his bid for the presidency in 1980.

The Newtonian principle that action and reaction are equal and opposite applies to psychology as well as physics. It is natural for Canadians to feel both a backlash of resentment, at being so overwhelmed by America, as well as a frontlash of ardent response. This is the emotional basis for the anti-American policies of Canada's Nationalist elite. And they might well calculate that with luck and judicious propaganda a wedge could be driven between the English-speaking peoples of North America, just as determined radical republicans in Ireland eventually succeeded in engineering a far more complete divorce from Britain than the limited internal autonomy advocated by the country's leaders in the generations before World War I. But Canada is not Ireland, and the U.S. is not England.

Every student of Canada must make a judgement on the ultimate significance of these perennial anti-American twitchings. On the evidence presented here, they are no deeper than the normal North American sectional squabbling. And, while American politicians have found it advisable to heed regional sentiment by selecting candidates who bring geographic balance to national tickets, and frequently run against Washington or New York, the basic integrity of the union is not threatened. "Anti-Americanism is as old as the country itself," veteran Canadian columnist Dennis Braithwaite wrote in early 1984 when the Liberal government was experimenting with the issue in the run-up to the federal election. "But despite this early conditioning, America is not all that unpopular in Canada today. Having grown up on America culture and consumerism, we have begun to take on the coloration of our Yankee neighbors. ... We winter in Florida, retire in California, swallow the products of Hollywood and Madison Ave. with our mothers' milk." Or, as Goldwin Smith put it in 1891: "Of the antipathy to Americans sedulously kept up within select circles and in certain interests, there is absolutely none among the Canadian people at large."

A further piece of evidence may be adduced. Although Americans might be pardoned for not noticing the difference, Canadian Nationalists actually have been distinctly reluctant to attack the U.S. openly in public debate. Indeed, they often indignantly disavow the very thought. Mel Hurtig, a leading Nationalist publisher, has complained that it "appears mandatory to repeat again and again: It's not necessary to be anti-American to be pro-Canadian." This, needless to say, is disingenuous. Canadian Nationalists constantly seek to exacerbate and exploit anti-Americanism, and their activities do poison and pervert the relationship. But it is true that their primary interest is manipulating and tithing their fellow Canadians, towards which end they aim to "manage" Canada-U.S. interaction rather than abolish it. In any event, they clearly feel that pro-American sentiment in Canada is sufficiently powerful to require handling with care.

There is, however, a sense in which all stereotypes are true. And in this limited sense, it can be admitted that, yes, it is (partially) true what they say about Canada. Compared to most of their fellow North Americans, Canadians no doubt are unemotional – or, more accurately, undemonstrative – and even taciturn. They are impressively tolerant, but inhibition probably accounts for some part of this, and can cause outsiders to overestimate their welcome and misjudge the natives' often-considerable subterranean sensitivities and resentments. Although many of the Fathers of Confederation were immigrants, for example, it is noticeable that few immigrants in recent years have been successful in elective politics, although they are very well represented in the professions, in commerce and particularly in the labor unions, seemingly a specialty of arrivals from the United Kingdom.

Canadians often say that they have an inferiority complex, and they may be right. They are deeply concerned about status, quick to suspect that others have an unfair advantage – the charge that some group is being made "second-class citizens" is a powerful one in Canadian politics – and their reluctance to admit each other's achievements is legendary. It's certainly tempting to extrapolate this defensiveness and caution into a cultural explanation for their high savings rates, relatively weak entrepreneurial sector and attachment to bureaucracy. This of course neglects institutional factors, such as differential tax rates and weak political control over the executive branch. However, the trait is sufficiently marked as to suggest that Canadians are wrong to regard the brawling game of ice hockey as their national sport. More appropriate is curling, imported from Scotland and played by both sexes and all ages in every community across Canada. Curling involves sliding a polished granite puck down an ice rink so that it comes to a halt within a circle marked at the end. But if you can't manage that, *it's just as good to block everyone else.*

Pierre Berton was entirely right to fasten on Scottish influence as the key to the Canadian character. This is strikingly apparent in John Kenneth Galbraith's evocative account of the southern Ontario Scottish farming settlements into which he was born in 1908. Although "one of the world's more egalitarian communities," the Scots "gave a good deal of attention to the question of precedence," status being determined by endless discussion among peers. While "certainly not averse to net income," the Scots were equally concerned with "minimizing gross outlay." They would avoid spending not just on consumption, but even for productive purposes whenever possible: "To spend either their own or borrowed money meant some risk of loss. The goal of their agriculture was a safe, one-way flow of income, the flow being in their direction." Exactly the same reflex caused another Scottish Canadian, Colonel John Maclean, to stunt the growth of his company and profoundly alter the future of the Canadian publishing industry by declining to acquire daily newspapers because financing any purchase might have meant issuing stocks or bonds; it remains a constant complaint of today's Canadian venture capitalists. According to Galbraith, the Scots took a perverse pleasure in negativism, stemming from the "moral and political cleavage" between them and Canada's "English-oriented ruling class. . . . One never joined, and one never overlooked any righteous opportunity to oppose or, if opportunity presented, to infuriate." And, finally, Galbraith's Scots were profoundly honest and law-abiding. "The nearest police officer with jurisdiction was twenty miles away; during the twenty years that I knew the community, I never heard that he had occasion to visit it."

Mackenzie King, of Scottish stock himself, certainly believed in the virtue of throwing a good block. "Far more has been accomplished for the welfare and the progress of mankind in preventing bad actions than in doing good ones," he once assured Lester Pearson. And it is uncanny how many of the feats upon which the Canadian Establishment now congratulates itself, like stalling the unification of the British Empire, orchestrating the U.N. attack on the Anglo-French Israeli Suez expedition – for which Pearson was to win a Nobel Prize – and even the National Energy Program, are essentially negative. Nothing was created, but somebody was prevented from doing something. Rather than a beaver, the Canadian heraldic beast could well be a dog in a manger, rampant.

Nevertheless, Galbraith's American editors had no difficulty recognizing the people he described, even if they constituted a kind of Canadian quintessence. "The Canadian Scotch," they told their readers, entirely accurately, "have much in common with the [New England] Yankees. . . ."

English Canada is a relatively small country. Its people are concentrated in a few large, fairly isolated cities. They quickly get to know their peer groups. Theirs is a comfortable if slightly incestuous way of life. One reason for the more casual attitude towards legal technicalities that distinguishes Canadian from American business is the greater familiarity among all parties, which often means they trust, or at least anticipate, each other. But it can also lead to potential abuses, particularly because Canadian shareholders are notoriously supine and slow to litigate. For example, controversy lingered for years after the giant Canadian holding corporation, Brascan Limited, took over a company substantially owned by Brascan's own management, a circumstance which a subsequent royal commission described as "a very manifest and yet apparently inescapable conflict of interest situation."

Brascan also illustrates the practical uses of Nationalism. Its chairman had been an early supporter of the Committee for an Independent Canada, and during this period, when for technical reasons the company was more vulnerable to a takeover bid, it took advantage of Nationalist provisions in Canadian corporate law to restrict the transfer of its shares to non-Canadians. "One of the results of this kind of by-law," the royal commission pointed out, "is to provide a further layer of insulation for the incumbent controlling group [in Brascan's case, its management] against any potential bidders for control." Any offer for Brascan seemed likely to come from the U.S., as it was thought to be too big to be swallowed by Canadian pools of capital. Subsequently, however, it was.

To paraphrase a prominent Canadian export, Marshall McLuhan, Canada is a national village. And it has the failings of a village: insularity, parochialism, complacency, lack of sophistication. It has been basking in the eye of the geopolitical hurricane for many years and, despite the presence of immigrants who know better, its political debate is naive and unworldly by the standards of North America. In 1945, when Igor Gouzenko defected from the Soviet Embassy in Ottawa with evidence of far-reaching espionage, Mackenzie King at first refused to believe him, wanted to send him back, and thought it worth recording in his private diary Gouzenko's extraordinary belief that "the Russian democracy was different than ours." At that time Mackenzie King was seventy years old and had first become prime minister twenty-four years earlier.

But any summary of national character, if it is honest at all, must inevitably sound churlish. Two alleviating points should be borne in mind. First, this delicate Canadian variant of the North American character has been disseminated more or less successfully right across the continent, just as the distinctive Canadian accent can be heard from coast to coast. (Etymologists report that American regional accents also show east-west patterns, reflecting migration from the different Atlantic coastal settlements.) This does provide a certain basis for some specifically Canadian cultural expression. Popular music is a good example. Canadian singers like Gordon Lightfoot found an audience in Canada even before Canadian-content airplay regulations, in the same way that country-and-western became spontaneously popular throughout the South. Both, of course, subsequently developed a wider North American appeal.

Unfortunately, this is not at all what the Canadian elite has in mind by "culture." It's too low-brow, too involved with other North American manifestations, and above all too unpredictable to be controlled. It offers no guarantees to "national newsmagazines" and the various other important pyramids erected to honor Nationalism (and Nationalists.) Like the very similar issue of free trade, the idea of cultural *laissez faire* is at once too ambitious, in that it supposes a Canada can exist without government splints and bandages, and not ambitious enough, in that it does not promise to duplicate America in miniature right down to the last toy bell and whistle. Nor, fatally, does it require the services of professional regulators.

The second alleviating caveat is, once again, that Canada must be viewed in context. In a famous scene in Carol Reed's film, *The Third Man*, Orson Welles denounces the Swiss on the grounds that, unlike Renaissance Italy, their bourgeois civilization has produced no great works of art – its supreme artifact, he says with contempt, is the lowly cuckoo clock. But of course the supreme artifact of societies like Switzerland and Canada is civilization itself: safe cities, clean streets ("antiseptic" or not), the implicit honesty that makes possible efficiency, the high degree of freedom. This humble combination is exceedingly rare in human history. New Yorkers appear to be losing the knack. Yet it is the prerequisite of progress. Leonardo comes later. As W.B. Yeats wrote:

How but in custom and in ceremony,
Are innocence and beauty born?

The fact that English Canada is a delicate variation on a North American theme is easily missed because of several specific distractions. One is that its expression on the federal level is diluted by the influence of French Canada. (The political culture of the Francophones is discussed more fully in Chapter Ten.) But at this point it is worth noting three areas where its presence on the national level can be discerned. These are: the much-vaunted Canadian attitude towards the state; towards authority; and towards political mores.

First, the French connection has greatly reinforced those English Canadians who were inclined to favor government intervention in the economy, a.k.a. socialism. This point was made very effectively in 1981, at the height of the Liberals' post-election reform frenzy, by Douglas Fisher, himself once a socialist MP. Pierre Trudeau, Fisher wrote in *Executive* magazine, had taken Canada "over the watershed from moderate and rather undeliberate interventions by the federal state into the economy. . . ."

Now when I see the shock of some Liberals, especially of many Liberal senators, who boggle (but without public protest) at the implications of the new constitution and the NEP, you wonder where the change came in the party of Bob Winters, Bud Drury, George McIlraith, John Turner and Bob Andras.

My answer to such wonderment now is that the shift in economic attitudes came out of Quebec and through a rather subtle or at least unnoticed change among French Canadians, now in their 40s and 50s. Essentially, ministers like De Bané, Pinard, Ouellet, Lamontagne and Lalonde were influenced by Lesage's, "Masters in Our Own House," by the Manicouagan power development, James Bay, etc., that is by the idea that a government must command the heights of the economy.

As Pinard, the Liberal House Leader, told me a short time ago: "A lot of us, guys like De Bané, Joyal, Dawson and Deniger (the latter three are able back-benchers) are Liberal social democrats. We don't get worried about differences between free enterprise and socialism; that's pretty old-fashioned."

What I've just portrayed is not to suggest that the readiness to nationalize and Canadianize is largely a French Canadian phenomenon. It isn't, and I can even think of a handful of Liberal MPs from Ontario and the Maritimes who shared or share the economic and social ideas of the New Democrats and the Parti Québécois. But now the overwhelming strength of capable French Canadians in the ruling party's ministry and caucus has shucked off the restraining influence and the old rapport with the business community of men like Sharp, Lang, Drury, Turner and Andras who were in previous Trudeau governments. . . .

Actually, this *dirigiste* tradition has even deeper roots in Quebec than Fisher implies. Its continued strength can be gauged from the fact that even Robert Bourassa's Quebec Liberals, in making renewed economic growth the center of their successful 1985 campaign to defeat the Parti Québécois provincial government, proposed to achieve this growth through massive state-directed "megaprojects."

The second aspect of French influence is more controversial. The authoritarian streak in the Canadian official character, which often surprises observers as much as a sudden bite from the country's heraldic beaver, can be said to have a certain Gallic piquancy. Observers agree that French Catholic society was hierarchical, prescriptive and collectivist by comparison with the English-speaking world, and the decline of formal religion has altered this less than might be supposed. There is, as Conrad Black noted in his biography of Duplessis, a "traditional Quebec view of collective over individual rights. . . ." In his book *Deference to Authority,* the American academic Canada-watcher Edgar Z. Friedenberg specifically attributed to Trudeau's Quebec background the paradox that, although "a professed civil libertarian," he "believes and has often affirmed that, in a serious conflict between the requirements of the state and the rights of the individual, the rights of the state come first." Similarly, the personal dominance Trudeau achieved over his party caucus, cowing them into terrified silence long after electoral expediency would have compelled the resignation of any normal leader, was unmistakeably reminiscent of the autocratic style of Maurice Duplessis, the strong man of the Union Nationale. His fellow Quebecker Brian Mulroney is similarly demanding detailed control over the activities of Tory MPs, although not yet emulating Duplessis' promulgation of a dress code.

Deference to authority is a habit that can also be traced to Britain, and Canada certainly remains closer to Britain than to the U.S. in its interpretation of the legal heritage common to the English-speaking world. Indeed, critics like Barbara Amiel and George Jonas have argued that since mid-century the attitude of Canadian judges to questions of due process steadily became so robust that it exceeded even the pro-prosecution sympathies of British judges, and was certainly diametrically opposed to trends in the U.S. In Canada, according to this argument, there is greater likelihood of both conviction and also possible injustice.

However, since civil libertarianism is a cause common to vocal middle-class liberals throughout North America, there was intense lobbying on these issues during the 1980-81 debate on "patriating" the constitution. The paradoxical result was that this crowning expression of Canadianism contained what Robert Sheppard and Michael Valpy described as "new protections . . . more akin to the U.S. model," although the full implications of these changes are not yet clear.

This pattern of Canada's conforming to the North American norm also asserts itself lower down the social scale. In the late 1970s, the great Canadian public greeted with stoic indifference several revelations of RCMP "dirty tricks" played on separatist and assorted left-wing groups some years earlier. Nationalist publicists such as Pierre Berton claim, with obviously mixed feelings, that this is a manifestation of that unique Canadian preference for order. But all the indications are that the American public is equally disposed to support its local police despite any amount of elite disapproval. There was, for example, much consternation when opinion polls showed solid majorities supporting the "police riot" during the anti-war demonstrations at the 1968 Democratic convention in Chicago.

A third aspect of the French fact, most controversial of all, is the question of governmental ethics. Canadian libel laws are so strict, and the Canadian press so servile, that there is little American-style investigative reporting on the peculation of politicians. But a further cause of this inhibition is that it too often involves the exposure of Francophones who have brought to the federal scene the worldly attitudes traditional in Quebec provincial politics. On a less contentious level, this clash of mores can also be said to have transformed the unwritten rules governing the Canadian version of British-style parliamentary life. In one typical episode at the end of the Trudeau era, Marc Lalonde refused to assume responsibility and resign after a former Liberal minister had apparently traded on their relationship. Pierre Trudeau, according to Richard Gwyn, "never learned these conditioned reflexes of Anglo-Saxons. . . . Trudeau does not play fair . . . he has no sympathy whatever for the underdog."

Any generalization about English Canada's character must also reckon with regional differences. It is highly significant that Canadian prime ministers must balance their cabinets to reflect not just the ethnic divisions in the Canadian state, but also the geographic divisions within English Canada, province by province. An Anglophone minister from Ontario simply will not satisfy Anglophone Western Canadians. No equivalent convention ever developed in the British version of the parliamentary system, although no less than four different nations – five, counting the Ulster Protestants – have been represented in the House of Commons at Westminster. Indeed, what Goldwin Smith called "localism" is so severe in Canada that, as he noted in 1891, "a resident in one electoral division in Toronto would be at a disadvantage as a candidate in another division, although the unity of the city, commercial and social, is complete." In Britain, by contrast, aspiring MPs are not expected to have any particular connection with the ridings they seek to represent, and are positively encouraged to earn their spurs by contesting hopeless elections in remote places. Even elected MPs in Britain will regularly switch to safer ridings at the other end of the country, which in Canada would inevitably evoke the damning charge of being a "parachute candidate."

Once again, geography emerges as the ultimate reality of Canadian politics. Even epochal ideological contests, as they are billed by Canadian standards, such as the Tory leadership conventions of 1976 and 1983, in fact turn out to be primarily about sectional loyalties, with delegates earnestly explaining, to anyone who will listen, the imperative necessity of a leader from *southeastern* Ontario, or wherever they happen to come from.

These differences between English Canadians are of course not significant compared with their common difference from the Francophones. But, as will be argued in Chapter Twelve, there are sufficiently serious and coherent patterns of divergence among Anglophones to raise the possibility that they reflect incipient nationalisms threatening the fabric of Canadian Confederation.

The most important single source of error about English Canada's national character, however, is the tendency to attribute to a unique Canadian culture many features that are actually the result of institutional accident. A classic example occurred in 1980, when Canada's Conservative government, headed by Joe Clark, was overthrown and replaced by its Liberal rivals under Pierre Trudeau. This was exactly the reverse of what happened in the U.S., where the conservative challenger Ronald Reagan ousted the liberal administration of Jimmy Carter. The Canadian nationalist claim that the two countries were now definitively "polarized" was obviously tendentious, since in 1980, as in every election since 1968, English Canada had given a majority of its seats to the Progressive Conservative Party. But the Nationalists were also overlooking another remarkable fact: if the U.S. electoral system had been the same as Canada's in 1980, House Speaker Tip O'Neill would have become the American prime minister. He would have repeated the feat, barely, in 1984.

O'Neill, a decidedly liberal Democrat, was the leader of the party that won a majority in the House of Representatives. Legislators are elected to the House from single-member districts of roughly equal population, making it the direct equivalent of the Canadian House of Commons. In both countries, this procedure allows the cities of the East to dominate the spaces of the West. But Americans are not constantly being reminded about their deep-rooted preference for strong government and social democracy, because the House is only one element in the U.S. government.

The American founding fathers were keenly aware of the possibility of domination by a tyrannical majority, and of the reality of sectional differences in a continental-sized polity. They repudiated a simple head-counting view of democracy by balancing the House with a Senate, to which each state, regardless of population, was entitled to send two members. This was a conscious effort to reflect the separate communities and interests within the U.S. For the same reason, the president was to be chosen by a College of Electors, who were to be adopted on a state-by-state basis. This rationale was confirmed as recently as 1979, when Senator Birch Bayh's attempt to amend the constitution to provide for the direct election of the president was decisively repudiated by the U.S. Senate. By contrast, the upper house of the Canadian legislature is appointive, and has become moribund.

This absence of regional checks and balances in the Canadian system of government explains why the federal Liberals, after rallying their constituency in Central Canada and returning to power in 1980, felt no compunction about launching their National Energy Program onslaught upon the West. In Australia the Labor government of Gough Whitlam, similarly based in the cities of the Southeast, began a similar campaign of state control and *de facto* expropriation directed against mineral resources located mainly in the West and the North. But its efforts were ultimately parried by the Australian Senate, which is elected. This led to the constitutional crisis of 1975, precipitating a general election which Labor lost. In the U.S., no Administration could have even begun to get such legislation through the Senate.

The flaws in Canada's governmental institutions extend beyond the problem of regional representation to the failure of the British-style Canadian parliamentary system itself. The parliamentary system has evolved enormously since the golden age of England's patrician liberties in the eighteenth century, when it provided an unparalleled focus for national debate, and admiring French *philosphes* developed their idealized analysis of it that so influenced the framers of the U.S. constitution. A case can be made that even in Britain the parliamentary system has not successfully adapted to mass democracy and the electronic age, but its deficiencies are much more apparent when it is grafted onto a North American country the size of the Canada of Confederation – Ontario and Quebec plus a Maritime appendage – let alone the continental polity Canada has now become.

Once elected, a Canadian prime minister need not worry about any mid-term elections demoralizing his troops. There need be no further confrontations with ungrateful voters for up to five years, and even then he can pick the time to suit himself, frittering the opposition's resources away with election scares if he chooses, as Pierre Trudeau did in 1978. Not only has Parliament become effectively unicameral, but the balance between the executive and legislative branches that so impressed the *philosophes* has also disappeared. And in the U.S., legislators are elected separately from the president and cannot simultaneously hold posts in the executive branch, which encourages them to develop independent power bases. By contrast, the Canadian prime minister is not only head of the executive branch but also by definition commands a majority in the legislature. He can select legislators for almost all the executive branch posts in his gift, sealing their loyalty. And the growth of government in the twentieth century has given him even more patronage power. Even when a party is defeated and goes into opposition, it still must retain a permanent leader to orchestrate its activities in Parliament. And that leader still retains significant patronage, in the shape of appointments to the tax-supported party bureaucracy and to the "Shadow Cabinet," whose members are guaranteed some publicity as their party's official representatives on the various issues.

Indeed, Canadian party leaders are now able to impose a more stringent discipline upon their MPs than is the case even in Britain. Thus in 1980-81 Ottawa had genuine difficulty understanding why British Prime Minister Margaret Thatcher could not override her backbenchers' scruples and guarantee the quick passage, through Westminster's House of Commons, of the legislation technically required to "patriate" the Canadian constitution.

A similar degeneration has affected the selection procedures for parliamentary candidates and for party leaders. In the heyday of the parliamentary system in Britain, such questions were efficiently decided by a consensus of local squires and party grandees. In that more deferential and socially cohesive climate, it was even possible for the British Conservative Party to sail along quite serenely until as late as 1965 without ever stooping to the actual election of a leader. When a new one was needed, the party went through a mysterious process of opinion-sounding, after which he was said to have "evolved."

In Canada, party bosses have made an unhappy compromise with the democratic ethos of North America, to the extent that candidates and leadership convention delegates are elected – not in American-style primaries, however, but at general meetings of the local riding associations. This places a premium on a relatively small number of people willing to show up and stay late at such affairs – often unrepresentative activists, members of a candidate's ethnic group and the recipients of financial incentives. The resulting brawls are becoming an embarrassment. The downfall of Tory leader Joe Clark was materially hastened by the prolonged controversy in 1982 when Peter Worthington, the popular Toronto newspaper editor and Clark critic, was deprived of a federal Tory nomination by a specially recruited squad of Greek immigrants, normally Liberal voters. In the subsequent leadership race, the forces of both Clark and Brian Mulroney openly packed and manipulated local delegate-selection meetings, enlisting children, motorcycle gangs and the residents of a shelter for derelicts. As long as the establishments of both major parties still believe that this imperfect situation offers them more opportunity to exert influence, they will not accept the logic of the less controllable primary system.

In the U.S., the establishment of the major parties was overthrown four times in sixteen years – with the nomination of Barry Goldwater in 1964, of George McGovern in 1972, of Jimmy Carter in 1976, and of Ronald Reagan in 1980. Two of these insurgents went on to win the general election. There have also been two important third-party movements: George Wallace in 1968 and John Anderson in 1980. It is Canada's political structures, rather than its traditions (which, particularly on the Prairies, have had a distinctive populistic streak) that make such insurrections more difficult.

The net effect of the parliamentary system's degeneration is to create a stagnant pool of professional politicians and bureaucrats, infused with enormous power, and to achieve an illusory stability by suppressing the reality of difficulty and dissent. Rationales for state power, such as Canadian Nationalism, quickly spring up in such an environment. And manipulation is all too easy.

It is sobering to reflect, for example, that Canadians never had an opportunity to vote directly or indirectly on their new constitution. The issue of its patriation did not figure in the 1980 federal election, which therefore can hardly be regarded as a mandate. Nevertheless, a deal was promptly done between provincial and federal incumbents, assuring a *fait accompli* long before the voters had to be faced again. The one point all the politicians agreed on was the absolute undesirability of any form of plebiscite on the constitution, both because it would infringe upon their own prerogatives and because it was too risky. "What we do not need in Western Canada is a referendum on language rights for Franco-Canadians," said Saskatchewan NDP Premier Allan Blakeney in 1981. Instead he wished to impose those "rights" by decree. When Trudeau at one point spoke of a referendum to break the deadlock, his Ontario Tory allies were appalled, and warned him they could not guarantee the support of voters even in Ontario, the Central Canadian heartland. Fortunately the shocking step of consulting the people proved unnecessary. Parliamentary leaders are able to ride down a lot of objections – Sir John A. Macdonald refused to submit Confederation to a referendum, saying the idea was "unBritish" – but at some point such tactics must threaten the legitimacy of the state.

The massive, "non-partisan" (and therefore inviolable) civil service that also has emerged everywhere as a concomitant of the parliamentary system further reinforces Canadian Establishment complacency. The federal bureaucracy instills the government of Canada with permanence, continuity and a grand imperviousness to crude electoral excitement. During the 1979-80 Clark government, for example, officials at the Department of Energy, Mines and Resources simply ignored Tory campaign promises to abolish Petro-Canada and to develop free-market energy policies. Instead, on their own initiative, they began analytical studies that formed the basis for the completely antithetical, inverventionist National Energy Program that was adopted by the Liberals as soon as they returned to office.

Naturally, the legislators and civil servants in the apparent center of this political Sargasso Sea become convinced that Canada depends upon them. No Georgia or southern California Mafia arrives in the federal capital every four years or so to disturb this assumption. The attentions of diplomats and journalists seem to confirm it. In subtle ways, the Ottawa political class begins to treat Canada as the unitary state for which the Parliamentary system was, after all, designed. For example, the distinguished anarchist intellectual George Woodcock, now based in Vancouver, who has written indignantly that "CBC News and Public Affairs programming has been subordinated to the Liberal government's 'National Unity' policy," claims that "CBC president [and long-time Ottawa bureaucrat] Al Johnson once asserted in my presence that Canada was *not* a confederal polity." Professor C.E.S. Franks agrees that it is the parliamentary system as much as any hypothetical Canadian "political culture" that "enables the executive to express a public interest beyond party and interest group ... this institutional feature has permitted Canadian governments to be more activist and welfare-oriented than American. ...." He has even warned against Senate reform on the grounds that it could "open up the political processes to every organized special interest in Canada ... and make the national government less able to act in a general public interest." Ottawa, of course, is uniquely able and willing to announce what constitutes this "general public interest" – as opposed to those noxious "organized special interests."

Ottawa's centralizing tendency was further illustrated by the "patriation" of the Canadian constitution in 1981. The constitution's written provisions will naturally require interpretation by the courts. On the face of it, this might appear to mean that the Canadian judiciary will acquire the power of the U.S. judicial branch to review and restrain the activities of the legislative or executive branches in accordance with the law. And to some extent this has already happened, in the areas of compulsory metrication and advocacy advertising. But this development might actually turn out to be a further step towards unlimited government and the concentration of power. The federal government retained the right to name judges automatically, without review by Parliament. This obvious threat to the principle of the separation of powers caused minimal protest, a measure of how little the Canadian public classes understand the theories of their own institutions. But it has raised the spectre, or perhaps the hope, that a future Canadian government will be able to appoint its partisans to the bench without the public scrutiny and periodic Senate donnybrooks that accompany judicial nominations in the U.S. Its legislative goals could then be achieved through the courts by the simple process of a series of judicial fiats decreeing them to be implicit in the constitution – the dreaded "judicial legislation" denounced by American liberals in the 1930s and by American conservatives since the 1950s. Indeed, this was specifically advocated by the authors of *The National Deal*, who concluded with the hope that Canadian courts will be able to achieve, through "creative" interpretation, the goals the conferring politicians were unable to attain, and the government of Canada might then be carried on with even less contamination by ordinary Canadians.

Although the parliamentary system shapes the way Canada presents itself to the world, a close examination reveals evidence that the country itself is slowly distorting the institution. The most obvious example is that irrepressible sectional divergences have compelled the institutionalization of regular interactions between federal and provincial governments. These now culminate in the "First Ministers' Conference," an annual meeting between the prime minister and all the provincial premiers. From the point of view of constitutional theory, the federal-provincial conferences are ad-hocery of the most primitive sort. They have no power to make or interpret laws and are unable even to reach substantive agreement most of the time. They serve merely to provide a legitimizing theatre for occasional bargains between bureaucrats. As Richard Gwyn commented in *The Northern Magus*: "It all amounted to a mysterious new kind of *national* government through which Ottawa and the provinces ran the country jointly – out of reach of Parliament and the legislatures." The conferences are not a cure but a symptom of sectional stress on political institutions not designed to deal with it.

Canada's parliamentary system is showing the strain also of representing a more pluralistic, heterogeneous society than that of Britain.

Paradoxically, the immediate effect of this is to sharpen party discipline. In Britain, the political, cultural and commercial elites are integrated socially, and they all live in London. It is perfectly possible to be an MP and simultaneously to pursue a career at the Bar, in the City or on Fleet Street. In Canada, by contrast, as in the U.S., the political elite is quite separate both socially and geographically from the commercial and cultural elites. And MPs must devote many more hours travelling between Parliament and their home ridings, which can be thousands of miles apart. Second careers are much less practical. So any Canadian MP contemplating rebellion knows he can be deprived of any hope of office and be marooned with a backbencher's salary by his wrathful leader. A British MP at least has alternatives, reluctant though most are to contemplate them. In the U.S., the institutions of Congress and the vastly greater staff support available to legislators effectively protect their independence and even make it into a thing of joy.

A subtler but ultimately more alarming cause of stress is that Canadian society insists on sprouting political leaders outside Parliament, despite the difficulties the parliamentary system places in its way. This would be unthinkable in Britain. It is a reflection of Canada's pluralism, marking it out as a North American society. In the past, these leaders have often been civil servants, such as Mackenzie King and Lester Pearson. But more recently Brian Mulroney was able to sustain himself as Tory leader-in-waiting after his defeat by Joe Clark in the leadership convention of 1976, until his defeat of Joe Clark in the rematch of 1983, although he held no elected office and was working throughout almost the entire period as president of the obscure Iron Ore Company of Canada in Montreal. One of his rivals, Peter Pocklington, was an Edmonton businessman who previously had had no known connection with any party at all. On the Liberal side, Finance Minister John Turner actually resigned from Parliament after he quit Pierre Trudeau's cabinet in 1975 and joined a Toronto law firm without in the least diminishing his own stature as Liberal heir-apparent. Another potential candidate, Donald Macdonald, did exactly the same thing in 1977. In Britain, by contrast, for a politician to leave the House of Commons would be tantamount to announcing his retirement.

One consequence of this pluralistic sprouting of leaders is that men who are parliamentary neophytes are constantly finding themselves in political power in Canada. This again would be unthinkable in Britain, where a long apprenticeship in the specialized and treacherous House of Commons environment is regarded as an essential preface to any ministerial career. A whole string of Canadian political catastrophes has been the result. In 1935, when C.D. Howe was taken into Mackenzie King's cabinet straight after his election, he promptly steered the National Harbours Board bill into an easily avoidable parliamentary bog, requiring a large part of the 1936 session for its extrication. In 1958, the Liberal defeat in the general election was partly ascribed, at least by Jack Pickersgill to the party's parliamentary rout by the veteran John Diefenbaker. The fateful debate on an ill-judged motion was advised by Pickersgill himself – a politician who had stepped straight from the Civil Service into the House and the St. Laurent Cabinet a mere five years earlier – and was proposed by Lester Pearson, who had just become Liberal leader. In 1963, Walter Gordon became Lester Pearson's Finance Minister directly after entering Parliament; his career never recovered its equilibrium after his disastrous handling of the subsequent nationalistic 1963 budget. In 1979, Joe Clark had been an MP barely seven years when he became Prime Minister of the minority Tory government; within months, he completely misjudged its situation in the House and was defeated on a confidence motion that he could have easily avoided.

Catastrophe may not be the word to describe the emergence of Pierre Trudeau as Prime Minister in 1968, when he had been in the House less than three years. But it was surely understandable that he never developed into a "House of Commons man." His contempt for the institution that had so little to do with his rise to power is obvious – he denounced Opposition MPs for being "nobodies" outside the House, and in a famous incident refused to apologize for mouthing obscenities across the floor. Not surprisingly, his years in office saw, in the name of efficiency, a relentless reduction in the powers and privileges of Parliament, and the unprecedented exploitation of "Or-ders-In-Council," a loophole which allows the direct promulgation of the details of legislation without debate. Over 40,000 were issued in the Trudeau era. Brian Mulroney is equally an outsider, and he is not likely to reverse this trend.

Even those politicians who have bothered to get elected to the House of Commons have their careers deeply affected by the extra-parliamentary dimension to Canadian politics. Both Pierre Trudeau and Joe Clark owed their elevation to forces outside the parliamentary caucuses of their parties – in Clark's case, to the contacts he developed in the party machine while working as an *apparatchik*. Canadian party leaders can avoid both the laser-like scrutiny of the caucus, which has its own specialized knowledge and concerns, and the larger furnace of a full primary campaign, with its unpredictability and intensity. Not for the first time has this Canadian compromise ended up with the worst of both worlds.

So dominated is Canadian public debate by Central Canadian interests that there has been little serious discussion of reforming the parliamentary system, least of all when Pierre Trudeau "patriated" the constitution in 1980, altering it in the process. Frustrated leftists have from time to time suggested that the House of Commons itself should be elected according to some version of proportional representation. This system would rescue both their own supporters, now trampled underfoot in the current method's first-past-the-post races, and also the small bands of Liberals and Tories usually imprisoned in one another's electoral strongholds in Quebec and the West respectively. Even some Liberals think it might bolster their position. But proportional representation would not solve the sectional problem, and it could destabilize the Canadian party system by making it easier for the smaller parties, notably the various regional separatists, to elect representatives. The major-party incumbents have taken extraordinary care to rig campaign financing and registration laws against their smaller rivals. The prospects for any reform that endangers these cozy arrangements are not good. Canada's parliamentary pathology is particularly tangled.

It will be a sad moment for Canada when the failure of the parliamentary system is finally acknowledged. U.S. government institutions are not perfect. Parliament certainly appears more flexible, for example. But somehow real change rarely materializes. A well-placed "no confidence" motion *could* have brought a Canadian equivalent of Watergate to an early end. But without an Ervin committee, such an issue could not have been developed. In fact, since the Pacific Scandal of 1872, no Canadian government has been defeated in the House because its elected members felt obliged to withdraw their support. Again, the rough and tumble of the House of Commons' Question Period does produce a pleasingly articulate breed of politician. But they all tend to say the same thing.

Ironically, Parliament's most ardent defenders are those who suffer most from its degeneration – the Anglophones, the Tories, the West, those excluded from power for various reasons. This is not just posturing: the parliamentary system is an important element in English Canada's heritage. But it is salt that has lost its savor. English Canada's desperate clinging to the system in the vastly changed circumstances of today is a symptom of continuing post-Imperial trauma. The recognition that, paradoxically, the spirit of parliamentary liberty has survived better in its American version than has its British-style direct descendant will be a sign that English Canada is finally recovering, and adjusting to its North American reality.

Despite all indications to the contrary, English Canada – like the epigraphic beaver at the beginning of this chapter – is still whole. It may not yet have realized this itself. But for the Anglophones to continue in the ideological cell designed for them by the architects of the modern Canadian state will require an endless effort of cultural self-abasement, an unceasing denial of past experience, present reality and very pressing immediate interests. Such an effort is profoundly unnatural. No free nation will make it indefinitely.

It is impossible to predict in detail the process by which English Canada will come to itself. It may happen all at once, or it may be led by one or other of the increasingly distinct sections within English Canada, to be discussed in Chapter Twelve.

Nations think in symbols. In recent years, Anglophone politicians have completely failed to develop symbols to help English Canada express itself and understand its situation. But symbols have a way of developing anyway. An earlier moment of national crisis is instructive in this regard. In 1849, while the economy of Upper and Lower Canada was staggering from the effects of Britain's repeal of the Corn Laws and the last remnants of the "Old Colonial System" of Imperial preferences, the Baldwin-LaFontaine Reform government, a predecessor of the Liberal Party, enacted the Rebellion Losses Bill. This provided compensation for losses incurred in the 1837 Lower Canada Rebellion, even to the rebels themselves. British Governor-General Lord Elgin signed the legislation, a step now celebrated as key to the evolution of Canadian self-government.

The Montreal Tories, surrounded by an alien majority, saw themselves betrayed. In the words of Donald Creighton, "they only knew that they had relied upon a British governor to veto or reserve the bill, and that a British governor had failed them. Their unquestioned assumptions, their traditional beliefs, their hereditary loyalties, lay strewn about in the broken confusion of a rout; and grief and fury had planted their angry banners on the wreckage." A Tory mob headed by prominent citizens, one of whom was the fire chief of Montreal, burned down the Parliament Buildings; three hundred of their leaders published an "Annexation Manifesto" advocating union with the very American Republic from which their Loyalist forefathers had fled. Lord Durham had predicted it in his report: the Montreal Tories, in order "that they might remain English, "had been persuaded they must "cease to be British."

The crisis passed. A reciprocal lowering of tariffs was negotiated with the U.S. The economy adjusted. The British began to take an interest in their colonies again. The idea of a confederation of all British North America, recruiting the other English-speaking colonies to redress the ethnic imbalance of Lower Canada, surfaced at a convention organized by Tories to discuss their plight, and they gradually came to believe that it would solve their difficulties.

Central Canadian pundits, like Charles Taylor in his *Radical Tories,* are continuously reminding today's Progressive Conservatives of the collectivist and Nationalist episodes in their past. But little is said about the earlier moment when the flower of the party saw the United States as the saviour of English Canada, although a future Tory prime minister, Sir John Abbott, signed the Annexation Manifesto, and although the problems to which it was directed – imperial implosion, economic dislocation, and the relationship between language groups – have returned.

Nevertheless, slowly but perhaps more surely than before, the U.S. is being drawn in to play a symbolic role in Canadian domestic debate. In 1980, during the U.S. presidential primaries, the *Financial Post* was amused to observe this process in action:

> Ontario's Tories have always been staunch supporters of the monarchy. Any Conservative politician knows he can get a warm response from an audience by stressing his devotion to the Queen and her continued role as head of state.
>
> Ontario Premier Bill Davis is no exception. In countless speeches to the party faithful he has maintained his unalterable commitment to maintenance of the monarchy. This past weekend he got strong applause from 1,700 Tories at a general meeting of the Ontario Progressive Conservative Party when he assured the audience that he would not accept any revision that replaced the Queen as head of state.
>
> But wait a moment. At another part of his speech the audience not only applauded strongly, they *stood* and clapped and clapped and whistled and cheered. What did he say? Well, he slammed External Affairs Minister Mark MacGuigan for his recent criticisms of U.S. foreign policy. Davis termed MacGuigan's comments "cheap shots" at "our American allies" and if the band had struck up the Star Spangled Banner everybody would probably have burst into song.
>
> The Tory strategists in the room will find it hard to forget that emotional response when planning for the next provincial election. The Queen may have to take second place in campaign speeches to fulsome references to Jimmy, or Ronnie (or Teddy, if he pulls a miracle).

Fittingly, the editorial was headed "A new loyalty?"

10

Quebec: Our Master, the Past

"Quebec is all our own;
They can't prevent it."
He said without a groan,
"I die contented."

– Brave Wolfe

However inadequate the Canadian Nationalist myth may be in explaining English Canada, it is considerably worse on the Anglophone-Francophone relationship. A classic example is Hugh MacLennan's novel *Two Solitudes,* perhaps the most celebrated literary expression of Canadian Nationalism. First published in 1945, this study of intertwining Francophone and Anglophone families in Quebec ends with the ritual proclamation that Canada had taken the "first irrevocable steps towards becoming herself," etc., etc., as she entered World War II in 1939. Nevertheless, it does have moments of real insight into the relationship between English and French Canada, as in this striking vignette set in rural Quebec in the fourth year of World War I.

It was a day in early July when Janet Methuen stood in Polycarpe Drouin's store with a letter in her hand from His Majesty the King, via the Canadian Ministry of Defence. She read it through, and when she had finished she lifted her head and looked around the store, seeing nothing. She began to walk forward and bumped into the side of the Percheron model, her arms hanging at her sides, the letter in one hand and the envelope in the other.

Drouin came from behind the counter. His voice was soft and kind, his face wrinkled, his eyes friendly. "You are all right, Madame?"

Janet turned her head rigidly and saw his tap-like nose and the wrinkles about his eyes blur and then waver into focus. She saw him look at the letter in her hand and immediately she lifted her chin. She was as pale as unbleached muslin.

"I get you a drink, maybe?" Drouin said.

She heard her own voice, like a scratchy phonograph in another room, "I'm quite all right, thank you." But she continued to stand without moving.

Drouin went to the kitchen behind the store and returned with a glass of water, spilling some of it in his hurry. When he offered it she gave him a frozen smile. "I'm quite all right, thank you," she repeated tonelessly.

Her mind kept repeating a phrase she had read months before in a magazine story: "I mustn't let people see it . . . I mustn't let people see . . . I mustn't let . . ." The words jabbered in her mind like the speech of an idiot.

Drouin looked sideways at the only other person in the store, a farmer who had come in to buy some tar-paper. Their eyes met and both men nodded. The farmer had also seen the long envelope with O.H.M.S. [On His Majesty's Service] in one corner.

"Get a chair, Jacques," Drouin said in French. "The lady wants to sit down." But before the man could get one to her, Janet went to the door and went out. The silence in her wake was broken as the chair hit the floor. Drouin shook his head and went around the counter. "That's a terrible thing," he said.

"Her husband, maybe?"

"The old captain says her husband is overseas."

The farmer scratched his head. "When I saw that letter this morning," Drouin went on, "I said to my wife, that's a bad thing, a letter like that. You never hear anything good from the government in Ottawa, I said."

The farmer was still scratching his head. "And she didn't cry," he said. "Well, maybe she doesn't know how."

Drouin bent forward over the counter in his usual jack-knife position, his chin on the heel of his hands. After a time he said, "You can't tell about the English. But maybe the old captain will be hurt bad," he added, as though he had just thought of it.

By global standards, despite the guilt and anger about it now officially built into the Canadian polity, the relationship between Canada's two "Founding Races" has been essentially humane. But it has also been one of deep incomprehension. The two cultures have collided, rebounded and continue sadly alone on their separate ways, the English drawn by their wider world, the French firmly rooted in the soil of Quebec.

Although *Two Solitudes* has provided the definitive catch-phrase for this notorious mutual isolation, its conclusion actually involves a blaze of meliorism that Goldwin Smith would have ridiculed as self-deluding "poetic talk": Francophone boy marries Anglophone girl and announces his intention to enlist as news comes over the radio that World War II has been declared (by the British, of course).

This fudges the Quebec separatists' fundamental question: which culture is to prevail – in the state, in the work-place, even in the marriage bed and particularly in the cradle? *Two Solitudes* is basically unconscious of the incisiveness of this question. However, when its final scenes of reconciliation take place in English, and when there is a vagueness about the language in which the French-speaking hero is writing his Great Canadian novel, an answer is implied that the Francophones just don't appreciate: assimilation. This blithe optimism is implicit in the book's title. It comes from a comment in a letter written by Rainer Maria Rilke: "Love consists of no more than this, that two solitudes protect and touch and greet one another." The tendency of modern Anglophone intellectuals to believe that nations are like individuals, and that people need only be nice to each other, has been an unmitigated curse to English Canada, rendering it helpless in its hour of political need.

Hugh MacLennan has paid a certain price for his naiveté. He never dreamed, he has said, that after twenty-nine years of living in the utterly peaceful Quebec countryside, a night would come when he and his wife would take turns sleeping "so that at least one of us would be awake should a car come up to the cottage filled with masked young men." More than half as many years again since the FLQ crisis, his apprehension is easy to ridicule. But his prominence in the cause of reconciliation between Canada's "founding races" would have made him a fine symbolic target. The moral is simple: Quebec confuses Canadian Nationalists.

MacLennan says he knew no French when he wrote *Two Solitudes*. Yet Francophones apparently accepted his portrayal of them without complaint. This comparative success illustrates a point often overlooked in the current Canadian obsession with the bilingualism panacea: speaking French is no substitute for reading history – *notre maître, le passé* (our master, the past), as Abbé Groulx, Quebec's leading nationalist intellectual between the two world wars, used to say.

Nor is knowing French a substitute for thinking politics. Much comment was attracted by John Crosbie's lack of French in the 1983 Tory leadership race, but the complete failure of Michael Wilson's bid was at least as significant. Wilson, a moderate Anglophone from Toronto, had indeed undergone the Stanfield-Clark ritual of painfully acquiring French in mid-life. Unfortunately, nothing he said in it appealed to the Québécois. "It's not just *speaking* French," Lise Bissonette, editor of *Le Devoir,* told Wilson after a frustrating editorial board encounter in which he had attempted to cling to the Ottawa establishment line on constitutional matters, while vainly seeking to distract attention to that Anglo-Saxon proxy for politics, "the economy." When the leadership convention was held, practically no Quebec support went to Wilson and he was eliminated on the first ballot.

The history and politics of Quebec are dominated by a single great reality: the emergence of the French-speaking nation. The process has been slow, complex and agonizing. There have been false starts, reversals and long periods of quiescence. But for over two hundred years its ultimate direction has remained the same: towards ever-greater self-expression, as the growing plant seeks the light.

In the case of Quebec, one of the myths of Canadian Nationalism is true: the Francophones are not just North Americans who happen to live north of the border and speak French. But they are not Canadians who speak French either. They may seem similar at first glance, but their cultural background is quite different, and the more closely it is studied the more completely different it appears. Christina McCall-Newman's epitaph on a failed 1977 fence-mending lunch between Pierre Trudeau and a group of Anglophone publishers is actually no more than the literal truth: ". . . they were, in effect, foreigners to each other. What they needed was a diplomatic briefing before they met."

Such a diplomatic briefing would begin like this: a vital force in Francophone culture has been its particularly rigorous version of the Roman Catholic Church. The Church was at one time all-pervasive in Quebec. Even as late as 1960, incoming Liberal Premier Jean ("Quiet Revolution") Lesage was credibly reported to have submitted a list of his proposed cabinet ministers to Cardinal Léger, the Archbishop of Montreal. Obviously, both province and priests have changed dramatically in recent years. Superficially, it might appear that North American norms have prevailed. But history is not so easy to shake off. The modern Quebec state, with its powerful bureaucracy, has replaced the Church as the authoritative Francophone institution. Its dependent cadres of intellectuals and white collar workers form a new clerisy. And the underlying message, preached most forcefully by the separatists, has remained constant: there are higher values than economics.

In the nineteenth and early twentieth centuries, the Church opposed Francophone migration to morally dubious towns or – worse – the United States. Monseigneur Louis-François Laflèche, Bishop of Trois Rivières until 1898, even urged Francophones to protect the purity of their faith by not learning English, the language of the Canadian commercial class. "We have the privilege to be entrusted with this social priesthood, granted only to select people," said Monseigneur Louis-Adolphe Paquet in his famous "Sermon on the Vocation of the French Race in America," preached in 1902 on Saint Jean Baptiste Day, an official holiday in Quebec. "Our mission is less to handle capital than to stimulate ideas; less to light the furnaces of factories than to maintain and spread far and wide the glowing fires of religion and thought." Sixty-five years later, in the manifesto that would precipitate his exit from the provincial Liberal Party and the formation of the Parti Québécois, René Lévesque echoed this theme of uniqueness:

> We are Québécois. What that means first and foremost – and if need be, all that it means – is that we are attached to this one corner of the earth where we can be completely ourselves: this Quebec, the only place where we have the unmistakeable feeling that "here we can be really at home."
>
> Being ourselves is essentially a matter of keeping and developing a personality that has survived for three and a half centuries.
>
> At the core of this personality is the fact that we speak French.

Quebec's Church is the key both to the initial success of Canada and to its ultimate failure. At the time of the Conquest of 1759, there were only some 60,000 French settlers in Canada, as opposed to 1.5 million English-speakers in the rest of North America. In 1755, on the eve of war, the British had simply uprooted and expelled the Acadians, a similar group of French colonists in Nova Scotia who had been refusing to swear allegiance, although Britain had been legally awarded the territory by the Treaty of Utrecht in 1713. The Acadians' fate inspired Longfellow's poem *Evangeline;* some eventually filtered back, but many ended up in Louisiana, where their descendants are still known as "Cajuns."

Nothing of the sort was attempted in Lower Canada. The new British authorities in Quebec did not even make any sustained effort at assimilation, much to the disgust of their more robust colonists to the south, who made short work of their own Dutch, Spanish and

French enclaves. Instead, the British groped their way by trial and error into an alliance with the Church and the land-owning seigneurial class. The first such effort came as early as 1774, when the British Parliament's Quebec Act confirmed French legal and landholding practices, permitted Catholics to hold civil office, established the Church by permitting it to collect tithes and also expanded the colony's boundaries at the expense of American aspirations in the West. This tolerance, exceptional for that age, materially encouraged the outbreak of the American Revolution the next year.

In the short run, this liberalism offered real advantages to a hardpressed Imperial power, and to its Canadian heir. The Francophones supported the British rather than the American cause when the revolutionary armies invaded Canada. In the War of 1812 the American thrust at Montreal was repulsed at Lacolle and Châteauguay by Francophone militia commanded by a seigneurial scion, Lieutenant-Colonel Charles-Michel de Salaberry. But the long-term result of the policy was that the Francophone community was not digested. Two hundred years later, Canada is choking on it.

"The *Entente Cordiale*" between Canada's founding races, Hugh MacLennan has observed, "though few Anglophones ever realized this, depended for its strength on the Vatican's calculation that it was in the general interest of the Universal Church" that it should exist. Having reached an understanding with the British civil power, Quebec's Catholic Church ceaselessly reminded its flock of their duty to Caesar. Bishop Briand threatened to refuse the sacraments to Francophones who did not rally to the British in 1775. Catholic priests denied burial to *patriotes* killed in the 1837 Rebellion. All six Quebec bishops publicly endorsed Confederation in 1867, greatly aiding George-Etienne Cartier in the struggle to hold his mutinous province in line. The archbishops of Montreal and Quebec City told their parishioners that they had a sacred duty to aid Great Britain, when World War I broke out in 1914. During World War II, Cardinal Villeneuve, the Archbishop of Quebec City, mounted a prolonged campaign of what Conrad Black has called "astonishing energy" to rally Francophones to the Allied cause, mercilessly crushing pro-Axis and neutralist sentiment among his clergy, and certainly contributing to the small but significant increase in Francophone volunteers. In Hugh MacLennan's words:

> When Pius XII held a high mass in St. Peter's for the [Francophone] Royal 22nd Regiment, just after the liberation of Rome, no French Canadian failed to get the the message. The Bloc

Populaire, [an anti-war left-nationalist group], which might otherwise have won the provincial election, was instantly doomed. When King's Liberals finally broke their promise never to impose conscription on Quebec, all stayed quiet in the province.

The Conquest, summarizes a recent historian of Quebec, Susan MannTrofimenkoff, had the effect of "catapulting the clergy into positions of power and prestige it had never known during the French Regime ... [the British] needed those links to the people if the transition from French to English, from surrender to acceptance, was to be made calmly. The clergy moved softly and spoke smoothly. Of all thue elite groups, it survived best."

There are, however, more things in heaven and earth than are dreamt of in sociology. The Catholic Church in Quebec was not merely grabbing for power but responding from the most profound belief. In an age of Liberation Theology, it is easy to forget that the prescriptive and hierarchical nature of Catholic Christianity naturally inclined it to the view that monarchy was divinely ordained, and that republics and revolutions were to be regarded at best with deep suspicion. The Church's very catholicism ran, xenophobic lower clergy notwithstanding, against the worldwide worship of nationalism that developed at the end of the eighteenth century. The Quebec Church in particular was absolutely appalled by the French Revolution, and its opinion of France never completely recovered.

Today, only traces of this attitude remain: cathedrals are still dedicated to Christ the King – or in the center of Montreal, to Mary, Queen of the World – not to Christ the Premier or Mary the Social Worker. Nevertheless, as late as the morning of the 1956 Quebec provincial election – Duplessis' last – Francophones listening to a program of morning prayers on CBC radio were informed in no uncertain terms that

sovereign authority, by whatever government it is exercised, is derived solely from God, the supreme and eternal principle of all power. . . . It is therefore an absolute error to believe that authority comes from the masses, from the people, to pretend that authority does not properly belong to those who exercise it, but they have only a simple mandate revocable at any time by the people. This error, which dates from the Reformation, rests on the false principle that man has no other master than his own reason . . . . it will have as a consequence the weakening of authority, making it a myth, giving it an unstable and changeable basis, stimulating popular passions and encouraging sedition.

"Think *that* over before you cast your vote!" commented Pierre Trudeau ruefully in a 1958 essay on anti-democratic and un-progressive trends in French-Canadian culture.

Indeed, this stark social philosophy had very definite implications about just who should be casting those votes. In 1940, when the Quebec provincial government was finally getting up the nerve to allow women the vote, Cardinal Villeneuve unhesitatingly con-demned the plan as "contrary to familial unity and hierarchy." Di-ffusing into the secular sphere, this heritage explains some unex-pected differences between Anglophone and Francophone politics. For example, Henri Bourassa, founder of *Le Devoir* and a prominent Quebec politician in the early years of this century, seems to be the very model of an anti-war, anti-imperialist radical of a sort familiar in Anglo-American progressive movements. He is much favored by today's English-Canadian Nationalists for his early advocacy of "au-tonomy" within the Empire. Yet Bourassa actually interrupted his campaign against conscription in World War I to direct his fire against Ottawa's intention to enfranchise women in federal elections, which, as Susan Mann Trofimenkoff has acidly observed, "he obviously considered a much more serious problem." He denounced the plan as a direct consequence of an alien Protestant individualism and another threat to Francophone society.

Despite appearances, and although it did its best, the Church in Quebec was not monolithic. It had complicated internal tensions, notably between the higher and lower clergy, and its relationship to its laity was much more subtle and less mechanical than outsiders realized. Cardinal Villeneuve's endorsement of the war effort did not mean, as some English Canadians assumed, that Francophones were now ready to accept conscription, which they had resisted vehe-mently in World War I. As Conrad Black has noted, Villeneuve "knew that there were limits on what could be asked of the fearful popula-tion, even for a good cause." He remained pointedly silent during the 1942 referendum on conscription, when English Canada voted 80% "Yes" and French Canada, 90% "No."

A significant challenge to the Church occurred in the nineteenth century. At that time, in Quebec as everywhere in Europe, the Catholic Church was faced with the spread of what might be loosely described as liberalism – secular, democratic, individualistic, liber-tarian, sometimes nationalistic and even agnostic or atheistic: an intellectual and political phenomenon closely related to industrializa-tion and the development of an educated bourgeoisie. The problem was peculiarly acute in Quebec because the province's British rulers had practically invented this new disease back in the mother country. And in that long-ago era, British institutions and ideas had perforce acquired real prestige among the Québécois: symptomatically, they were constantly referring to their rights as British subjects, sometimes indeed to discomfort Anglophones, but quite often in quarrels entirely among themselves.

The Church reacted, as it had to the Protestant Reformation three centuries before, by rallying and reorganizing its own forces. This new counter-reformation movement eventually crystallized into a conservative ideology called "ultramontanism" – because its French exponents had been accused of looking over the mountains (the Alps) to Rome. There was a renewed stress on centralization and discipline, culminating in Pope Pius IX's proclamation in 1864 of the *Syllabus of Errors,* which condemned a great deal of what was going on in the contemporary world. And in 1870 Rome reiterated the doctrine of papal infallibility. The leaders of the Quebec Church were fierce ultramontanes. Simultaneously, they were launching a vast program of expansion which greatly strengthened their position in society. There was only one priest for every 2,000 Quebec Catholics in 1840; by 1880 there was one for every 500 – and they believed more than ever that they had an obligation to make their presence felt.

In every Catholic country in Europe, throughout the nineteenth century, a cultural civil war raged between the Church and the local liberals. In Quebec, a particularly bitter battle was fought to suppress the *Institut Canadien,* a mildly free-thinking Francophone adult education association in Montreal, whose members included a future Liberal prime minister of Canada, Wilfrid Laurier. *Institut* members were actually refused the sacraments in 1869. It took a six-year lawsuit that went all the way to the British Privy Council (at the time functioning as Canada's Supreme Court) before one of them, Joseph Guibord, could be given burial in a Catholic cemetery, guarded from the mob by one thousand of the Queen's soldiers and encased in concrete lest the faithful feel tempted to dig him up. The Church then deconsecrated the ground.

Under these circumstances, anti-clericalism became almost an inverted religion among some scarred Francophones. As late as 1944, the president of the newly formed provincially owned Hydro-Quebec electric utility, T.D. Bouchard, took the opportunity offered by his elevation to the Canadian Senate to launch a searing and lovingly detailed attack upon what he said was the obscurantist propaganda taught as history in Quebec's Catholic-controlled schools. Only after leaving the seminary, he claimed, had he "learned that Canadians of

English descent were not all cloven-footed and did not all bear horns. . . ." Uproar resulted, and he was fired.

The civil war within world Catholicism was already settling down towards the end of the nineteenth century. A major irritant had been removed when, despite the help of a *zouave* regiment of volunteers from French Canada, Pope Pius IX lost his fight to prevent the absorption of the Papal States and the city of Rome into the new unified Kingdom of Italy. In 1878, Pope Pius died, and his successor, Pope Leo XIII, was perceptibly more moderate. What divided Quebec Francophones now began to seem less important than what united them. And what united them was, in Pierre Trudeau's words, "but one desire – to survive as a nation. . . ." Quebec's *bleus,* locked into the Conservative coalition, were unable to escape the taint of association with the party of Anglophone patriotism. Once the issue of Francophone nationalism became paramount, they were doomed. Subsequent elections in Quebec have usually been contests to find the French-most party, with the Liberals easily able to prove that they were more French than the Tories, running into trouble only when confronted with totally Francophone competition like the Union Nationale – or the Parti Québécois.

Since then, social and economic conservatism has only surfaced in federal elections in Quebec when it has been able to find an unimpeachably Francophone outlet. This happened in 1962, when Quebec suddenly returned, to general amazement, twenty-four MPs to the House of Commons who professed allegiance to the Social Credit movement. Social Credit, the monetary theory developed by British engineer Major Clifford Hugh Douglas, had been the ideological expression of a powerful protest movement in Western Canada during the Depression, but on a federal level it had long been in decline. The Quebec Créditistes, however, had only nominal links with the Anglophone movement. They were authentic products of Francophone Quebec, a rural, right-wing, pro-small business, often unilingual group with close links to their constituents, usually quiet but given to making anti-Communist remarks and generally disturbing Ottawa's liberal orthodoxies. Above all, the Créditistes were loyal Québécois. In the 1979 Parliament, the Créditiste leader Fabien Roy was, according to Jeffrey Simpson, in *Discipline of Power,* "a Quebec nationalist, the closest politician to the Parti Québécois in the House of Commons." Tory Prime Minister Joe Clark's government was in a minority and could have used Créditiste support, but instead Clark was blindly hostile to them, convinced that if they "faded in Quebec their supporters would find a new home with the Conservatives." He was wrong, of course. In the 1980 federal election, they actually voted for the Liberals – "a party more deeply rooted in French-Canadian society than the Conservatives," Simpson concluded with deadpan understatement.

Canadian conventional wisdom maintains that when the Conservatives hanged Louis Riel in 1885, they made a crass blunder that brutally shattered Quebec's trust in them. But this is to confuse symptom with sickness. "The break-up of the Conservative party in Quebec was well underway before the ghost of Louis Riel consigned it to electoral oblivion," Susan Mann Trofimenkoff has written. The danger had been briefly apparent as early as the 1872 federal election, when the decision of the New Brunswick provincial government to end support for its Catholic schools enabled the enterprising Quebec *rouges* to form an alliance of their own with outraged nationalists and ultramontanes, and to defeat George-Etienne Cartier in his own riding. That coalition was short-lived, probably because of poor leadership, but Riel's execution offered another opportunity. "Honoré Mercier, leader of the Quebec Liberals . . . had in fact been looking for such an issue for years."

As it happens often when a new nation is learning its symbols, things took time. At first, the Métis uprising had been universally condemned in Quebec. No one justified the taking of arms against legally constituted authority. A Francophone militia unit assisted in its suppression. But the Francophones' underlying alienation from the surrounding Anglophone polity found expression in doubts about the severity of Riel's punishment, then about the details of Ottawa's Prairie policies, and finally about the justice of its cause. Mercier's Parti National coalition of Liberals, Catholics and nationalists formed the provincial government in 1887; in the federal election of that year, the Conservatives' federal majority in Quebec plunged to one. In the 1891 federal election, it vanished completely.

It was only during the mid-nineteenth century, when the Catholic civil war was still raging in Quebec, that there was a viable alliance between Anglophone Conservatives outside Quebec and Francophone Conservatives within the province. As often happens in civil wars, one Francophone faction secured its position by making a deal with a foreign power. In this case, the Francophones who had traditionally supported the Church, Cartier's *bleus,* whose opponents were the *rouges,* chose to link up with John A. Macdonald's Ontario Tories. This was the origin of the Conservative electoral coalition that achieved Confederation and dominated Canadian politics until the end of the nineteenth century.

Ever since, Anglophone Tories have peered into Quebec hoping for the return of this Francophone federal Conservatism, like medieval travellers on the cliffs of Cornwall scanning the Atlantic in the hope of seeing the fabled lost land of Lyonesse rising again far out among the waves. These Tories naturally assumed that their French-speaking fellow-citizens arrived at the truth of Conservatism by contemplating the majesty of the law, the sanctity of private property and various other noble topics, just as they had themselves. And no doubt this helped. Ultimately, however, the Francophones' motives were their own, and quite different.

An electoral alliance of this type no more requires a shared political culture than does a strategic alliance between sovereign states: in the 1911 federal election, the last hurrah of the Tory coalition, "Conservative" candidates were even able to take diametrically opposed lines in Quebec and English Canada, arguing respectively that the Liberals' Navy Bill was excessively or insufficiently pro-British, while agreeing only that it was a "bad thing." Equally, however, such an alliance could last no longer than the needs it served. And in the end, as the civil war within Catholicism was resolved, the cultural base for Francophone support for the federal Tories in Quebec began to sink away. In its place remained only the deep waters of Francophone nationalism.

In fairness to English-Canadian Conservatives, it should be noted that many of them were convinced that they caught a glimpse of at least the steeples of Lyonesse surfacing in 1958, when the minority Conservative government of John Diefenbaker called a federal election and suddenly and unexpectedly won a majority of Quebec's seats, the first since 1887. The Tories were not precisely sure what they had done to conjure up this magical response – besides already being in power in Ottawa, a not inconsiderable factor in a patronage-minded province. But it reinforced their belief that the right combination of incantation and incentive would summon Quebec back. Hence, nearly twenty years later they turned to Brian Mulroney. And in 1984, under his leadership, the miracle seemed to happen again.

The real explanation for Diefenbaker's sweep, however, lay once again in Quebec's unique politics. Premier Maurice Duplessis, fresh from his fourth consecutive provincial election victory, finally felt strong enough to commit his formidable Union Nationale organization to wreaking vengeance on his Liberal enemies in Ottawa. This was a cherished end in itself for Duplessis, and did not at all imply endorsement of Diefenbaker's policies, particularly on federal-provincial relations. In Conrad Black's account:

Duplessis himself selected the candidates, and oversaw the effort. They would concentrate on 50 ridings of the province's 75, the others being conceded to the Liberals. Duplessis authorized $15,000 for each of the constituencies, the extraordinary sum of $750,000 in total . . . .

The Liberals did not realize that beneath the surface, homing toward the election like a grim torpedo, was the whole party machinery. . . . In the 50 selected counties, every home was visited at least twice by Progressive Conservative canvassers, in almost every case veterans of the Union Nationale campaigns who knew well their constituencies. For hundreds of thousands of Quebeckers, this was the first physical evidence they had ever seen, on their doorsteps, of a Conservative Party. The old financial tricks were replayed on a modest scale – gifts, favours, promises. Diefenbaker was already in power; Duplessis had been there since time immemorial. Thus, there was no lack of credibility in such a tactic . . . .

Every one of Duplessis' fifty ridings returned a Conservative MP. Characteristically, Diefenbaker in his memoirs took credit for the victory and nowhere mentioned the Union Nationale's role.

The explanation for Brian Mulroney's victory in Quebec is essentially similar to that for 1958. The support of a provincial government with its own agenda, in this case the Parti Québécois, was equally essential although other factors also played a part . It is also significant that although Duplessis had been continuously in power since 1944, this was the first time he had seen the chance to defeat the Liberals. In other words, it takes just the right combination of winds and tides to uncover the steeples of Lyonesse. They are not likely to be visible for long.

By the late nineteenth century, the Francophones were beginning to reject political values derived from the Anglophones' ideological hegemony and, under their leaders' tutelage, develop values of their own. Riel was necessary for this process. But if he had not existed, he or something like him would have been invented. The frictions unavoidable when two nations coexist in one state made it easy – and inevitable.

And these frictions were increasing as the nineteenth century drew on. "Our people don't want English capital nor English people here – they have no ambitions beyond their present possessions, and never want to go beyond the sound of their own church bells," Louis-Joseph Papineau, *patriote* leader of the 1837 Rebellion, had said. This could easily be arranged while the Francophones stayed down on the farm and the Anglophones gathered in the towns – Montreal had an English-speaking majority for much of the nineteenth century, and until the 1860s Anglophones comprised about 40% of the population of Quebec City, now almost entirely French. But as urbanization proceeded, the two communities increasingly found themselves inspecting each other's faults at distressingly close quarters.

Democracy exacerbated division. As the British colonial authorities conceded representative government, Canadian politicians began to compete directly with one another for power. Ethnic and religious appeals were quickly found to be the most rewarding ways of marshalling votes – for the very good reason that they corresponded to real divergences of interests and values among the electorate. And as the limited governments of the early Victorians went out of fashion, and public policy became increasingly interventionist, there was simply so much more to argue about. The redistributive effect of taxation and transfer payments immediately developed acute ethnic implications in a heterogeneous society, which was why Goldwin Smith predicted, not unpresciently in view of Quebec's current severe tax rates, that "the commercial Protestants at Montreal . . . [run] no small risk of being despoiled by the needy financiers of a separate race." But on a more elemental level, frequent contact with the machinery of government forces you to think about symbolic and substantive issues of political power in a way that would not occur if all you ever saw were your neighbors. No one complained about the language in which welfare checks were issued when there was no welfare – when MacLennan's Polycarpe Drouin could truthfully say that "you never hear anything good from the government in Ottawa."

The fact that Francophone Quebec is different has been used by Quebec nationalists (and paradoxically also by Canadian nationalists) to make Anglophones feel guilty. The relationship between Anglophones and Francophones in Canada is often compared with the systematic discrimination by whites against blacks in the American Deep South. Usually, this is a polemical ploy, as when Pierre Vallières, theorist of the FLQ, called his 1969 book about the plight of the Francophones *Nègres blanc d'Amérique* – "White Niggers of America." To a surprising extent, however, English Canadians will acknowledge its validity. They cite as supporting evidence the prevalence in polite Anglophone society until very recently of slang and stereotyping about Francophones.

Actually, this merely serves to illustrate the mildness of the Quebec situation. Apart from the fact that the Francophones were themselves accomplished name-callers, what American blacks faced was far more serious: statutory discrimination enforced by the full power of the state. But in Quebec since Confederation, the state apparatus has always been entirely in French hands. There has never been an Anglophone premier of Quebec, although the Anglophone minority there is comparable in size to the Francophone component in the overall population of Canada, which elected its first French-Canadian prime minister in 1896. Indeed, even before Confederation, the first prime minister of the united provinces of Canada East and Canada West under "responsible government" was a Francophone, Louis-Hippolyte LaFontaine. It is ludicrous to suppose that anything like the discrimination experienced by Southern blacks would have been tolerated for a moment. The Anglophones no more had the machinery to prevent Francophones from entering the professions or commerce than it had to keep them out of politics. And in fact there have always been some Francophones in these areas – such as Pierre Trudeau's father.

It is possible to argue, of course, that although the institutions necessary for effective discrimination did not exist in Canada, the private attitudes and actions of the Anglophones were still enough to inflict injustice on the Francophones. This assumption was behind the 1967 Royal Commission on Bilingualism and Biculturalism's focus on salary and rank disparities between Francophones and Anglophones in the federal civil service. The difficulty Francophones faced in the civil service, however, or at any rate the one addressed by the resulting bilingualism policy, was not discrimination against Francophones as such, but the fact that at the higher levels they had to work in English. Francophones who were prepared to speak English could always in effect resign from their race in working hours, unlike the American blacks. And many did so with great success, including four sons of Colonel de Salaberry who entered the British Army, two prime ministers of Canada, Laurier and St. Laurent, and an outstanding Imperial proconsul, Sir Percy Girouard, the military engineer who built the railway that made possible Kitchener's conquest of the Sudan, and who ultimately became governor of Kenya.

For Francophones who are not prepared to speak English, this is of course no consolation whatever. What concerns them is not just opportunity for individuals, but the survival of their collective culture. Hence the wholesale promotion of the minority in government and industry (which might, at least in theory, do the trick in the case of American blacks) will not solve the Canadian problem. It might even exacerbate it, by threatening assimilation, something no amount of bilingual road signs or cornflakes boxes can wholly prevent.

Anglophones accept the charge of discrimination for a variety of reasons, often personal and psychological rather than political. But it is important to note that their meekness subtly detracts from the Quebec nationalist case. If discrimination is the problem, then ending discrimination could be the answer – not a sovereign Quebec. Far less comforting, because unappeasable even by the most abject confession of guilt, is the inexorable quest of a nation to find political expression in its own state. However, Quebec's Francophones are a nation, not a minority group. Only political power can satisfy nationalism. And only in Quebec can Francophone nationalists see their way to political power in sufficiently pure form.

This concept of "societal" or "pervasive" discrimination is controversial throughout the English-speaking world. One of its weaknesses is its inability to explain why some victims prosper anyway, notably Asiatics and Jews – and historically Montreal was the center of Canada's very successful Jewish community. Another is that there may be other causes of disparities in ethnic groups' economic performances, besides discrimination on the one hand and the unacceptable possibility of differing abilities on the other. The American economist Thomas Sowell, himself black, leads a school of thought that cultural factors, such as differing ethnic attitudes towards education and work, play a crucial role. This sort of argument is often dismissed as "blaming the victim." But whether or not mitigating factors are admissible in any trial of English Canada, they cast an interesting light on the past and future of French Canada.

The traditional Francophone attitude to education has been bluntly summed up by June Callwood:

> Quebec's schools, operated by the clergy, served the church's hope that French Catholics would stay away from the English-dominated cities. Stressing dogma and piety, then tended to turn out illiterates who couldn't compete for skilled jobs. Even higher education, reserved for sons of elite Canadiens [Francophones], produced classical scholars rather than engineers, economists, or scientists.

In 1867 the new Quebec provincial government set up an education ministry, but eight years later it was forced by Church pressure to disband it. Education was not compulsory in Quebec until 1943; the province assumed direct responsibility for it only in 1963, in one of the major victories of the Quiet Revolution. So low were Francophone educational standards in general that English-speaking Catholics rebelled: the complaints of the Catholic bishop of London, Ontario, triggered the reform of French-language schooling in that province, which further stimulated Quebec's nationalist fervor during World War I.

In recent years, a considerable boom in French college-level technical and commercial education has encouraged federalists, who think business will absorb energies that might otherwise go into politics. But this may be deceptive. The policies of successive Quebec governments have almost certainly induced English-Canadian employers to hire Francophones, although often while simultaneously withdrawing all non-Quebec functions from the province. They may also have been influenced by the fact that the head of Montreal's Francophone business school, the Ecole des Hautes Etudes Commerciales, was the brother of a prominent Parti Québécois cabinet minister. A whole species of Francophone service companies has emerged to mediate between business and government. But, in the words of two pessimistic Anglo-Quebeckers, "these young Francophone executives . . . are learning that the way to succeed in business without really trying is to support francization."

It is not yet clear that this new attitude to education is much more than an update of the Francophone elite's traditional respect for professional credentials and dependence upon government favor, which Susan Mann Trofimenkoff has traced back to the early nineteenth century and beyond, to before the Conquest. Nor is it apparent that it must involve a change in the way Francophones feel about their nationhood. Indeed, it should intensify it, by ending the inferiority complex that some Francophones believe their community has secretly suffered from when comparing itself to the Anglophones, the same complex they have blamed for the community's deep suspicion of political change. This makes sense. Nationalism, after all, is supposed to be a bourgeois phenomenon.

The traditional attitude of Francophones towards work has also been distinctive. That they had a different opinion of the rat race from the rest of North America has long been recognized even by such disinterested outsiders as the Prudential Insurance Company of Newark, New Jersey. Its corporate historian notes with wonder that, "One man in the city of Quebec refused a transfer to Lévis, across the river, just five miles from his home, because he would be leaving the community in which he had not only lived but worked – refused even though he could have commuted from his home to Lévis easily. In October 1973, there were 30 such refusals on the desk of Jean Paul Labonte, Prudential's regional vice president in Quebec." These career paths were in sharp contrast to that, for example, of Robert Beck, subsequently to become Prudential's chairman. He had already moved fourteen times in twenty years and was still only forty-seven.

Sensibly, Prudential reacted by treating Quebec as a completely alien civilization. By the mid-1970s, every Prudential employee in Quebec was a Francophone, and 410 of its 485 Quebec agents could speak only French. They probably would never be chairmen of Prudential. But one day they might well be citizens of a state of their own.

The differences between Anglophone and Francophone economic cultures may well pre-date their Canadian manifestation. In 1976, Alain Peyrefitte, a former member of Charles de Gaulle's cabinet, published *The Trouble With France,* a best-selling analysis of *Le Mal Francais,* the French sickness. Peyrefitte argued that centralism, uniformity and hierarchy had been recurrent themes in France's history, ultimately going back to five centuries of Roman rule and emphatically reaffirmed by the influence of the Catholic Church, by the mass flight of France's Protestants after the Edict of Nantes was revoked in 1685, and also by the French Revolution (which "lived up to its etymological original as a return to its point of departure: the all-powerful bureaucracy"). This had given France formidable durability and identity, but at a real price in individual economic initiative. "From [the Revolution] until now, there has not been a single private bank of any importance in France that was not founded by Protestants or Jews," wrote Peyrefitte, incidentally throwing light upon Anglophone domination of Montreal's financial community in St. James Street (now *Rue St.-Jacques*). Peyrefitte explicitly regarded French Canadians as a transatlantic confirmation of his general thesis about France, not as victims of colonial oppression: "Their troubles stem less from law or politics than from [their own] attitudes." Quebec's story is particularly poignant in view of What Might Have Been: "Ah! If Richelieu and Louis XIV had let the French Protestants migrate to the New World," Daniel Johnson told me when he was Quebec's premier, "the first men on the moon would have spoken French, not English." But in fact the colony's rulers preferred purity to prosperity, and made great efforts to keep refugee Huguenots out. This precedent should be borne in mind when assessing the likelihood that any Quebec government will favor the various imaginative proposals that Montreal should be taken out of politics and made an international free city, an "enterprise zone" exempt from the more onerous provincial tax and language requirements.

All issues of guilt or innocence, superiority or inferiority, are in the end irrelevant in Quebec. It is simply unnatural that two nations should live together in the same state. The differences between Anglophones and Francophones are in themselves, and in all innocence, quite sufficient to make conflict certain. And it can be predicted with absolute confidence that these differences are not going to go away. What is astonishing is not that the communities have continual crises, but that they have got along so peaceably for so long. Emotions would be lowered and recriminations minimized if both sides could agree on the concept of a no-fault divorce, if I may indulge in the anthropomorphism favored by English-Canadian intellectuals. Good fences make good neighbors – and sometimes even reasonably harmonious ex-spouses.

Although national survival is the essential theme of Francophone history, the idea of an independent Quebec state has come to the forefront of Francophone political debate only relatively recently. Despite some nineteenth-century mutterings – Parti National leader Honoré Mercier endorsed separatism shortly before his death – there was much less precedent for it in that age of Empire. Maurice Duplessis welded Francophone nationalists with the surviving *bleus* into the electoral coalition that kept the Union Nationale in power until 1960, but according to his biographer he "had never spoken of or, so far as can be ascertained, even positively considered separatism in his conscient life." Yet his defense of Quebec's rights within Confederation was so militant that at least one prominent observer, the historian Mason Wade, suspected him of plotting it. Post-war decolonization, however, made independence an unavoidable issue in Quebec. It was not a coincidence that the FLQ, the Quebec urban guerrilla movement of the 1960s, merely adapted the name of the Front de la Libération Nationale, their counterparts in the struggle to wrest Algeria from France.

The emergence of Quebec separatism is a fascinating demonstration that ideas, symbols and ideology have consequences. Historically, Francophones were in the habit of referring to themselves as *Canadiens* (Canadians) and to their English-Canadian fellow citizens as *les Anglais,* the English. This carried the innuendo that the Anglophones' Greater British loyalties disqualified them from being *real* Canadians like the Francophones. But it also left the Francophones morally disarmed, committed to a polity in which they were heavily outnumbered. English Canadians flew the Union Jack. The Francophones had no distinctive banner of their own except what Hugh MacLennan has described as "a defaced French *Tricolor* with the letters V and N interwoven in the middle of the central stripe," invented in Quebec to mark the Anglo-French Crimean War alliance, or, most often flown in the countryside, the yellow and gold colors of the Vatican City.

But in 1948, the Quebec provincial government of Maurice Duplessis adopted a provincial flag. Significantly, its heraldry was exclusively that of France, New France and Catholicism: the *fleur-de-lis,* the blue field, the white cross. As Susan Mann Trofimenkoff has said: "The flag proclaimed in 1948 what nationalists had been saying for years, but what politicians would not utter until the 1970s: Quebec was a separate place, a homeland, distinct from the rest of North America." And then, around 1960, the Francophones suddenly and mysteriously stopped calling themselves *Canadiens* – or *Laurentians,* the term favored by some nationalists in the 1930s – and became, according to themselves at least, "Québécois." They were coming to regard themselves no longer as a minority in the whole of Canada, but as a majority in one of its parts.

It was as if an acute political intelligence had made a brilliant but ruthless move. At one stroke, it established the principle that Quebec was a European-style nation-state, implicitly reducing its non-French minorities to the status of ethnic anomalies, and thus morally disenfranchising them. Indeed, to the Parti Québécois, they were literally invisible persons. In an interview with *Barron's* in 1982, René Lévesque brushed off any suggestion of economic dislocation in Quebec and began enthusing about a businessman in his riding who was about to travel to Hong Kong to inspect his branch plant there. "That was unthinkable for us twenty-five years ago," he concluded.

"Us being French Quebeckers," began his interviewer, mindful of the enormous commercial and financial enterprise of Montreal, the traditional metropolis of Canada, "because obviously the English Quebeckers –"

"Yes, a home-grown boy," interrupted the Premier of All the Quebeckers, missing the point in his eagerness to discuss another Francophone success: Bombardier Incorporated's sale of subway cars to New York City, with a little help from the export-subsidy schemes of both provincial and federal governments. "One was made to feel as if six generations of forebears in the area counted for nothing," said one Anglophone participant in a Quebec provincial government colloquium for "minorities" in 1979. He was right. They didn't.

Ideologically alert Anglophone Quebeckers have denounced this change of nomenclature as a "semantic fraud" designed to legitimize the Francophones' exclusive claim to all Quebec. They pointed out that Anglophones were the original settlers of large areas of the province: the Ottawa Valley; the Eastern Townships; the "northern townships" along the foothills of the Laurentians; the Gaspé; and the north shore of the St. Lawrence river adjacent to Labrador. On top of this, the northern two-thirds of the province was part of "Rupert's Land," the vast territory sold by the Hudson's Bay Company to Canada in 1870 and only subsequently assigned to Quebec as an administrative convenience, largely at the behest of English-speaking provincial bureaucrats in Quebec City. This includes the site of the great provincial hydro-electricity project at James Bay (now *la Baie James*), and the territories of Inuit and Cree Indian groups whose second language is English. By contrast, the Francophones were historically concentrated in the relatively small area north of the St. Lawrence, between Montreal and Quebec City. They moved from it into other parts of Quebec only reluctantly and with considerable prodding by the organizers of the Church and provincial government colonization schemes.

Reflecting this reality, there have been suggestions that if Quebec seceded, some of its Anglophone areas could in turn secede, just as West Virginia did when Virginia joined the Confederacy in 1860. Then the city of Montreal could be divided and it would form an "eleventh province," to be called West Quebec. (In fact, after the rebellions of 1837 the governor of Upper Canada, Sir Francis Bond Head, suggested that Montreal should be annexed to Upper Canada, a proposal which Goldwin Smith thought "more sensible than the plan of union" between the Canadas that was in fact adopted.) René Lévesque has dismissed this possibility in terms that indicate a basic contempt for the Anglophone cause: "Westmount [the upper-class Anglophone district of Montreal] is not a nation." Others have argued that Quebec should be partitioned on separation, with Canada retrieving Rupert's Land and retaining the south shore of the St. Lawrence as a sort of Danzig Corridor, linking Ontario to the Maritime provinces. But although this type of approach was advocated in a controversial *Maclean's* article by Canada's pre-eminent historian, Donald Creighton, and examined in formidable detail in a 1980 book, *Partition* (one of whose co-authors was William Shaw, a leading Anglo-Quebec legislator), it quickly passed into the limbo the Canadian political class reserves for things about which it would rather not think. As for Quebec separatists, the only boundary revision they seem prepared to contemplate is a reversal of the 1927 Privy Council judgment that Labrador belonged to Newfoundland, a detail that Quebec government maps of the province consistently ignore.

But this "semantic fraud" also concealed a wrenchingly hard decision for the Francophones. It meant they were finally abandoning the dream of a French Canada. It had seemed so close to realization. The memory of the *voyageurs* was dear to a history-conscious people. All across North America, in a great arc from New Orleans, Louisiana, through St. Louis, Missouri, Coeur d'Alene, Idaho, and on out to La Vérendrye's camp in the foothills of the Rockies, were tantalizing reminders of past glories. Some Francophones even continued to hope that their remarkably high birthrates might one day actually restore them to numerical superiority in Canada – *le revanche des berceaux,* the revenge of the cradle. The possibility was seriously discussed as late as 1950, when Francophones made up 30% of Canada's population and foreign immigration was popularly supposed to be at an end.

This lingering wishfulness underlies much of the emotional attraction Francophones felt for the federal Liberals' bilingual policy and its chimerical vision of a Canada-wide phantom French-speaking nation. "The Rocky Mountains are part of our heritage," René Lévesque was told by a colleague, Yves Michaud, as he was preparing to break with the provincial Liberals in 1967. "Marquette and Joliet . . . we were there first." In the 1981 referendum campaign in which the Parti Québécois sought a mandate to negotiate its version of separation, "[Federal Justice Minister] Jean Chrétien lost his voice shouting about 'my Rockies'," according to the authors of *The National Deal.* A majority of Francophones apparently still hankered with Chrétien after those Rockies and voted *Non* – barely. But Yves Michaud did eventually join the Parti Québécois.

Earlier generations of Francophone nationalists, for example Henri Bourassa, had supported Francophones in distress wherever they were to be found – in Ontario, Manitoba, even in the U.S. And today, a natural human desire to have one's cake and eat it too leads many Francophones to sympathize both with the Parti Québécois' legislative suppression of the "English Fact" in Quebec and simultaneously with the federal Liberals' legislative sponsorship of the "French Fact" in Canada at large. The comedian Yvon Deschamps quite accurately satirized their ideal as *"un Québec independant dans un Canada uni "* – an independent Quebec in a united Canada.

But although many English Canadians do not realize it, the Parti Québécois nobly rejected this double standard. In return for a free hand in Quebec, it explicitly renounced any interest in the fate of Francophone minorities elsewhere in Canada. It did not even claim those Francophone areas contiguous to Quebec. "It could happen," commented Lévesque on the possible acquisition by Quebec of northern New Brunswick. "But we are not looking for it. We have a lot of land. Young Franco-Ontarians or Acadians are coming to Quebec to make their future. I think that is a better solution in the long run than territorial rearrangements." The strategy the Parti Québécois proposed for the Francophone nation is the same as that of Kemal Ataturk, who salvaged modern Turkey from the collapse of the Ottoman Empire by coldly abandoning Turkish communities in the periphery and concentrating all efforts on the defense of the Anatolian heartland. Anglophones mistakenly assume that the intense interest Quebec separatists show in the perennial language conflicts elsewhere in Canada means that they are rooting for the pro-bilingual side. In fact, they are merely checking in to confirm their opinion that the policy is unworkable and absurd.

The idea of an independent Quebec was also, to a much greater extent than English Canadians realize, a profoundly defensive move for the Francophones. For nearly two hundred years, Francophones had consoled themselves that their rapid reproduction guaranteed them increasing influence in Canada. After Confederation, massive immigration into the Anglophone community had maintained the overall demographic balance, but Francophones were able to use their local superiority in Quebec to achieve a majority in Montreal and to take over previously Anglophone areas like the Eastern Townships and the Gaspé, an enjoyable process often organized by the Church. By the middle of the twentieth century, after the Depression and World War II had choked off immigration for a generation, the Francophone component of the Canadian population had expanded to the upper limit of its historic range.

But then two deeply shocking developments occurred. First, a new and huge wave of immigration hit Canada and Quebec. These immigrants overwhelmingly chose to integrate into the English-speaking community. Secondly, Francophone birth rates suddenly began to fall, to the point where the fertility of Quebec as a whole is now discernibly lower than in the rest of Canada. This was a particularly important cultural event, because it could only mean that in the privacy of their homes Francophones were finally rejecting a central doctrine of their Church, and were using contraception. Canada's demographic balance was destabilized, and the Francophone proportion of the country's total population slid into a decisive decline. In Quebec, the impact was particularly alarming. By the mid-1960s, demographers at the Université de Montréal were predicting that by the year 2000, if current trends continued, the city would once again be dominated by its English-speaking population, as it had been in the nineteenth century. Cruel necessity compelled the Francophones' convulsive response.

Starting with Lesage, successive Quebec provincial governments, of every party, have intervened forcefully to arrest and reverse these trends. The province is now growing steadily more French. Federalists claim that this proves the Francophones were able to find all the tools they needed to protect "their language and culture" within Confederation – or nearly all, since the constitutionality of their more draconian measures is still in doubt.

But it is crucial to note that this federal complacency has already conceded the nationalists' case. The essential principle has been abandoned: that individuals in Quebec should voluntarily decide among themselves in which language they will work and educate their children. Instead, this decision is to be made for them by a political collectivity which claims to speak for Francophones. This collectivity happens to be the provincial government of Quebec. And it says, on behalf of Francophones, that it's not enough that they themselves should speak French – everyone else, at least for official purposes, should too. By accepting this, Canada's federalists in effect admit the existence of a Francophone nation and its identity with the Quebec state. From here on, everything else is just a matter of degree, and time.

Whether or not the rest of Canada realizes that it has inadvertently given away the farm, Francophones universally take for granted that they now possess a farm. An American expert, Alfred O. Hero, has put this well: by 1981 a "widespread consensus had developed among culturally, socially and politically alert Francophones living in Quebec that their society and its provincial institutions had become the only effective embodiment of their language and culture on the North American continent likely to endure over the long term." This consensus exists regardless of party. It was Jean Lesage who in 1964, when he headed the Liberal provincial government, formally enunciated the doctrine that "Quebec is the political expression of French Canada."

Pierre Trudeau's life-work was to convince Francophones that both they and the Anglophones could simultaneously look to the federal government in Ottawa as their supreme instrument, and that the provinces were merely administrative units in which Anglophones and Francophones were just plain Canadians, or should be.

But his effort has failed. In his wake, rhetoric abounds about "equality" at the federal level. In a democracy, however, there is a fundamental contradiction between majority rule on the one hand and "equality" between two discrete groups of such different size on the other. This incompatibility is particularly acute in a federal system of theoretically equal jurisdictions, a single one of which contains and is controlled by the smaller group. Jane Jacobs put it bluntly:

> The issue of how to combine the duality of French and English Canada with federation of ten provinces remains insoluble because it is inherently insoluble. To adopt the theory that the country consists of two peoples highly unequal in numbers, and yet equal, or nearly so, in their powers over the country as a whole, is to make federation unworkable. But to retain workable federation means that Quebec's claim to equality with English-speaking Canada in the organs and organizations of the government cannot be satisfied.
>
> Lévesque and his colleagues are the only political leaders in the country who have admitted that this constitutional problem is insoluble . . . .

In practice, quietly and step by step, even Trudeau's own allies are yielding to the inevitable. A particular embarrassment was the Task Force on National Unity, the very study that Trudeau initiated as a tension-lowering ploy after the Parti Québécois' 1976 election victory. In 1979, despite, or perhaps because of, the fact that the co-chairman was Jean-Luc Pepin, a prominent Francophone federal politician, the Task Force recommended the heresy of "special status" for Quebec, the much-derided *deux nations* approach that Trudeau must have thought he had driven from public life in 1968. According to Gwyn in *The Northern Magus,* the report "was promptly shelved by official Ottawa, and a peevish Trudeau shunted Pepin into the transport portfolio after the 1980 election, a job as far away from mainstream constitutional issues as possible."

The Francophones' common assumptions about Quebec mean that when they debate the province's future in Confederation, they are not at all addressing the question Anglophones fondly imagine. As early as 1965, Peter Desbarats provided the definitive description of this phenomenon in *The State of Quebec*:

Non-Quebeckers tend naturally to see Quebec in their own terms. They know that there are separatists in the province. They assume that other French Canadians are neutral or anti-separatist.

This neat classification misses the basic point completely. Quebec is not composed of a "Quebec First" element opposed by a "Canada First" element. With the exception of the English-speaking minority, Quebec is populated almost entirely by the "Quebec First" element.

Opposition to official separatism in Quebec rarely stems from any regard for the Canadian nation. It comes from those who are as deeply committed to the "Quebec First" philosophy as the separatists but who believe that separation from the rest of Canada would be against the interests of Quebec . . .

French Canadians . . . are exasperated by English-Canadian attempts to classify them neatly as separatists or anti-separatists. The French Canadian himself is conscious of no such clear-cut division. He recognizes, in the official separatist, a brother "Quebec Firster" whose goal is the same as his: the development of the French-Canadian group.

And this spirit of fraternity extends a long way. In 1964 René Lévesque, then a Liberal provincial cabinet minister, told Montreal students that Quebec's negotiations with English Canada should be carried on "if possible without bombs or dynamite." English Canadians were distressed at what they saw as an implied endorsement of the FLQ's sporadic terrorist violence in Quebec. The *Montreal Star* was particularly critical of the ambivalence of the Francophone media: "[Lévesque's speech] set off a shock wave in English Canada. It should have set off a shock wave in French Canada." This provoked a violent quarrel with the editor of the French daily, *La Presse,* Gérard Pelletier, a committed federalist who shortly was to go with Pierre Trudeau to the House of Commons in Ottawa. Desbarats comments that the *Star* editors were merely illustrating their complete "isolation from their French-speaking neighbors":

René Lévesque was among the leading protagonists of a communal adventure that affected every French-Canadian during the Sixties. So were the terrorists. French-Canadian readers of *La Presse* might quarrel with Lévesque's tactics, as they might abhor terrorism, but they knew instinctively that all the main actors of the "quiet revolution" were expressing, in total, all the varied and conflicting tendencies of the whole group. As far as the terrorists were concerned, most French-Canadians neither condemned them outright nor made heroes of them. They were "all in the family."

In the end, however, the irrepressible force of the idea of a politically distinct Quebec arises not only from abstract questions of ideology, identity and allegiance but because, unlike Canada's official bilingualism policy, it is based on solid social reality. In their daily lives, the two nations are already separate. And they are becoming more so all the time.

"More than they ever were," Peter Desbarats wrote in July 1976, "French Canadians of Quebec are on their own. . . ."

And that was four months before Quebec elected its first separatist government.

11

Quebec: We Shall Have Our French State

The road to progress lies through international integration; nationalism will have to be discarded as a rustic and clumsy tool.

– Pierre Trudeau

The disappearance of nations would impoverish us no less than if all peoples were made alike, with one character, one face. Nations are the wealth of mankind, they are its generalized personalities: the smallest of them has its own particular colors and embodies a particular facet of God's design.

– Alexander Solzhenitsyn

Notre état français, nous l'aurons [We shall have our French state].

– Abbé Lionel Groulx, 1937

The Parti Québécois governed Quebec for nine years. It was eventually defeated in 1985 by the Quebec Liberals under a born-again Robert Bourassa. This seemed to mark a convenient breathing-space after the quarter-century of national excitement in Quebec that began with the election of Jean Lesage and the inauguration of the Quiet Revolution in 1960. Quebec society had been transformed, and in every area of Quebec life Francophones were indisputably *maîtres chez nous* – in charge. A period of consolidation seemed natural and inevitable.

A common and comforting view of the PQ in power is that it achieved a species of pyrrhic victory: by establishing French primacy in Quebec, it removed the causes of discontent that brought it to power in the first place. By winning the battle, it lost the war. In fact, of course, Quebec's ingenious nationalists still have many complaints about the province's position within Canada, and the "patriated" constitution does pose serious legal threats to any *deux nations* approach to Quebec's uniqueness. But any consideration of a pyrrhic victory must include the question of which side is King Pyrrhus' – and which side the Romans'? By conceding the principle of a French Quebec, Canada's federalists may have stalled the separatist offensive, but not along a line that can be easily defended, should separatism revive.

If, in the mid-1980s, you were in an English-language bookstore in Montreal and wanted to buy that last Ross Macdonald (he was Canadian-born, after all) the clerk would direct you to the shelves marked *Romans Policiers*. In a city with as many English-speaking citizens as San Francisco, it was a crime, since the Parti Québécois succeeded in making French the only official language in the province, to use English signs in an English bookstore. Or Chinese ideographs in front of a Chinese restaurant, or Hebrew for a kosher butcher. Enforced by a special provincial government agency that welcomed informers, Quebec's language law was applied with fanatical zeal. Stop signs were replaced with ARRET, although such signs in France employ the English word. Safety instructions on Quebec ski lifts were only posted in French and English versions were ordered covered with plywood, although the entire clientele might well be American tourists. The program bore a haunting resemblance to the federal government's equally doctrinaire insistence on bilingual signs, regardless of need throughout the rest of Canada – except that Quebec, unlike Ottawa, had awarded itself the right to intervene in purely private transactions between citizens.

This suppression of the English fact in Quebec was not limited to its visible symbols. Language was used as a lever to overturn an entire community. Anglophone professionals were in effect disbarred from practicing if they failed to pass French proficiency examinations administered, somewhat controversially, by the provincial authorities. After the PQ victory in 1976, casual laborers who had worked every summer for twenty years on roads in Anglophone areas (for instance, parts of the Gaspé and Pontiac County), found themselves denied employment by the new government because they could not speak French. Businesses above a certain size were required to operate internally in French and receive official certification that they did so; employee "francization committees" were to be established to meet in working hours and supervise the process; it was legally hazardous to deny employment to any unilingual Francophone. And practically all children were to go to French-language schools unless they could show that at least one of their parents was educated in English *in Quebec* – Anglophones from other Canadian provinces were treated exactly like foreign immigrants. Politics, in short, was now in command of the Francophone capitalist class.

These policies involved daunting questions of ethnic and linguistic definition and distinction, all to be settled by administrative fiat. And they quickly shaded into questions of race. Francophones traditionally regarded their language as the property of what Arthur R.M. Lower, writing about Quebec as it was in 1900, described as "a band of blood brothers." Notwithstanding their later indignation about immigrants' tendencies to assimilate into the Anglophone community, at the beginning of the century Francophones had been distinctly reluctant to share their schools with strangers. When Montreal's immigrant Jews were accepted *en masse* by the Protestant (English-speaking) school system at the turn of the century, according to Canadian Jewish Congress archivist David Rome, "French Quebec was rather pleased to see them enter the English fold rather than its own . . . . [Francophones] were happy to have the alien non-Catholics, non-Protestants out of their kin." Significantly, even immigrant Catholics found it easier to learn English and assimilate into the Anglophone minority. Today, while the name of Parti Québécois leader Pierre-Marc Johnson is evidence of some intermarriage, the linguistic designation retains a more specific ethnic connotation than is usual in North America. Certainly many Canadian firms have concluded that, to extrapolate from Lise Bissonette, it is not enough for their Quebec representatives to *speak* French – they literally must *be* French . . . or, as René Lévesque would say, "a home-grown boy."

Quebec's language legislation had unavoidable parallels with the Third Reich's Nuremberg Laws, as Montreal's large European refugee community did not fail to point out. Francophones angrily objected to all such imputations. A less emotive comparison might be with Malaya's efforts to regulate its Chinese business class. For a society that calls itself free, however, the spectacle Quebec presented was not a pretty one.

Nevertheless, the Parti Québécois did not amount to a radical departure in Quebec's history. There was a basic continuity between its policies and those of its predecessors. Every Quebec provincial government since the 1960s had been preoccupied with legislation, progressively more restrictive, dealing with language and education. In Quebec's National Assembly – the name the Union Nationale gave to the provincial legislature in 1969 – the provincial Liberal Party, the only opposition group, made it clear it would not substantially repeal the Parti Québécois measures.

Neither was the use of the Quebec state apparatus to alter the balance between language groups a new development. It was one of the barely hidden motives when Jean Lesage's provincial Liberal government expropriated Quebec's private hydro-electric power companies and merged them with the French-speaking provincial-owned utility, Hydro-Quebec – itself initiated by the 1944 government takeover of Montreal Light, Heat and Power Consolidated. Lesage's move so delighted the veteran nationalist Abbé Groulx that for only the second time in his eighty-four years he emerged to vote when the Liberals called a provincial election on the issue in 1962. Quebec's power industry, the core of the province's economy, had been essentially created by Anglophones – Francophone colleges graduated no electrical engineers until 1943. But some fifteen years later, the inevitable was well underway. During hearings on the Parti Québécois language legislation, Dr. R.E. Bell, the principal of McGill University, reported that the school's Faculty of Engineering had cancelled a proposed program in hydraulics because the management of Hydro-Quebec, the main local employer of hydraulics engineers, had made it clear that no Anglophone graduates need apply.

At the other extreme, the Quebec civil service did not use French at all until 1910, when it became bilingual. Yet, as the Quiet Revolution was slowing down in 1964, Peter Desbarats could already note that "an English-speaking Quebecker in the Quebec civil service is much more of an oddity than a French Canadian on St. James Street . . . . This situation is so well understood that it almost never occurs to an English-speaking Canadian to apply for a job in the Quebec civil service." By 1979, only 0.7% of the Quebec service was Anglophone, as opposed to some 13% of the province's population. Quebec's Allophone 6.2% (those who speak neither French nor English) actually contributed more of its civil servants – a whole 0.9%. Intriguingly, this pattern is repeated in the Quebec branch of the federal civil service. By contrast, the proportion of Francophones in the federal civil service as a whole is slightly higher than in the population of Canada at large. In the Ontario civil service, Franco-Ontarians fill their proportionate 5% of civil service posts.

The Parti Québécois was always quite open about its intentions. René Lévesque was a cunning and careful leader, and one of a number of battles he fought against the movement's radical wing was over its insistence that a Parti Québécois government should withdraw all provincial funding from English-language schools. But he shared the radicals' ultimate goal: a purely French-speaking Quebec, with Anglophones absorbed – or evicted. In such a society, education in English would be an expensive luxury that diminishing numbers could afford. The problem would liquidate itself. Indulging in a flight of futurology with Peter Desbarats, in a 1969 interview that Canadian newspapers refused to carry on the grounds that it made separatism appear too credible, Lévesque imagined the situation after independence, which he guessed would have been achieved by 1972:

> So we left the English school system pretty well alone, tax-supported, and basically what's going on is, I guess, the normal thing .... it will take a while for younger people, while keeping their English set-up from elementary school to McGill, to learn French. But they will have to learn. It's a French-oriented society!
>
> And some every year (as used to happen) are leaving because it's not the kind of society they want. The others, the majority are staying and making careers in Quebec. I think that eventually everyone will be assimilated.

Nearly twenty years later, Quebec's independence is slightly behind schedule. But the Quebec Anglophones are switching or leaving right on cue.

The specific policies of the Parti Québécois were merely the visible tenth of an iceberg, to be washed over by variations in enforcement and even melted somewhat by the unpredictable rays of Canada's Supreme Court. But institutionally and ideologically, the entire mass of Francophone society underlay the visible expression of a separate society in Quebec. It is hard to see how a successor government could alter legislation designed to facilitate this – even supposing one had the will.

The decline of the Quebec Anglophones became unmistakeable with the election of the Parti Québécois. In his lifetime, a European historian said recently, the British have ceased to be Romans and have become Italians. The fate of the Quebec Anglophones is even more striking. They were Romans; they are becoming Anglo-Argentinians. Their reaction to the transformation of their historic home is an object lesson in the processes of political dispossession.

For the Quebec Anglophones, just as for the Francophones, ideas have had the most profound consequences. But rather than arousing and rallying the Anglophones, the effect of their beliefs has been to induce passivity and paralysis, sometimes masked by piety and a certain self-congratulation. There is nothing inherent in their situation to explain this failure. For example, the Ulster Protestants, who form a community of about the same size, have responded with remarkable political energy whenever they perceive their existence to be threatened, generating a range of leaders, organizations and tactics which, whatever else can be said about it, is undeniably wide. By contrast, even at this late hour in their collective existence, the Quebec Anglophones have not organized a political party to defend their interests at either the federal or provincial level. At both levels they vote Liberal, although the provincial Liberals were the authors of highly restrictive language legislation and the federal Liberals have made it clear that they will not risk annoying the Francophones by interfering with the despoliation of their fellow Quebeckers.

The Quebec Anglophones offer the rationalization that they are, after all, outnumbered in the province. But other minorities in the same situation behave very differently. Italy's German minority in the South Tyrol and its French minority in the Valle d'Aosta are both represented by their own parties, as are Finland's Swedes and – the last of a once-great faction – the Irish Catholics left in Ulster after the partition of 1922. There is a lot to be said for this strategy, even in terms of immediate political gratification. The cohesion of a minority can give it disproportionate power in negotiating alliances with majority factions absorbed in fratricidal conflict. This, as Goldwin Smith noted with disgust, was exactly why the Francophones themselves were not drowned after 1840 in the united legislature of Upper and Lower Canada, as Lord Durham had expected. But far more important in the long run, a minority that develops its own political organizations has a focus for its own existence, and a path to the future. And no majority can be expected to take a minority seriously if it does not take itself seriously enough to develop a tangible expression.

Like a dog on the operating table licking the hand of the vivisectionist, the Quebec Anglophones hope that their meekness will curry a little favor. They receive any hint of compassion with pathetic eagerness. They shrink from organizing politically because to do so would challenge directly the ideological hegemony that the Francophones have established in the province. But this amounts to unilateral moral disarmament. In a polity where the supreme good is the protection of Francophone "culture" – which in Canada has become an unexamined term of art increasingly synonymous with "nationhood" – it is too late for the Anglophones to protest when a minor technicality turns out to be their own elimination.

Intense moral pressure of this type is an accepted feature of newly independent states, where nationalism is the essence of legitimacy.

Thus Kenya can demand affirmations of loyalty from its white and Asian minorities, expelling those who decline to take out citizenship; the Protestant minority in Eire must offer allegiance to Dublin, whereas Belfast – or, more accurately, London – hesitates to exact it from the Catholics of Ulster. English Canada once exerted this hegemony over Quebec, reacting with sincere outrage when it was challenged, as over conscription, and receiving homage from Francophone politicians in the form of profession of Greater Britishness. Now the snowshoe is on the other foot.

The Protestant churches in particular illustrate the effects of this hegemony in a way that would have sent John Knox or Cotton Mather into pulpit paroxysms. "We recognize there is something new and, to some, even exhilarating in the Canadian situation today," said the Protestant United Church general executive in a statement issued within days of the Parti Québécois' 1976 victory. This victory was to compel the departure of many of its members from the province their forefathers largely built.

> ... the crucial factor in the shaping of future political structures must be the deliverance of French Canadians from any sense of subjection ....
>
> ... we also call attention ... to collective rights, to the rights of communities and peoples. In this we include the right to take what measures are necessary for collective survival and fulfilment. We call for safeguards of both individual and collective rights in a situation full of conflicting interests. At the same time, we are convinced that the defense of self-interest is not necessarily the way of the Gospel, which testifies to the dying of self and to being born for others.
>
> ... there is the opportunity, by way of referendum, for *the people* of Quebec to make a choice ... to have some measure of control of its destiny ....
>
> To the English in Quebec, whatever its future in or out of Canada, there is an additional opportunity to discover and demonstrate the role of a responsible minority.

"We have only gone a little way into this uncertain place – this *terra incognita* that is 'the new Quebec,' " wrote Dr. Douglas Hall, a Protestant academic in McGill University's Faculty of Religious Studies. "We recognize that we are strangers in this land. We have a great deal of listening to do before we can earn the privilege of speech." Symptomatic of this responsible minority's self-abasement before presumed majority susceptibilities, the main umbrella group for Quebec Anglophones calls itself (in the tortured Franglais fashionable among enlightened Canadian institutions) Alliance Québec.

Among the several reasons for the Quebec Anglophones' inability to defend themselves, one of the simplest and strongest is honest error. For quite a long time, it just didn't dawn on them that they were a threatened minority. They thought that they were part of the larger English-speaking world, whether British Imperial ("It is hard to imagine any city in the world with more places and institutions named after Queen Victoria," wrote William F. Shaw and Lionel Albert about the Montreal of their youth), Canadian Federal, or plain American, North. Tellingly, the student politics of Montreal's Anglophone universities in the 1960s were basically the same as those of their Canadian and U.S. counterparts, with no obvious concern that this generation of graduates was to pay the price of francization.

Or, in the rich sociologese of Professor Michael Stein of McMaster University, there has been "a gradual and intensifying state of dissonance between the strong residual 'majority group' self-perception which Anglophone Quebeckers had retained from their past, and their growing awareness of the reality of their current 'minority group' status and political impotence."

Anglo-Quebeckers were not helped to any greater understanding of themselves by their English-language press, which was heavily staffed with temporary imports from the rest of Canada. These outsiders have been accused by David Thomas, a bilingual Anglo-Quebecker, of maintaining "anxiety and ignorance" among Quebec Anglophones. But actually they tended, even more enthusiastically than the average Canadian mediacrat, to embrace the Liberal Establishment's ideology, with its compulsive sympathy for Francophones and complacency about separatism, because they did not identify with those who will suffer the consequences.

And this compulsion was powerful. As an example, David Waters, a producer for the Canadian Broadcasting Corporation, has reported that in the 1960s the CBC's Montreal English-language television outlet decided that "Quebec coverage meant coverage from the perspective of the overall Quebec society and not just from that of the more limited interests and concerns of the English community." As fears over the Liberal government's language legislation mounted, the CBC "aired an exhaustive series explaining the social and political realities surrounding the language problem," whereas a privately owned rival's radio affiliate actually organized a petition signed by

600,000 mainly Anglophone Quebeckers that called on Ottawa to use its constitutional powers to disallow the bill (vainly, however, and in the name of bilingualism). Not surprisingly, CBC-TV ratings fell precipitously. Waters felt that this proved the superiority of Canadian-style public-enterprise media over the private sector, which made "hucksterish managerial decisions" and had a crass commercial incentive to "identify with [its] public." But similar reflexes existed throughout the media industry. When the publisher of the Montreal *Gazette* wrote a front-page editorial denouncing the Parti Québécois just before the 1976 election, over a third of his editorial staff paid for a simultaneous advertisement disassociating themselves from it, apparently in large part because of its tone. The paper's regular editorial page "serenely" described the separatism issue as a "bogey." None of this, needless to say, prevented René Lévesque from denouncing the English media's "common front" against him.

Another reason for the Quebec Anglophones' inertia is that, ever since Confederation, they have played little part in the politics of their province. In 1958, in a famous anti-Duplessis polemic, *Le Devoir* editor André Laurendeau attributed this to the practice (developed by British colonial authorities to a high art) of indirect rule through a *roi nègre*, a "nigger king." But it is hard to see what else the Anglophones could have done. Duplessis himself used to decline flatly to discuss politics at all with his Anglophone contacts in the business community: "I'll take care of that. That's only of concern to us, as French-Quebeckers. That's my responsibility. Don't worry about it." Anglophone politicians such as George Marler, who was acting leader of the provincial Liberals at one point in the 1940s, quickly found that Francophone xenophobia imposed what Duplessis' biographer has described as very definite "limits of ambition for an English-speaking Quebecker, no matter how fluently bilingual." Most, like Marler, turned their attention to federal politics.

The result of this situation was that the Quebec Anglophones developed the habit of depending blindly upon whatever Francophone leaders they thought were the most sympathetic: in recent years Robert Bourassa when he was Liberal premier; then subsequently Claude Ryan, his successor as Liberal leader – and, of course, at the federal level, Pierre Trudeau. This invariably leads to disappointment, a cyclical pattern now clearly visible with Robert Bourassa, Mark Two.

To a great extent, Quebec Anglophones opted to flee rather than to fight. Unlike the French-speaking Québécois, the Anglophone community in Quebec, while it remained about the same relative size, traditionally experienced a high degree of demographic turn-over as immigrants arrived from overseas and from the backwoods and the native-born struck out for Ontario and the West. They were Canadians, after all. Since the Quiet Revolution, despite some Quebec government quibbling, it is clear that augmentation has ceased, emigration has accelerated, and the Anglophone community is being undermined to the point of collapse.

Between 1971 and 1981, the population of Canada rose 11.6%, to 24 million; Quebec Francophones increased 7.9%, to 5.25 million; but Quebec Anglophones declined 8.8%, to 810,000. The erosion has been heavily concentrated among the young. The number of Quebec Anglophones between twenty and forty-four years of age in 1981 was 17% lower than the group between ten and thirty-four years of age in 1971. In 1978, a survey of Anglophone junior colleges and universities showed that 37% of the graduating class were definitely leaving and a further 17% probably leaving, wrote Shaw and Albert. Ironically, knowledge of French was high in these groups – suggesting that the increase in the number of bilinguals in the rest of Canada may be more of an exogenous accident than a sign of spreading enlightenment. As a result of this exodus, Quebec Anglophones are beginning to have difficulty maintaining effective community institutions, which in turn provides added incentive to leave. *Le Devoir*'s Lise Bissonette suggested in 1982 that if trends continued, the English-language school system in Montreal would have lost half its pupils by mid-decade, close to the "critical threshold" where service in some areas would become impossible. Symbolically, the *Montreal Star* – the hammer of Lévesque and *La Presse* – ceased to publish in 1980.

In the last analysis, the Quebec Anglophones were the ground-zero victims of Canadian Liberalism, which was largely developed by (and for) their own leaders. Long before the Quiet Revolution, the Quebec Anglophones' "First Commandment," according to Peter Desbarats, was "Thou shalt not criticize the French Canadian – publicly." Projected onto the national scene, this became what Christina McCall-Newman called the Liberal Party's "major shibboleth." In Quebec, more than anywhere else in Canada, can be observed at close quarters the devastating effect on Canadian Anglophones of government-promoted multiculturalism, combined with the excision of the British connection. The editors of a recent study of the Quebec Anglophones, themselves English-speaking Quebeckers who now work in French, illustrate this when they venture, to say:

> One suspects that a late awareness of the heterogeneity of the
> English-speaking population – an awareness which has emerged in

answer to the question "who are we?" – has caused [Anglophones] to draw back from an energetic expression of the merits of their great cultural tradition.

. . . is there not to be found in the British tradition as embodied in the existence and history of substantial communities in Quebec, or perhaps (even more pertinent) as experienced by all Quebeckers via their participation in political, legal and economic institutions of British origin, the elements of a cultural tradition worth acknowledging and drawing inspiration from?

. . . We are not suggesting that English-speaking Quebec should identify with the British cultural tradition – heaven help us, we would instantly be condemned as dinosaurs, "more English than the Queen," a new "ultramontanism" . . . .

Quebec Anglophone leaders have displayed a marked tendency to think that the rest of English Canada should help them by making concessions from which they will be the chief beneficiaries. Liberalism provided a rationale for subjugating English Canada to their local concerns. Accustomed to submitting to the Francophones provincially and confining their hopes to the federal sphere, many Quebec Anglophones became among the most ardent believers in Pierre Trudeau's bilingualism panacea. Even Lionel Albert, William Shaw's co-author, dropped his work with the Preparatory Committee for an Eleventh Province to concentrate on promoting free-choice language zones throughout Canada; Alliance Québec publicly supported the extension of bilingualism to Manitoba during the controversy in 1984.

It should also be noted that some Quebec Anglophones themselves benefit personally from Ottawa's institutionalized appeasement of Québécois nationalism. Despite stereotypes, they are an even more bilingual group than the Quebec Francophones – some 47% of Quebeckers whose home language is English told the 1981 census-takers that they could also speak French, compared to only 28% of those speaking French in the home who claimed to speak English as well. Federal bilingualism benefits them personally, even as provincial unilingualism extinguishes them communally. Significantly, the most privileged Anglophones in Quebec have been the quickest to seek an individual accommodation, sending their children to French schools and offering no leadership to immigrant Catholics defying the law in their struggle for an education in English.

But Liberalism has turned out to be a Faustian bargain for the Quebec Anglophones. It offered them a period of unnatural influence at a time when their metropolis of Montreal was already faced with increasing competition from Toronto and the West. However, a key component of Liberalism was guilt, and in order to purvey it throughout English Canada the Quebec Anglophones had to accept it themselves. When Québécois nationalism arrives to claim their souls, they will have no answer.

The English-speaking community in Quebec will continue to disintegrate, as some individuals are absorbed completely and many more leave. A significant minority will remain in the Quebec elite, like the Anglo-Argentinians, irritating the Francophones with their continued economic success and, notwithstanding their perfect French, their indefinable other-ness. And a few, poor and outcast, will huddle in rural isolation or urban ghettos, still loyal to the language of their ancestors – relics, like Eire's Georgian mansions and New Delhi's viceregal edifices, of an empire upon which the sun never set.

While Quebec Anglophones have acquiesced to Francophone nationalism, the Liberal Establishment has simply tried to ignore it. The moment the very name of Quebec is mentioned, to paraphrase Sydney Smith, the Canadian elite and its friends seem to bid adieu to common sense and behave with the fatuity of idiots. This makes the future of Quebec a treacherous topic for discussion. Indeed, federalist fatuity often takes the curious ostrich-like form of ignoring Quebec altogether. In 1979, ex-Privy Council Clerk Michael Pitfield attended a conference in upstate New York to advise St. Lawrence University on its respected Canadian Studies program. He actually argued that any special consideration of Quebec should be excluded, on the highly unacademic grounds of the delicate political situation. In 1982, the editors of the Atlantic Council's authoritative survey, *Canada and the United States: Dependence and Divergence,* felt obliged to append a note to Alfred O. Hero's perfectly sensible essay on Quebec, recognizing "that the issue of Francophone Quebec and its relations with the rest of Canada is a highly sensitive matter charged with emotion." It also recorded the objections of some members of their working group, not merely to Hero's conclusions but to the presence of any special chapter on Quebec at all. In 1983, the former U.S. Ambassador to Canada co-authored a book on Canada and its relationship with the U.S., *Canadian-American Relations,* that contained no discussion of Quebec and in which the word "separatism" nowhere appeared.

A similar irrationality, albeit carefully cultivated, was central to the strategy adopted by Ottawa to defeat the Parti Québécois' 1980 referendum seeking a mandate to negotiate "sovereignty-association" with the rest of Canada. The premiers of the nine Anglophone provinces were repeatedly trotted out to say that no, no, a thousand times no, they would *never* discuss the details of any settlement if Quebec dared to vote in favor of the Parti Québécois proposal. Federal Tory politicians who hesitated momentarily before ruling out all such negotiations were brutally clubbed into line by their leader, Joe Clark. This ploy was ridiculous and irresponsible – ridiculous because the economic relationship between Quebec and the other provinces, particularly Ontario, is far too important to be severed in a fit of pique; irresponsible because the refusal to respect such a vote inevitably invites violence. Only months after the provincial general election of 1970 and the usual spate of short-sighted speculation that separatism had "peaked," the FLQ kidnapped James Cross and Pierre Laporte, throwing Canada into a crisis as grave as any experienced in the democratic world since World War II.

Yet the Anglophone premiers' response was based on a certain emotional reality. Ordinary Canadians have been encouraged to think that the secession of Quebec would be an almost physical cataclysm, that the province would be replaced by a void in the center of the continent, or at the very least vanish behind a high wall. Jane Jacobs in her book *The Question of Separatism* skewered a fine example of this alarmism:

> From time to time the press reports sentiments like this: a proposed new corridor road across Maine would speed truck and tourist traffic between the Atlantic Provinces and central Canada and it would take on added importance – here is the kicker – in the event of separation from Confederation.
>
> The man who said that is the past president of the Atlantic provinces' Chamber of Commerce. Of course, much traffic between Quebec and the Maritimes already runs through Maine because the route is shorter and more convenient in spite of the nuisance of crossing international boundaries. There spoke a man who accepts such border crossings with equanimity, even with some enthusiasm – yet is dismayed that people and goods could traverse an independent Quebec.

So many prominent people have so much at stake in the Canadian federal system that virtually no normally reliable source can be trusted on the question of Quebec separatism. Thus the charitable might assume that when in early 1976 Prime Minister Trudeau said that "separatism is dead," he was risking making a fool of himself in the higher cause of Canadian unity. But the disturbing probability is that he really believed it himself, and was as shocked as anyone at the Parti Québécois' crushing victory in the provincial election that fall. Even back in 1964, as a disinterested academic observer, a reporter found him "serenely confident that separatism was a declining force." This was four years before the Parti Québécois was formed. His confidence is of course still serene, but his judgment can reasonably be treated with caution.

Certainly the editors of *Maclean's*, with deadlines to meet, had every incentive to anticipate the 1976 election result. But they did not, and had to spend some desperate days tearing apart and rewriting the magazine as a result. In retrospect, however, there is little excuse. In the 1966 provincial election, when the Union Nationale defeated the Liberal government, two separatist parties that later merged into the Parti Québécois had obtained 8.8% of the Quebec vote. In 1970, when the Liberals under Robert Bourassa returned to power, the Parti Québécois won 23.1%, and seven seats. In 1973, when the Liberals were easily re-elected and the Union Nationale completely wiped out, the Parti Québécois won 30% of the vote but, due to the vagaries of the single-member-constituency first-past-the-post electoral system, only six seats. Almost completely unnoticed at the time – comment centered on the Liberals' 104 seats and Lévesque's loss of his second bid for a seat under Parti Québécois colors – this was the decisive breakthrough. Quebec politics were now polarized. In 1976, when the Parti Québécois was finally elected, it had 41% of the total vote and 47% of the Francophones. In 1981, after the referendum, it was re-elected with 49% of the vote, and a remarkable 57% of the Francophones. Even in 1985, when the Parti Québécois lost power and once again became the victim of the first-past-the-post system, it still received 39% of the total vote, and almost half the Francophone vote.

It is in this context that the result of the May 20, 1980 referendum must be judged. Some 59.6% of Quebeckers voted "No." This, of course, meant that very close to half the Francophones had actually approved. In particular, young Francophones, whose support for separatism is strong, approved by a substantial margin. Although this cannot be automatically extrapolated into an eventual separatist majority as the population ages and the federalists die off, it does put the federal cause in Quebec under a certain pressure. And, of course, the Guards regiment of Quebec federalism, the Anglophone community, is rapidly disbanding.

Following the federalist victory in 1980, it has become common in Canada to view the whole referendum episode with complacency. But at the time, the result was far from a foregone conclusion. During the February, 1980 federal election, which was to return Pierre Trudeau to office, Ottawa's secret polling in Quebec showed that the prospective No vote was falling precipitously, and that 52% of those questioned would support sovereignty-association, with only 37% opposed. Independent polls in March confirmed the trend. According to Robert Sheppard and Michael Valpy: "Panic seized the senior mandarins in the Langevin Block, where the Prime Minister's advisers ply their craft, and took hold of the upper reaches of the federal Liberal Party . . . . Convinced that the federal side was about to lose the referendum, [senior privy council officials] were anxious that the Prime Minister not become too involved in the campaign, lest he give it greater credibility." One aide even urged Trudeau to declare that he himself would vote Yes on the grounds that the question posed was too vague, in the hope that this would render the proceedings a farce.

Instead, Trudeau threw every ounce of federal and Liberal Party resources into the fray, shouldering aside Claude Ryan, then the leader of the Quebec Liberals, and incensing the Parti Québécois government, which had framed its referendum legislation to equalize expenditure by both sides. As chronicled by Sheppard and Valpy, the federalist campaign was a frank, crude and deafening appeal to Francophone self-interest. "Throughout March . . . the economic arguments dominated the new media. Ministers rarely missed an opportunity to turn up in Quebec towns, no matter how small, to publicize the latest federal grant and to talk about medicare, old age pensions, and family allowances. It was the politics of fear, performed extravagantly. . . ." Over $3 million in federal advertising money was employed wherever TV spots, billboards, and brochures could be put to use, as well as massive covert aid from the budgets of Crown corporations and departments of state, and amusing little tricks like the inclusion with all federal family allowance checks of anti-drinking pamphlets that by amazing coincidence happened to have the same slogan – "*Non merci*" – as the federal referendum campaign. There was certainly grass roots enthusiasm for the federalist cause, at least in Quebec. Parents in the English suburbs flew their children home from universities in other provinces, and even from the United States, so that every vote would count on the day. The fact remains, however, that the federal effort was a systematic exploitation of "the conservative elements in the Quebec psyche – [of] the old, the scared, and the infirm, who wanted the comfort of the status quo with only some modest betterment," orchestrated by a political clique that happened to have control of the Canadian public purse, and liked it that way.

Although I may appear to be breaching the professional cynicism of the political journalist, it is highly instructive to consider what the politicians were saying about Quebec separatism. Appeals to self-interest are of course an honored aspect of democratic politics. Robert Bourassa himself, as leader of the provincial Liberals prior to 1976, based his entire political strategy on *le fédéralisme rentable,* profitable federalism, arguing that Quebec stood to benefit from Canada's natural resources and Ottawa's various programs for redistributing wealth. But once again, this implicitly conceded the separatists' case. Federalism was justified as a material means, not a moral end in itself. As Claude Ryan observed tartly, long before he became Bourassa's successor, "If I were an English Canadian, I would be humiliated and ashamed of such an argument. I would see in it an expression of weak support for the real values of federalism. I would also see the half-disguised expression of an unhealthy ambition to get fat at my expense." In a truly stable federal state, any area must be prepared to make sacrifices for the common good. Western Canada was certainly a net economic loser in Confederation during the 1970s, but although its elected leaders moaned they stolidly (and somewhat unimaginatively) eschewed any thought of separatism, which probably explains why no one took any notice of them. Bourassa would not and could not commit Quebec to such sacrifices. If the province were a net loser in Confederation, as the Parti Québécois economists promptly maintained it was, the federalist cause would be finished.

Even more ominous was what Claude Ryan said when he became leader of the provincial Liberal Party, the only political party available to those clustered at the federalist pole of Quebec politics. As editor of *Le Devoir,* Ryan had unimpeachable nationalist credentials, and had even advised his readers to vote for the Parti Québécois in 1976 because of his disapproval of the Bourassa government's ethics and efficiency. But Ryan had always been an advocate of special status for Quebec. His position was that federalism had to be "renewed," and he eventually issued a "Beige Paper" outlining Quebec's requirements. Jane Jacobs describes this episode well:

In the latter part of 1979, as Ryan began showing the proposals to premiers in other parts of Canada to try to line up their support, little winds of disquiet began to blow across the land; nothing much, just hints of doubts. In the meantime, the Quebec government issued its White Paper on Sovereignty-Association and announced that the Referendum was only months away. English Canada could not afford doubts about the Ryan proposals; anticipation of them built up, and at length, in January 1980, they were published with great fanfare . . . .

Muted consternation! Consternation because of what they were. Muted because for English Canada to say forcefully that it found them unacceptable might undercut the *Non* vote in the Referendum. Ryan was reported in the press to be "rattled by the polite but generally noncommittal response" from the politicians of English Canada. His position was that they must understand that the Québécois are not pleased with the status quo, and that if his proposals for duality or something like them are not accepted, he cannot answer for the disillusioned reaction in Quebec.

Apart from such minor details as the abolition of the monarchy, Ryan's proposals basically called for an enhancement and entrenchment of Quebec's veto in federal affairs through various institutional reforms. Combined with his insistence on Quebec's autonomy, the increase in Quebec's power could have been so great that one academic commentator, J.D. Morton of the University of Toronto, compared Ryan and Lévesque to a Mutt and Jeff team of detectives working over a suspect: ". . . the goals of the two actors seem remarkably similar . . . ."

Although the federal Liberals and their allies did not accept Ryan's strategy, they did appropriate his tactic. As Pierre Trudeau said at the rally in Montreal's Paul Sauvé Arena that climaxed the campaign, "I know that I can make a most solemn commitment that following a 'No' vote we will immediately take action to renew the constitution and we will not stop until we have done that. And I make a most solemn declaration to all Canadians in the other provinces; we, the Quebec MPs, are laying ourselves on the line, because we are telling Quebeckers to vote 'No' and telling you in the other provinces that we will not agree to your interpreting the 'No' vote as an indication that everything is fine and can remain as before."

This ingenious maneuver meant that the federalists could glorify all the advantages of Confederation while dismissing any disadvantages as technical difficulties that would shortly be corrected, please keep your seats. The details were soothingly unspecified. Or, as Joe Clark told the inhabitants of Shawinigan, bathetically, during the referendum campaign: "The Canada that Mr. Lévesque wants to separate from no longer exists." Rene Lévesque must have felt that he was arguing with a plate of jello.

It took René Lévesque eighteen months to this counter dialectical play. On November 5, 1982, Trudeau and the premiers of the nine English provinces signed an accord to patriate the constitution. But while achieving some of the federal Liberals' symbolic, Canadian Nationalist, centralizing and bilingual goals, the agreement was unable to accommodate Quebec's Francophone nationalism. It did not give Quebec the veto power her politicians of all shades had been holding out for, and it meant that collision between the province's language law and the new federal provisions was inevitable. Lévesque, who had been excluded from the final negotiations, withheld his signature and denounced the agreement as "betrayal." Ryan echoed his opposition. "Few can ignore the dismay and cynicism that swept through Quebec at its isolation," wrote the devoutly pro-federalist Robert Sheppard and Michael Valpy, "and not be worried about the future."

"It would be optimistic in the extreme to think that we can avoid a new crisis on the question of separation in a very few years," wrote former privy council clerk Gordon Robertson, the grandfather of federal-provincial diplomacy, directly after the November 5 agreement. "The Constitution Act, 1982," he said subsequently, "is clearly not the 'renewal' most Québécois thought they were voting for" in the referendum. In the next separation crisis, however, the difference will be that the federalists will not be able to play the renewed-confederation card again. They may not even have a Francophone prime minister, and a disproportionately Francophone federal government, to do their playing for them.

The struggle for Quebec's divided soul in the next few years will be interesting. Both federalists and separatists in Quebec have to approach their fellow Francophones with care. The federalists know better than to confront French nationalism head on, as they showed by their cautious reaction to the Parti Québécois and their penchant for presenting their Canada-wide policies as the expression of a Greater Quebec – at least to the Québécois. Indeed, in a sense the federal Liberals actually need the separatist threat to justify their existence: in the run-up to the 1979 federal election, it was only with the greatest reluctance that Trudeau and his aides accepted Anglophone Liberals' insistence that the party could not rely on scaring English Canada into line if they campaigned once again on "National Unity," and they proved quite unable to come up with a replacement. On the other hand, Quebec is not grindingly oppressed in Confederation, and Francophones clearly feel that they have a lot to lose by getting out. Opinion polls in recent years have generally shown the proportion of them favoring outright unconditional independence stalled at bout one-fifth to one-quarter, an ambivalence distressing to both federalists and separatists alike. René Lévesque demonstrated his awareness of this ambivalence by developing his comforting concept of sovereignty-association, by undertaking not to separate in 1976 without a referendum, by the elaborate wording of the referendum proposition itself, and by compelling the PQ to reverse its decision to run on the separation issue in the 1985 provincial election.

But the Francophone elite in Quebec is a small family, and when some show a trait as dramatic as separatism, it can be assumed to be part of some inheritance that they all share. In the referendum, one of the "No" voters was the brother of René Lévesque, while a sister of federal Health Minister Monique Bégin and a nephew of federal Justice Minister Jean Chrétien voted in favor. In 1982, when Bourassa was re-elected provincial Liberal leader, a major rival was Daniel Johnson, Liberal Member of the National Assembly and brother of Pierre-Marc Johnson, the Parti Québécois cabinet minister who subsequently succeeded Lévesque as Premier and led the PQ against the Liberals in the 1985 provincial election. Both are the sons of Daniel Johnson, the former Union Nationale premier who had also flirted with separatism, publishing a book before his election entitled darkly *Equality or Independence?* Even those intimately involved in this little world have trouble figuring out who draws the line where. During the FLQ Crisis in 1970, Pierre Trudeau and Marc Lalonde, apparently quite sincerely, justified their imposition of the War Measures Act by leaking the story that a group of prominent Francophones were preparing to seize the opportunity to set up a "provisional government." One of the alleged plotters: the very same Claude Ryan they were later to embrace as the savior of federalism and the provincial Liberals; and who later still turned into one of the most pessimistic Quebec critics of their patriation package. (Meetings had indeed been held during the October Crisis, but the participants say they were innocent; Anglophone puzzlement lingers on.)

Perhaps even more significant for the coming years, in 1967 Robert Bourassa had been one of the very last to leave the group of Francophone provincial Liberals contemplating separatism with Lévesque, allegedly reneging on a pledge to quit the party with him. And according to Peter Desbarats, "Bourassa's decision went against the personal sentiments if not the political instincts of his wife," although she was a daughter of the Simard clan, French Quebec's leading industrialists.

The immediate political future of Quebec nationalism is in doubt. Although losing the 1985 election, the Parti Québécois at least maintained its claim to the Union Nationale's role as the political expression of the Francophone identity. The party began in Montreal, but its main bases of support are now the totally French-speaking rural areas like Chicoutimi and Lac St. Jean, the former

Union Nationale strongholds that returned the heaviest "Yes" votes in the referendum. The PQ was always a sort of nationalist Popular Front, in which various factions were held together by René Lévesque's heroic efforts. His departure may well be followed by a period of turmoil, with separatists impatient with gradualism and socialists dissatisfied with the mixed-economy approach and both experimenting with parties of their own.

There can be no doubt, however, about the long-term outlook in Quebec. The movement towards a nation-state has been the primary trend of Francophone history. Within it, minor trends may oscillate, including the defeat of referendums and even of separatist governments. But the long-run direction will eventually reassert itself. René Lévesque may turn out to have been just another Honoré Mercier, the Quebec premier who led the nineteenth-century nationalist surge that so much alarmed Goldwin Smith. But if Lévesque was Mercier, someone else will be his Lévesque.

This cycle cannot be resolved within the current Canadian Confederation. Even if Ottawa were prepared to allow Quebec to become a unilingual enclave within Canada, the centrifugal forces already operating in the province could well carry it out of Confederation, which is why Pierre Trudeau opposed this solution. But if Ottawa intervenes, it will antagonize Francophone nationalism. Whatever happens, the prognostication remains the same: more trouble.

And Quebec's nationalists have the advantage of the offensive. One lost referendum would be fatal for federalism. But René Lévesque in the Paul Sauvé Arena on the night of the 1980 referendum could simply tell the weeping crowd *"à la prochaine"* – until the next time.

On the question of sovereignty-association, Quebec's Francophones have ample cause to shrug their shoulders expressively about the sheer emotionalism of their Anglophone fellow citizens and their notorious obsession with saving face. In English Canada, the much-ridiculed concept never received the attention it deserved. Essentially, sovereignty-association envisaged Quebec and English Canada each as sovereign states with separate membership of the United Nations and the other trimmings, but linked by free trade and free movement of travellers; by mutual membership (along with the U.S.) in the commission overseeing the operations of the St. Lawrence Seaway and in military alliances like NATO and NORAD; and by a common currency. Some other joint legal and bureaucratic institutions were proposed, including even a possible superparliamentary assembly. In a fairly interdependent world, this would have been by no means an exceptional arrangement. In fact, it sounds distinctly like the European Economic Community, except that the EEC is supposed to be moving towards further integration and actually does have a superparliamentary federal legislature, although both the intent and the institution are fairly nominal.

The militant ignorance that prevailed upon this subject in Canada was exploited by Pierre Trudeau when, during the referendum campaign, he taunted the separatists that they lacked the courage to advocate independence openly, saying that they "risked humiliating Quebec, just as Irish patriots in 1916 would have humiliated Ireland had they said to Britain, 'We will be independent on condition that you have an economic association with us.'" Which is of course exactly what Ireland did say in 1921, when the Irish Free State came into being under a treaty that established extremely close links with Britain, including free trade, free movement, a common currency, a shared monarchy and even the right of citizens to vote in each other's elections. This was literally sovereignty-association. Only over a period of years did Ireland's radical republican faction dismantle the association aspect, finally declaring a republic and withdrawing from the British Commonwealth in 1948.

In an era when the Republic of Nauru (population 8,000, area eight square miles) can occupy a seat at the United Nations, it is comical to find any debate about the viability of an independent Quebec (population 6.4 million, area 595,000 square miles, even without Labrador). From a strictly theoretical point of view, free trade and the free movement of labor and capital should eventually enable a community with the high education levels and social stability of the Québécois to achieve an acceptable level of economic activity, regardless of political boundaries. This would be true even unilaterally, if the rest of Canada actually did erect tariff barriers: Switzerland (population 6.3 million, area 15,941 square miles) and Sweden (population 8.3 million, area 173,732 square miles) have traditionally avoided major trading blocs for political reasons. In effect, Quebec's lowered income from exports would be counter-balanced by cheaper imports.

Actually, Lévesque could have afforded to be more radical. A key advantage of independence for Quebec would have been the power to issue its own currency. This could then float against other currencies to a level equilibrating Quebec's exports and imports, indirectly cutting costs in export industries to competitive levels and spreading the burden across the economy. By contrast, Canada at present is not an optimum currency area. The Canadian dollar must respond to the trade patterns of regions very different from Quebec, and the resulting exchange rate can be an unhappy compromise. Lévesque was seeking to reassure the nervous when he espoused a joint currency. "I have to admit that, very frankly, it was mostly political," he said in 1982, adding that he had been impressed by Jane Jacobs' arguments against it.

Economic development is ultimately caused by the attitudes and organization of a country's people, not its natural resources. The most successful post-war economy, Japan, has no natural resources at all. But they can help. And Quebec has an abundance: minerals, timber and especially hydro-electricity. Robert Bourassa was correct to point out that the energy-deficient northeast United States is a natural market for Quebec's power – which Ottawa's energy regulations, designed to favor consumers in other Canadian provinces, might well impede. Similarly, Parti Québécois officials were critical of the National Energy Program, the Foreign Investment Review Agency and other artifacts of (English) Canadian Nationalism, which they saw as antithetical to the province's need for capital and jobs.

What passes for economics in federalist anti-separatist polemic is usually the discussion of transfer payments – the subsidies from Ottawa to governments, individuals and industries in Quebec. On the face of it, these appear substantial. For example, Quebec gets about half the fiscal equalization payments provided by Ottawa to the provinces under a formula meant to establish a uniform standard of public services across Canada. Of course, Quebec pays federal taxes too, and the net balance is not easy to calculate, particularly if an effort is made to account for implicit subsidies, like the tariff protection for Montreal's textile trade, or the National Energy Program's rein on oil prices, that kept them below world levels. Some of these policies, coincidentally, benefit Ontario as much as Quebec. Observers of the referendum debate (economic round) came away with the impression that both sides were about even, and concluded that this meant the balance of payments was even too. Playing against type, Jacques Parizeau, the PQ Finance Minister, said that the federal oil-price subsidy to Quebec since 1974 had tipped the balance, but that the total only amounted to a dozen beers per head; Robert Bourassa said the tally was about even, but that Canada's natural resources were worth waiting around for.

The real point about transfer payments, however, is that they are mixed blessing for an economy. They provide the wherewithal for immediate consumption, but they distort prices and incentives and can easily result in workers being frozen into uneconomic occupations that they would be better off leaving, such as marginally profitable textile operations that survive only because of tariffs. (In fact, the distortions and disruptions of both levying and disbursing what Goldwin Smith called "the necessary blackmail for Quebec" may make its total cost far greater than the benefits Quebec actually receives. This is the wedge that American "supply side" economists like Professor Arthur Laffer argue government activity drives between consenting economic partners. Both, they maintain, could profit from its removal.) The biggest problem Quebec would face in independence would be transitional dislocation – kicking the Canada habit. Otherwise, its difficulties are not insoluble – which is not to say everyone in the PQ would have liked the solutions.

However, Quebec must make some of these economic transitions anyway. Its obsolete forest products industry must be reoriented to meet competition from the non-union, technically advanced operations in the U.S. Southeast. Something must be done about Montreal. Irrespective of Quebec politics, Montreal has lost its hinterland to Toronto, and seems to be going into a decline like that of Vienna after the partition of the Hapsburg Empire left it stranded in little Austria. Even if these problems can be solved within Confederation, the Québécois might easily reason that while they're at it, they might as well sovereignty-associate too.

It is the issue of Quebec's separation in itself that seemed to upset people however. In 1977, Pierre Trudeau even told a joint session of the U.S. Congress that it would be "a crime against the history of mankind." Washington was understandably distracted by the spectacle of Margaret Trudeau attending a White House dinner in a short dress and with a run in her stocking. But someone should have remembered that it was an American president, Woodrow Wilson, who used to talk about the principle of self-determination, and imposed it on a reluctant Europe after World War I. Trudeau's worldview was in essence the one opposed by Alexander Solzhenitsyn in his Nobel Prize address, part of which forms this chapter's epigraph: "Nations are the wealth of mankind, they are its generalized personalities: the smallest of them has its own particular colors and embodies a particular facet of God's design."

There was nothing inherently ignoble or illiberal about Quebec separatism. And for English Canada, it was a solution, not a problem. The opportunity was missed by a degenerate leadership. But it will recur.

How could Quebec leave Confederation? Canadian reluctance to think about separation extends to a denial that any mechanism exists by which it could be achieved. An "impasse" was all that voting "Yes" in the referendum would accomplish Pierre Trudeau said during the Throne Speech debate in the House of Commons after the 1980 federal election. Even if the Parti Québécois won its mandate to negotiate, he implied, there would be no one with whom it could negotiate. But in fact the Canadian Confederation is surprisingly vulnerable.

Rhodesia resolved its "impasse" with the British in 1965 by a unilateral declaration of independence – "UDI." But Rhodesia had a small but formidable army, and could certainly have defended itself. Quebec has no army, and many federalists assume that a separatist vote can be frustrated by just ignoring it. This was the scenario predicted by the authors of *Partition*. And there is some Canadian precedent. In 1867, Nova Scotia elected anti-Confederation majorities to both its provincial legislature and the federal House of Commons in Ottawa, but both the Canadian and British governments ignored them until the Nova Scotia leader, Joseph Howe, was bought off in 1869 with a cabinet seat and renegotiated financial terms.

There is even an Antipodean analogy. In 1933, the state of Western Australia voted to secede from the Commonwealth (= Confederation) of Australia. The move was eventually blocked by a joint committee of the British Houses of Parliament, then technically the ultimate legal authority in Australia, as in Canada. The committee concluded that it could not agree to separation without the Australian government's approval. But it would be unwise to attribute too much to this legalese. Probably more important was the fact that Western Australians, perverse even by Canadian standards, had simultaneously elected an anti-separatist government, and that the separatist movement began thereafter to subside gradually.

Similarly, Howe succeeded in "pacifying" the Nova Scotians for some time. Subsequently, in a period of renewed economic unrest, the opposition provincial Liberal Party won one term of office on a secessionist platform in 1886. But in the federal election two years later, the Conservatives were able to make a stand on the Imperial connection. As June Callwood notes uneasily, the Conservatives "made windy speeches about loyalty to the Queen, waved the Union Jack, and left the impression that a vote against Tories was a vote against the British Empire"; they won decisively enough to undercut the secessionists again.

By contrast, in 1905 when the Storting, the Norwegian legislature, passed the resolution that unilaterally declared the country's independence from Sweden, it was after nearly a century of separatist agitation, and a referendum subsequently approved the step overwhelmingly. Originally the Storting had been purely symbolic, but it had established its authority in a long series of direct confrontations with the Swedes. Norwegian separatists mostly controlled it, but periodically divisions among them allowed Norwegians who favored the union with Sweden to win elections. As in Canada, the unionists had a competing ideology not unattractive to ambitious Norwegians: Scandinavianism, the view that all the Nordic countries should unite, as Italy and Germany did in the course of the nineteenth century. The playwright Ibsen, a Norwegian, was one of its proponents. But in the last of innumerable crises, the unionists succumbed to patriotic pressure and turned against the Swedes. There was a threat of force, which the Norwegians probably could not have resisted, but in the end, with the encouragement of the countries' neighbors, a peaceful settlement was negotiated. For sovereign states, Norway and Sweden are now associated unusually closely, cooperating in such areas as customs and immigration, social security and various scientific and industrial projects.

Like Norway, Quebec has been developing towards symbolic and substantive independence for a long time. It is not inconceivable that a determined government in Quebec City could stage confrontations – for example, over language legislation – and mobilize a consensus of Francophones in its support. Singapore Prime Minister Lee Kuan Yew's continuous disputes with the Malaysian federal government, together with his consistent encroachment upon its diplomatic prerogatives, eventually caused the Malaysians themselves to initiate the legislation that led in 1965 to Singapore's departure (population 2.5 million, area 239 square miles) from the federation, and to its full independence.

Even short of force, there are many passive resistance options that could then be employed. In 1974, for example, the Ulster Protestants were able to compel Westminster to drop its attempt to finesse them into a united Ireland, by calling a general strike. Such a situation would raise the interesting question of whether Canadian Anglophones are as liberal as the Swedes. Are they prepared to coerce Quebec by witholding welfare payments to mothers and children?

But all such speculations are unnecessary. The obvious course for those wishing to separate from a parliamentary union is that followed in the nineteenth century by the Irish Nationalist Party in the British Imperial Parliament at Westminster. Although it is often forgotten, the Nationalists completely succeeded in their objective: by 1914 a "Home Rule" Act giving Ireland its own legislature had already been passed by the British Parliament. Home Rule was not implemented only because of the outbreak of World War I, during which the radical republicans staged the 1916 Easter Rising and took control of the Irish movement.

The Irish Nationalist strategy was simply to elect Irish Nationalists to the House of Commons. There they formed a sufficiently large bloc to hold the balance of power between the English parties, and they were able to insist upon their prize. The Nationalist strength at Westminster was not fully achieved until later in the nineteenth century, as the franchise became progressively more democratic. W.E. Gladstone, however, attempted to pass Home Rule Bills in 1886 and 1892. He failed because of the militant opposition of the Ulster Protestants to any arrangement that would leave them at the mercy of the Irish Catholics; because many in his own Liberal Party suspected that devolution, once begun, would be unstoppable; and because the British electorate, not yet resigned to Imperial decline, did not support him when the Second Home Rule Bill, having been approved by the Commons, was rejected by the House of Lords in 1893. But in 1914, Prime Minister Herbert Asquith's Liberal government was preparing to use troops against Ulster.

The effectiveness of the Irish Nationalists arose not merely from their numbers, but from their systematic obstruction of the business of Parliament, particularly under the leadership of Charles Stewart Parnell. Almost any number of determined separatists could accomplish disruption. Sir John A. Macdonald felt "an enormous sense of relief," according to his biographer, when in 1867 Joseph Howe proved too much of a gentleman to employ such tactics. In 1984, Quebec had 75 of the Canadian House of Common's 282 seats, far too large a bloc to be ignored. Moreover, there is always the possibility that if the separatists were numerous enough, they could boycott Parliament, and, as the legally elected representatives of their province, set up a competing assembly. In Ireland, the radical republican party Sinn Fein did this after carrying all but one of southern Ireland's seats in the British general election of 1918.

Intervention by Quebec nationalists in the federal elections is the Sword of Damocles hanging over the Canadian political order. Its effect would be immediate and deadly. For example, in the spring of 1982 when the federal Liberals were governing, with a majority over the Tories and NDP combined that was barely in double figures, Parti Québécois organizers were estimating they could carry twenty seats in the province. Since the electoral strategies of both establishment parties is currently predicated on winning in Quebec, any such seats would come directly out of the government's majority. But the main

threat is obviously to the Liberals, Quebec's traditional representatives in Ottawa and the Parti Québécois' only real rival for Francophone affections. Even to campaign against Quebec separatists in a
federal election would be seriously embarrassing for the establishment parties. It would be a French-ness competition that they would
not be able to win by subtly drawing attention to the ethnicity of the
opposing leader's name. They would be forced to spell out how much
their policies favor Quebec, something that would arouse considerable interest in English Canada.

Why the Parti Québécois has avoided federal elections is one of the
great mysteries of Canadian politics. Its supporters sometimes reason
that to do so would be inconsistent with their separatist principles.
This excess of Gallic logic never troubled Irish Nationalists. The
diversion of resources from the provincial effort is also cited. It is no
doubt true that the struggle would have been costly and terrible: the
Liberals in particular would have been fighting for their lives, and
many Québécois who have been quite happy voting for both the
Trudeauvian and Lévesquian visions of French grandeur would be
reluctant to choose between them. But the fact remains that the
federal Liberals are the mortal enemies of the Parti Québécois, and
sooner or later they must close with them.

In 1982, Lévesque was quoted as saying that the party "should
participate deeply in the next federal election." A separatist Parti
National was set up to field candidates federally. But as it turned out,
and in keeping with Lévesque's cautious style, the PQ supported the
Tories in 1984. Lévesque apparently concurred that the Liberals were
the Parti Québécois' main enemy, even at the cost of allowing the
federal myth a further lease on life. The PQ was rewarded with
substantial covert support from the Tory government in the 1985
provincial election. Only its defeat has delayed an answer to the
absorbing question of who was fooling whom in this paradoxical
alliance.

Quebec was in a funny mood in the 1984 election. Some 3% of the
votes went to the PN anyway – and a very solid 3% to the Rhinoceros
Party, a Francophone joke party founded by Quebec's well-known
short story writer and separatist Jacques Ferron. Altogether 6% of the
electorate was too alienated, or too amused, to vote for a major party.

A more disturbing, and yet almost universal, route to Quebec
separation is terrorism. This is a second great mystery of Canadian
political life. In the 1960s, with the FLQ and allied groups active,
Quebec seemed to be conforming to the pattern of terrorist violence

then becoming universal throughout the modern world. In the seven years prior to the October Crisis in 1970, about one hundred bombs had exploded in Montreal. But during the succeeding decade, there was not one anywhere in the country. The silence has been eerie and uncanny. In the same period the Italian Red Brigades, the Baader-Meinhof Gang – even the Symbionese Liberation Army – have set countries on their ears, with no more access to popular support and often much less. Perhaps the Francophones were merely deferring to authority. Ottawa's violent reaction to the crisis and the imposition of the War Measures Act certainly shocked Quebec. Some 490 Québécois found themselves arbitrarily detained, many for no more than being known separatists. In the next year, membership in the Parti Québécois fell from some 80,000 to 30,000; Pierre Vallières, who was suspected of writing the FLQ's strategy paper, *The Role of the Advanced Guard,* renounced violence and became a community organizer on a federally funded project.

Another possible explanation is that perhaps the mounting electoral success of the Parti Québécois has literally disarmed separatist sentiment. If so, English Canada has something to thank René Lévesque for. Instead, Ottawa has gone back to sleep. A small number of motivated individuals – unimaginably small, there may only have been forty to fifty FLQ activists – could wake it up in a hurry.

Terrorism works. It polarizes communities and forces political consciousness on them; it also sharply raises the price of the status quo. And in Quebec at the moment, it would be pushing on a door that is already ajar. The running-down of Canada's armed forces in the Trudeau years is an indulgence internationally, because Canada's geopolitical position is underwritten by the U.S., but it has serious but little-noticed domestic implications. After the Liberals unified Canada's army, air force and navy in 1968, it was hard to figure out exactly who was assigned to what, but the Institute for Strategic Studies in London has estimated that ground combat and direct support units amount to some 13,000 men, only a portion of whom are available for carrying a bayonet. "If we were attacked tomorrow, it's doubtful if 3,000 'fighting' soldiers could be mustered in Canada, excluding NATO," Peter Worthington has written. This might be enough for a brief show of force in the streets of Montreal, but not for a protracted urban guerrilla war. In comparison, in recent years up to 20,000 British regular soldiers have been stationed in Ulster, which has a land area of less than 1% of Quebec and a quarter of its population. The majority of this population is ethnically distinct from the Irish Republican Army, opposes it vehemently and has to be restrained from taking matters into its own hands.

Moreover, however surprising this judgement may be to Americans familiar with their own Civil War and unfamiliar with the Canadian situation, in the end it is just not very likely that English Canada would fight to keep Quebec in Confederation. Pierre Trudeau himself set the tone by saying repeatedly that he would never use force in Quebec. Apart from English-Canadians' essentially tolerant civic culture, twenty years of bickering and bilingualism have served to underline the cost to Confederation of Quebec, which in any case, for most of them is a faraway place they know very little about. In many respects, the situation in Canada resembles that in the higher reaches of the federal Liberal Party in the late 1970s: Francophone and Anglophones were bored with each other, and tired of each other's problems.

What would an independent Quebec be like? After all the excitement – probably not very different from what exists now. For the Americans, it might even be better. For the Québécois, at least at the moment, the Gringos live in Ontario; Americans are absolved. Indeed, Francophones have regularly discussed annexing themselves to the U.S. in preference to Canada since before the *patriote* leader Louis-Joseph Papineau made annexation the center of his political program when he was allowed to return from exile and re-entered public life in 1847. While in power, Parti Québécois leaders seemed to enjoy outflanking Ottawa to the right on such issues as American investment; economics minister Bernard Landry said publicly that he would like to see the whole of North America a common currency area. Francophones have the highly developed Canadian migratory instinct for the beaches of Florida in winter (they congregate around Fort Lauderdale), a force of nature with which no government could trifle. "I don't feel any hang-up when I cross the border," René Lévesque once said. "In fact, I feel less hang-ups than when I cross the 'border' west into Canada."

The Parti Québécois were avowedly social democrats. ("What the hell does that mean? It's a European term, social democrats. Let's say progressives, North American style." – R. Lévesque.) In power the PQ's policies were not notably more collectivist than those of other Canadian provinces – or of Washington State. In his second term, Lévesque caused considerable histrionics by forcing Quebec teachers, strong Parti Québécois supporters, to disgorge a pay increase in the name of fiscal rectitude. Moreover, in Quebec, economic philosophy has been completely subordinate to the national question. The state takeover of the hydro-electric utilities or of part of the asbestos industry – the only move by the PQ – cannot be judged except in the context of political promotion of the French fact. The Parti Québécois was a popular front: a significant minority of the party's supporters were distinctly more conservative than the official line, economically and politically. Roderique Biron, a businessman and leader of the Union Nationale, personified this tendency when he switched parties, won election to the National Assembly in 1981 and entered Lévesque's cabinet as minister of Industry, Commerce and Tourism. Separation might allow Quebec's latent conservatism – long obscured by Nationalist tensions – to resurface.

Nevertheless, there is undeniably a radical left tendency in Quebec life. Ironically, its presence in the Parti Québécois was even reinforced by the minority of ideologically motivated Anglophones who were attracted to the separatists for just this reason: both of the Anglophones Parti Québécois MNAs elected in 1981 were labor union militants, one a British immigrant. However, whether from policy or principle, Lévesque fought tenaciously to maintain his moderate credentials. As the Parti Québécois was organizing itself in 1968, he maneuvered to frustrate any agreement with the left-wing separatists in the Rassemblement pour l'indépendance nationale while happily merging with the right-wing Ralliement National, led by a former Social Credit federal MP. When RIN members voted to dissolve their organization anyway and join the Parti Québécois as individuals, he was "enraged." Subsequently, he put down several left-wing revolts within the party.

But unlike France or Italy with their large Communist parties, Marxism is an unelected trace element in Quebec politics, as it is in the English-speaking world. This is the province where Maurice Duplessis was able to make a political issue out of Canada's alleged importation of "Communist eggs" from the Soviet bloc, and to insist that the collapse in 1951 of the bridge he had built and named after himself in his home town of Trois-Rivières was, or at any rate might have been, the work of saboteurs. "Under any scenario for Quebec," writes Alfred O. Hero, "the likelihood of a Castro, Allende, or Sandinista-type of regime is virtually nil." It might also be added that at one time much of the controversy about radical leftism in Quebec centered on the activities of one Pierre Elliott Trudeau.

During the referendum, some Liberals issued warnings about the authoritarian and racist possibilities of a sovereign Quebec. There is, not surprisingly, a racial tinge to Québécois nationalism, and the political culture of Quebec is of course not that of the American Civil Liberties Union. It was second nature for Quebec MP Yvon Pinard to justify Marc Lalonde's tight control of the Quebec federal Liberal caucus to Christina McCall-Newman by saying, "We are so large a family, we need a father to guide us." More seriously, there have been several episodes of European-style Francophone anti-semitic agitation in the past, and although there has been no evidence of it under the Parti Québécois, Quebec's Jews have been among the quickest to bail out of the province.

But it is also possible to argue that in an independent Quebec, ethnic tensions would be lessened, just as Lévesque himself has predicted that the Parti Québécois will split on economic issues once the national question is resolved. And Quebec is a democracy already. In other words, what you see now is probably what you would get after independence.

The fundamental point is that Quebec is not a Third World state. "After all, we're supposed to be Latins," said Lévesque with a dubious shrug, talking about his province's relations with Mexico. But it's not obvious. With his white hair and fierce blue eyes, he looked like a Viking dwarf. And in fact, aside from being America's neighbor, Quebec has little in common with Mexico, or with any Latin American state.

Since World War II, the emergence onto the global scene of so many "international basket cases," in Henry Kissinger's phrase, may have raised questions about the absolute virtue of self-determination. But a better parallel to the Quebec situation is again probably to be found earlier in the century, in the independence of Ireland – also Catholic, ethnocentric, brooding over real and imagined past wrongs, but with a long experience of free institutions. Eire may not be the polyethnic "brilliant prototype for the moulding of tomorrow's civilization" Pierre Trudeau once said Canada should become. But, despite its irredentist problem to the north, it has been a respectable bourgeois democracy. And one more of those would do the world no harm at all.

"Friendly islanders welcome you with open arms and recount tales of the lifestyle, describing the long winters and icy treks across the St. Laurent [sic] when they row, pull and tug their boats across the frozen waters."

There is some poetic license in the Quebec government tourist board's description of Ile-aux-Coudres, part of the Charlevoix region that lies along the St. Lawrence immediately northeast of Quebec City. On the other hand, it doesn't at all exaggerate the area's physical beauty. The countryside and villages have achieved an aesthetic harmony rarely seen in North America, and there are spectacular views.

As it turns out, the Coudrians repeat the pattern found all over

Charlevoix. They are perfectly correct, but totally incurious. Neither American license plates, a reporter's grunts, his wife's Parisian French, nor the fact that they are the only visitors so early in the year attract any comment. It is like living in a Chinese restaurant. When addressed socially, the natives appear vaguely disturbed, as if accosted by a tree.

There are worse ways for people to treat outsiders. Refugees from New York City, where even insiders live lives of constant paranoia, do not complain. "They were living on another planet," a New York colleague remembers from his visit to the Charlevoix of thirty years ago, when it was totally dominated by the Church. Now the Quiet Revolution has come and gone. And Charlevoix is returning to isolation, remote even from the American television stations, all English signs removed by order of the Parti Québécois. Even the name of the town of Murray Bay has vanished completely from official literature, replaced by what the tourist pamphlet says pointedly was its original French name of Malbaie, although the few Murrays in the telephone directory there seem to be Francophones. This is a significant and, for Canada, an ominous development. The nationalism of the Québécois now seems to increase in inverse relation to alien intrusion.

It is hard to see the Québécois – sitting outside their homes on a spring day in a seemingly endless line of lawn chairs from Montreal to Quebec City, soaking up the sun as if newly liberated from under a glacier – as a revolutionary force. But theirs is a revolution of inertia. Their mere continued existence is the rock upon which Canadian Confederation will founder.

Perhaps this seems exaggerated. If so, worse is to come. Our trip's whimsical purpose is to inspect Baie Comeau, the mining town far down the St. Lawrence where Brian Mulroney, the new Tory leader, was born. But after three hours' hard driving, with night falling, we call a halt at Tadoussac, a pretty town at the Saguenay River's mouth built by long-forgotten Anglophone entrepreneurs. Baie Comeau is several hours of twisting coastline road away.

At this waystation I am struck by the thought that the leader of English Canada's political party spent his formative years so very far from the reality of English Canada. It's as if René Lévesque had hailed from the darkest Toronto suburbs, or as if the president of the United States had been born into the minor aristocracy of Europe.

Part Three

The Maple Leaf Forever

12

The Other Fault Lines

When a large, cohesive minority believes it can transfer its allegiance to a neighboring state, or make a go of total independence, it will be inclined to disassociate itself from a consensus the terms of which have been altered in its disfavor.

– Pierre Trudeau

"Canada" originally meant Quebec and Ontario (a.k.a. Canada East and Canada West, a.k.a. Lower Canada and Upper Canada) and the term has not really stretched to cover the other provinces. Federal cabinet ministers getting out of their limousines in the House of Commons' parking lot in Ontario can look across the Ottawa River into Quebec. Unconsciously, they assume that what is good for Quebec and Ontario is good for Canada. "Like most in the East," writes Richard Gwyn of Pierre Trudeau, "he accepted as a given that Canada was composed of two economic nations, an industrialized, urban heartland in Quebec and Ontario and appended to its east and west, a resource-dependent periphery."

Given all the poetic talk about Canadians' intimate relationship with their landscape, this "given" was psychologically rather obtuse. The rest of Canada is not a peripheral fringe but a vast area. Its inhabitants are separated from Central Canada by salt water, great mountain ranges and thousands of miles of muskeg and prairie.

The inhabitants of the Prairie provinces of Manitoba, Saskatchewan and Alberta, for example, share a unique and unforgettable winter heritage: flat horizons, enormous brilliant sky, whipping snow and cold so intense that, despite the block heaters in every garage, the steel frames of automobiles chirrup when they are started up and their tires feel lumpy. Some four million people live here in a self-sufficient world the size of Western Europe, with their own metropolitan centers, universities and vacation spots in Hawaii and San Diego. To them, the "heartland" is not the center of Canada at all, but an increasingly remote abstraction off in left field somewhere. And to the west across the Rocky Mountains, gazing on the Pacific with what the rest of Canada regards as a weird surmise, are the mellow British Columbians, who feel themselves even further removed.

Far from the eruptions of Quebec, it is in such places that the fault lines in Confederation are becoming increasingly visible.

In the fall of 1980, after the federal Liberals' return to power and their imposition of the National Energy Program, reports began to filter back to Central Canada that the natives on the western frontier beyond the Ontario boundary were unusually restless. Several organizations had sprung up advocating that the West – the Prairie provinces, British Columbia and the federally administered Yukon and Northwest Territories – separate from Canada. The two most important were the Western Canada Concept Party, begun in British Columbia and headed by Doug Christie, a Victoria lawyer; and the Western Canada Federation Party, based in Alberta and led by Elmer Knutson, an Edmonton farm equipment millionaire. Both these parties argued that, to adapt Joe Clark's Shawinigan comment during the Quebec referendum campaign, the Canada to which they had wished to belong no longer existed. The conditions of Confederation had been changed, and they wanted out. Less active but worth a footnote was the Unionist Party, which directly advocated joining the U.S.: it was founded by Dick Collver, until 1979 leader of the Saskatchewan Progressive Conservatives, who shortly afterwards acted on his beliefs and moved to Arizona.

Suddenly, Christie and Knutson were attracting crowds of thousands to their meetings. Prominent Western figures were expressing sympathy, notably Carl Nickle, a well-known oilman and former Tory federal MP, who had even been considered a candidate for Lieutenant Governor of Alberta the previous year but who told a luncheon gathering of 700 Calgary businessmen in October that after the NEP he had "sorrowfully" become a separatist. At the same time, the *Edmonton Journal* ran a poll showing that a startling 23% of Albertans supported an "independent West." There were angry exchanges in the House of Commons in Ottawa when Tory leader Joe Clark drew attention to the phenomenon. He was immediately accused of thereby "aiding and abetting" it. Pierre Trudeau offered the helpful opinion that Western separatism was "nil and non-existent," being at root "a fight about money" in no way comparable with Quebec's grievances. This naturally inspired redoubled efforts to prove him wrong.

By early 1981, the furor appeared to be dying down. Polls showed support for outright separation was falling, although only to the unpublicized but statistically significant level it had steadily enjoyed for some time before 1980. The attention of the Toronto media was distracted by other controversies, such as Trudeau's drive to patriate the constitution. Central Canadian Establishment opinion reassured itself that the movement was "ebbing" and that separatists were after all just "losers," as Richard Gwyn put it that year in *The Northern Magus,* "fighting the late twentieth century."

Not for the first time in Canada, this complacency was premature. What was happening was typical of a popular political movement in its early stages. In the 1950s and 1960s, the Quebec separatist movement had shown exactly the same cyclical rhythm, characterized by intense factionalism and confusion over its precise objectives, just as the Westerners now displayed. And, as two University of Alberta political scientists observed in a prescient collection of essays published in 1981, "what the polls cannot show . . . is that in at least one western province – Alberta – the dominant political and economic elites are in the process of 'contracting out' of the federal system. . . ."

This process was taking tangible institutional form. Like Jean Lesage's Quebec before it, the oil-rich province under Tory premier Peter Lougheed was attacking the federal connection by incessantly quarrelling with Ottawa over the disposition of tax revenues and constantly scheming to assume control over aspects of certain common functions like the grain marketing system, medical insurance and – ominously – the police power, previously exercised under contract throughout much of the province by the RCMP. Even if this scheming was merely the bureaucratic imperialism evident in recent years in every Western province, it strengthened the logic of the separatist case, just as it had done earlier in Quebec.

On February 17, 1982, the Central Canadian elite was given a hint of how premature its complacency might have been. Gordon Kessler, the WCC candidate, was elected to the Alberta legislature in a smashing by-election victory in the rural Olds-Didsbury riding. Kessler had campaigned largely in opposition to federal-provincial compromise on the constitution. The Canadian Establishment's reaction was characteristic, "PM blames 'hate' campaign for separatist win in West," was the banner headline in the *Toronto Star,* promoting Pierre Trudeau's claim that anti-French "racism," unchallenged by Lougheed, was responsible for the result. By implication, the victory was therefore illegitimate and should be ignored.

Western federalists could not afford this luxury. "If I were the premier, I wouldn't give this group six months to get organized," said

Alberta's former Social Credit leader Bob Clark, who had held Olds-Didsbury for twenty-one years until his retirement precipitated the by-election. "I think he would be wise to go [with an election] right now." After some preparation, Lougheed did call an early election, and won overwhelmingly. Kessler, who had become the leader of the WCC in a savage internal battle, lost his seat. His party shattered into splinter groups. But despite competition from other separatists, the WCC still polled 11.9% of the Alberta vote – significantly better than the Quebec separatists did in 1966.

Olds-Didsbury alarmed Western politicians because they knew that their region had a long history of political volatility. Repeatedly, it has been swept by "prairie fires" of political protest that have utterly consumed governments previously regarded by conventional wisdom as totally safe. For example, Lougheed himself had taken over the Alberta provincial Conservatives in 1965 when they were in opposition and almost defunct and in 1971 had completely destroyed a Social Credit regime that had been in power thirty-six years. Back in 1935, Social Credit had come from nowhere and shockingly incinerated the United Farmers government, itself the heir of an agrarian protest movement that had immolated a long-established Liberal government in 1921.

In case anyone missed the point, in April 1982, Saskatchewan Premier Allan Blakeney's eleven-year New Democratic government was unexpectedly annihilated by the Progressive Conservatives in an early election called, according to Robert Sheppard and Michael Valpy, "to nip the western separatist movement in the bud. . . ." Attorney General Roy Romanow, the Crown Prince of Saskatchewan socialism and co-author of the final compromise during the constitution patriation struggle, was defeated narrowly by a twenty-two-year-old girl who worked part-time in her father's gas station. The new Tory premier, Grant Devine, previously unable to win a seat, had been leading his party from the Legislature gallery. The WCC polled 5% – but then the Liberals, who after all had governed the province until 1971, only got 7%. Blakeney's progressive and pan-Canadian views had made him a favorite with the Central Canadian Establishment, and his downfall was deeply disturbing to them.

In fact, the Central Canadian elite has long been plagued by periodic suspicion about the West. Pierre Berton conceded in *Why We Act Like Canadians* that, partly due to massive American immigration, "western Canada, like Quebec (although to a lesser extent) is a separate state within a state." In 1945, Prime Minister Mackenzie King actually believed that the Americans "could take peaceful possession of part of Canada with a welcome from the people of B.C., Alta. and Saskatchewan. . . . I felt perfectly sure that once the Western provinces became alarmed in the matter of their security, they would look to the United States for protection, not to Canada or the Commonwealth." "Goldwin Smith thought it was a fatal mistake to stretch our mandate beyond the Lakes," noted John Holmes in his recent Bissell lecture at the University of Toronto, "and I sometimes wonder if he was right."

The feeling is mutual. Western Canadians have voted against Ottawa with a persistence so stubborn that it is hard to avoid the impression that they are trying to send some kind of message. They have conducted prolonged experiments with minor parties. When Western Canada went for John Diefenbaker's Progressive Conservatives in the 1958 federal election, it was the last time it aligned itself with a Canadian government until the brief Clark interregnum in 1979. In 1963, the new Liberal government of Lester Pearson was not even the second choice of Western Canadians: they returned 47 Tories, 11 New Democrats and 10 Liberals. Even in 1968, Trudeaumania could only evoke 27 Western Liberals – 16 from the distinctive subculture of British Columbia – as against 25 Tories and 16 New Democrats. Since then, the Liberals have virtually ceased to exist as a Western party. The two thousand miles from the Ontario boundary to the Pacific returned only two Liberals in the great Trudeau victory of 1980 – both from Manitoba, and one from a Francophone enclave near Winnipeg. There were no Liberals in any of the provincial legislatures.

Paradoxically, while Ottawa was being acclaimed for its affirmation of the collectivist Canadian genius in contradistinction to the conservative Republican administration in Washington, Western Canada quietly produced in British Columbia the most radical *laissez faire* regime in North America. Particularly after 1983, when his Social Credit Party was re-elected with an increased majority, Premier Bill Bennett began to perform such unnatural acts as abolishing rent control, firing civil servants and actually rolling back the welfare state, with much more enthusiasm than anything seen south of the border, and all without provoking revolution.

Since the federal Liberal Party in essence is Canada, or at least the Establishment's idealized version of it, the West's revulsion is an unmistakeable symptom that something is rotten in the Canadian state. Nor is there an obvious cure. When the Liberals were strong on the Prairies, earlier in the century, they were unashamed exponents of unhyphenated Greater British Anglophonism – it was a Liberal government in Manitoba that in 1890 abolished provincial support for education in French. In that era, when economic liberalism meant free markets, the Liberals appealed to the abiding Western resentment of the payment of import duties to support Central Canadian industry. Because of Quebec's susceptibilities, they were inclined to defend provincial autonomy against Ottawa. Laurier did this when he sought a compromise solution to the Manitoba Schools dispute rather than disallow the legislation, as the federal Tories were being urged to do by their *bleu* allies. None of these options is open to the modern Liberal Party. Its Central Canadian Francophone and New Class elite demands protectionism, bilingualism and a strong, centralized state – as Brian Mulroney discovered when he began to negotiate continental free trade.

In some ways, Liberal policies towards Canada are a reprise on the national stage of the drama that took place inside the party after its defeat by John Diefenbaker. Walter Gordon and Keith Davey reformed the party apparatus, concentrating power in a Leader's Advisory Committee in Ottawa controlled by themselves, and bypassing the provincial Liberal organizations. The new Liberal machine was unquestionably effective. But powerful Liberal leaders in the West, such as Premier Ross Thatcher of Saskatchewan, were soon frantically opposing the personnel and policies it forced upon them as being too left-wing and Central Canada-oriented for their constituencies. They were ignored – and within twenty years were an extinct species. The Liberal overhaul of Canada, along distinctly similar lines, has lagged behind the party reform by rather more than a decade.

Any Liberal Establishment elite apprehension about the West can easily be justified. Unlike Quebec, the West is a clear economic loser in Confederation. Western Canada is a colony in the purest mercantilist sense . . . well, fairly pure. Its development has been channelled by political power in directions contrary to natural economic forces but concordant with the perceived interests of a distant metropolis. Historically, the West has never been allowed to buy freely where it wished, but has had to pay the Canadian tariff on imports. This gave Canadian manufactured goods a price advantage, and thus in effect subsidized Central Canadian industry. Federal government intervention also prevented the West from selling its principal product, oil and gas, where it wishes – in the world market. Instead, Western oil and gas was compulsorily diverted to the Canadian market, where it could only be sold at prices Ottawa fixed well below prevailing world levels. In effect, it was expropriated. Additionally, Ottawa intervened to inhibit the importation of foreign capital, particularly into the oil industry, making the West more dependent upon expensive Central Canadian capital and upon various government incentives. And having tied down the oil industry in this way, Ottawa proceeded to penetrate it with its own organ, Petro-Canada, the federal government oil company. Petro-Canada was specially favored by such methods as direct subventions from taxpayers, a "Canadian Ownership" levy on all gasoline purchases, the right to claim a share of or "back-in" to any discovery on federal land and – hotly denied but undeniable – a preferential access to government information, including a say in framing the National Energy Program itself.

The energy imbroglio is new, but the tariff problem is almost as old as Canada itself. "Western Canada has paid for the development of Canadian nationality, and it would appear that it must continue to pay," wrote Harold Innis, a pioneer of Canadian economic history, in 1923. Estimating the cost of tariffs and import quotas is a Canadian national sport, played with particular feeling in the West. Some years ago, a study suggested that trade barriers caused the average Canadian family to pay $100 more a year for clothing alone; a British Columbia study put the total cost per household in the province at over $1,000 a year. The Canada West Foundation has estimated that in 1983, Ontario alone received a subsidy amounting to $56 a head; the cost to Westerners and Maritimers was at least as large. Not surprisingly, federalist economists are noticeably reluctant to challenge directly the confident assertion by Western separatists that Western living standards would rise 30 to 50% with independence and free trade.

The federal connection has not been a completely one-way street for the West. Manitoba and Saskatchewan appear to be net beneficiaries under the federal government's fiscal equalization program. But the amounts involved are relatively small, reflecting their joint population of a mere 2 million, and British Columbia and Alberta are heavy losers. In fact, these two provinces in combination with Ontario support the other seven in terms of this program. Some Western industries benefit from tariffs, for example in Winnipeg. But an independent West could presumably protect these if it wished with a more selective tariff, and still enjoy freer trade overall. And Western Canada may well institute a more optimal currency rate to float upwards to regulate the inflow of investment capital attracted by its energy projects, rather than suffer excessive disruption of its internal price relationships. It would not have had to suffer the side-effects of the Bank of Canada's monetary expansion in the mid-1970s, which was designed to revive depressed Central Canadian industries; in the

West the same depressant – energy price increases – had proved to be a stimulant. Alternatively, an independent West could even opt for the greater efficiency and stability provided by the U.S. dollar, as Bernard Landry advocates for Quebec.

It is also true that Ottawa, like Washington, played a role in fostering domestic oil production in the long-gone days when international oil companies – the "Seven Sisters" – controlled the world oil trade and held prices low. But the way in which this was done offers a telling insight into the political economy of Canada. The Canadian markets west of the Ottawa valley were reserved for Western oil and the importation of the cheaper foreign oil was banned. This meant that Western oilmen were denied Montreal, then Canada's greatest city, and that Quebec consumers enjoyed lower-cost energy than even their fellow Central Canadians in Ontario – some 10% less by 1970. At the same time, Canadian officials campaigned to get the U.S. to accord honorary American status to more Canadian oil and accept it in their own protected market wherever it was competitive. Then the OPEC cartel began to take hold and world prices began to rise. Ottawa flip-flopped: Western oil was now so welcome everywhere in Canada that exports must be restricted – although of course it could only be sold in Canada below world prices. For technical reasons, Quebec could not quickly tap into Western oil supplies – so its continued import of foreign oil was subsidized by the federal government to reduce Quebec's energy costs to the level of the domestic oil price.

Artificially low energy prices are something of a poisoned chalice for an economy. They offer a transient advantage over other industrial competitors, but by blurring price signals they narcotize the natural process by which economies adjust to changed circumstances. However, this philosophical point was of little interest to Westerners. They just felt that Ottawa had been reluctant to help them when they were down, and now had robbed them when they were up. And it did not escape their attention that the only consistent theme in federal public policy was sedulous attention to Quebec.

Not all of the West's economic complaints are valid. It is easily provoked into defending those of Ottawa's redistributive devices from which it appears to benefit, such as farm subsidies and regulated freight rates, although this contradicts its general case for economic freedom. And that very free play of economic forces itself might well dictate that certain industries and commercial activities not be located in the West, which is after all a long way from the main markets of

North America. This was not a conclusion acceptable to former Alberta premier Peter Lougheed. He predicated his political career on the Alberta government's intercepting oil revenues and using them to develop petrochemical and other enterprises in the province. This was one of a number of signs that he conformed to the mixed-economy orthodoxy found among politicians throughout the capitalist world, and fatally lacked the imagination to mount an effective defense of the West.

Western populist moaning, however, should not be dismissed too quickly. Westerners have traditionally resented banks, for example, on the grounds that they drew savings out of the region. This ignored what economic theory says is the banks' function: to allocate resources efficiently where the return is highest, maximizing overall prosperity. But in Canada, this fine theory was contaminated by the fact that the banking business was a federally sponsored cartel, dominated until recently by five nation-wide giants, all based in Central Canada. Complaints about their rigidities and monopolistic inclinations were by no means restricted to Westerners. For years, the banks' most outspoken public critic was the head of a Montreal brokerage house, Richard D. Lafferty. Even E.P. Taylor, now the doyen of Canadian tycoons, was apparently the intended target of a power play at the beginning of his brewing career when his bank, which also had links with his competition, suddenly withdrew his credit line. And Western alienation at its most unreasonable is after all no more so than Canadian Nationalism at its most rational, which has been the fashion of the age. The two particularisms even share many of the same forms: for example, companies incorporated under Alberta law must have a quota of native (home-grown?) directors, just as their federally incorporated counterparts are required to sport certified Canadians.

Less dramatic than separatism but perhaps more ominous for Confederation, the careful polls of the Canada West Foundation consistently showed 50% to 60% of Western Canadians agreeing that the West could survive without the rest of Canada, even in years when support for outright separatism was in single digits. This Western consensus poses a grave dilemma for the Canadian Liberal elite. Hitting a mule with a two-by-four might get its attention, and even its acquiescence. But the mule might also decide to walk away – especially if it knows its halter is untied.

The best-known two-by-four to be wielded for some time was of course Ottawa's National Energy Program, introduced in 1980 with the ostensible purpose of Canadianizing the energy industry and ensuring Canada's energy self-sufficiency. Abolishing the NEP has been the Mulroney government's chief claim to pro-Western and conservative credentials. But in fact the fall in world oil prices had already undermined the NEP, forcing even the Liberals to make repeated concessions to producers in the West, and also in the East where development of the Hibernia field off Newfoundland had been stalled for years by jurisdictional disputes. Nevertheless, the NEP is worth studying as a classic case of aggression against the West by the Central Canadian establishment, a prime example of Pierre Trudeau's ability to create facts.

The NEP's different victims all had different complaints about it. And they were all right. From the U.S. standpoint, the NEP was a blow to American oil companies in Canada. As with Canadian companies, Ottawa was intervening to "back in" to a part-ownership of their discoveries, and to expropriate through royalties and taxes the so-called windfall profits they were about to receive because they had had the foresight to acquire assets whose price was rising. But U.S. firms also facing buy-Canadian provisions were not eligible for the same exploration incentives offered Canadians, and were severely constrained in their future exploration and other activities. Historically, the U.S. companies had been crucial to the development of the oil industry in Canada. They had actually committed more resources to it than prospects warranted, precisely because it seemed so much like home. Now they were not only deprived of opportunity, but the immediate value of the assets they had built up in Canada was being deliberately destroyed, while they were being pressured to sell out.

Both the oil companies and many Canadian Nationalists expected some action out of Washington in response. The NEP proved, however, to be a crisis ideally suited to the Reagan administration's political style. It did nothing. And in the end, of course, the NEP did go away – sort of.

From the Alberta government's standpoint, the NEP was Ottawa muscling into its revenue sources. From first to last, the attention of the Lougheed government was riveted by this issue, with little time for the Canadian companies and none at all for the Americans. After long negotiations a compromise was reached with Ottawa which oilmen regarded as a deal between thieves – in fact, a series of deals, progressively readjusted, because as the economy worsened the industry fell into an ever-deeper swoon, so that eventually even public officials in Alberta and Central Canada became alarmed.

From the oil industry's standpoint, the NEP was socialism. Canadianization was merely a mask for Ottawa-ization. There was always a hollow ring to the official clamor about the question of ownership. Since Canada is a sovereign state with the power to make laws and above all to tax, who actually owns its industry is economically irrelevant – except that where foreign investors assume risk and finance commercial activity, they free Canadian capital for other purposes. And even the chairman of Petro-Canada has been known to admit that the only reason foreign ownership levels in the Canadian energy industry were so high in the first place was that the federal tax system had not favored Canadian private investors as the America system had done. Even so, the fact was that, prior to the NEP, less than 10% of the Canadian petroleum industry's total revenue after operating expenses was actually going to foreigners.

Ottawa's proposed solution to this non-existent problem was even more suspicious. Petro-Canada was backing into Canadian as well as foreign discoveries; it was competing with Canadian corporations as well as American – for example, outbidding Calgary's Turbo Resources Limited to buy a chain of service stations in British Columbia that had been Canadian-owned anyway. And the NEP's definition of foreign ownership was so stringent that it caught in its net Dome Petroleum Limited, at that point Canada's outstanding corporate success story. This was because, although Dome was incorporated in Canada, headquartered in Calgary and very definitely run by its all-Canadian management, its stock was actively trading in the U.S. (having been vigorously promoted there by that same management, whose personal fortunes and pension funds were completely invested in it). Additionally, the NEP sought through regulation and incentives systematically to subordinate the private energy industry to political ends. It encouraged the consumption of natural gas rather than oil, to meet official conservation goals. It aimed to shift exploration to the federally controlled territories, partly because taxes on any resulting production would not have to be shared with troublesome (and Tory) provincial governments; and partly because its framers thought Ottawa knew better than the companies where oil could be found. The authors of the NEP did not believe that price could balance the supply and demand for energy: they believed that power should.

In the last analysis, the National Energy Program was really a National Political Program. By subjugating the burgeoning, politically deviant West, it served the needs of both the elected and permanent governments – where the two can be distinguished, not always easy in Canada. To a remarkable degree, the NEP was the creation of an identifiable group of federal civil servants in the Department of Energy, Mines and Resources who were explicitly motivated by considerations of what they called "equity" – that is, a disapproval of Alberta and the oil companies getting rich and a determination to make them share the wealth with the federal government and its clients. This was the culmination of an attitude that had been developing in Ottawa for many years. Federal officials had begun to equate the national interest with the welfare of the government machine, disregarding any impact on the real economy. For example, back in 1978, one civil servant was quoted in the *Financial Post* as justifying Petro-Canada's purchase of Calgary-based Pacific Petroleum Limited from the U.S. on the grounds that "the $1.4 billion expenditure *gives Ottawa assets,* as opposed to a *straight payout* in the form of such incentives as tax concessions." (Emphasis added.) These tax "concessions," of course, inspired oilmen to find oil and thus added to Canada's total wealth. But buying Pacific Petroleum added nothing to Canada's energy reserves, employment pool or revenue base. It merely used taxpayers' money to transfer already-discovered reserves into the hands of the federal bureaucracy – "Ottawa," like the man said. It would be hard to conceive of a more blatant expression of class interest.

A fine summary of the NEP was provided by a foreign Canada-watcher, Professor Charles Doran, director of the Center of Canadian Studies at Johns Hopkins University. In his 1984 study of Canada-U.S. relations, *Forgotten Partnership,* Doran noted that "a possibility not entirely to be discounted is that Ottawa never really was much interested in petroleum self-sufficiency." Both elected and permanent governments in Ottawa were strikingly indifferent to the NEP's effect on investor confidence, even after the collapse of the capital-intensive "megaprojects" that were supposed to develop the West's huge but technically daunting unconventional oil reserves and provide work for years to come. Professor Doran drew a distinction between the "real" and "announced" agendas that the bureaucracy and the Liberal Party hoped to fulfil via the NEP, and concluded: "Ottawa needed to defend the interests of central Canadian consumers and industrial users, a defense Ottawa pursued under the disguise of 'equity.' "

In all the excitement over the NEP, it has been quite forgotten that Ottawa had just finished hitting the West with another two-by-four. In 1977 it allowed a coalition of nationalists, environmentalists and "native people" activists to block the oil companies' plan to build a natural gas pipeline from Alaska down the Mackenzie Valley and on to the American Midwest. This would have been the world's largest construction project, and in an earlier moment of enthusiasm Jean Chrétien, then Minister of Indian and Northern Affairs, aptly compared it to the building of the transcontinental railway in its long-term benefits to the region. Ottawa compromised on a technically incomplete but politically brilliant alternative marketed by Alberta Gas Trunk Lines' Bob Blair. Blair was an outstanding example of the bisectoral entrepreneur produced by government encroachment on business, equally functional in both positions. The inevitable delay while plans were drawn up, and concurrent drastic changes in market and financial conditions, make it quite possible that this window of opportunity for the West has been slammed for a generation, perhaps for good, although Blair was able to "pre-build" sections of the pipeline directly affecting his company. But at least this fiasco affected only what might have been. The NEP injured what actually was.

In this context, it would be unwise not to note the real cultural antagonism between entrepreneurs and bureaucrats that pervaded the relationship of the West's energy industry to Ottawa. Although the oilmen were often derided, they made Calgary something of a magical place to those not distressed by the spectacle of others' wealth, an atmosphere well caught in Peter Foster's *Blue-Eyed Sheiks*. Rodeo riders and ranch hands, along with a variety of enterprising immigrants from Canada and the rest of the world, really had become millionaires. They gave the city the liberated atmosphere of a Cossack encampment on the marches of a gloomy autocracy. They were part of an intimate but international network that, without even a tip of the stetson to Toronto or the Department of External Affairs, was directly connected to Denver and Dallas, to the Persian Gulf and Indonesia. With their private jets and their business cards inscribed in Arabic on the reverse, they were a type not seen since the palmy days of Victorian Imperialism: confident Canadians. By contrast, the architects of the NEP had spent their formative years in academia and the bureaucracy. Edmund Clark, head of the Ministry's division, had been an active member of the Union for Radical Political Economists at Harvard where, writing as a "socialist scholar," he completed his Ph.D. on "Public Investment and Socialist Development in Tanzania" before joining the civil service in 1975. The two factions had practically nothing in common, except citizenship in what was nominally still the same country.

Economic exploitation of the West poses obvious dangers for Confederation. Nevertheless, the Central Canadian Liberal Establishment is locked into policies that exacerbate the situation by adding to economic insult an element of continuous cultural goading. Most important, Ottawa's institutionalized preoccupation with the French fact collides head-on with the Western way of life: in 1981, only 86,665 throughout the West told the census-takers that they spoke French at home – as opposed, for example, to 95,070 who spoke German. Only about 6% of the seven million Westerners claim to be proficient in both official languages, so that bilingualism in the federal civil service and other areas seriously damages most peoples' prospects of a career in the civil service. Adding insult to injury, they must periodically open their newspapers and confront stories like the one that appeared in the Victoria *Times-Colonist* on October 22, 1983, at the height of the pitched battle in Manitoba over the NDP government's plan to make Manitoba officially bilingual. In the article, Marc Roy, president of the cultural organization for the province's 45,000 Francophones, urged that B.C. should also become a bilingual province: "Sooner or later, each province will have to recognize that the price to pay for a united Canada is the recognition of French language minority rights," he was quoted as saying. His public relations director predicted that the 45,000 French-speaking British Columbians could easily increase tenfold to 500,000 in the next decade . . . a lot of Quebecers . . . are going to move to B.C. for many reasons." Roy went on to say that despite "B.C.'s strong Anglophone tradition" French education should be "made the right of all British Columbians" and they should have "the right to correspond with the provincial government in French as Francophones do now with the federal government." Notwithstanding his peremptory tone, Marc Roy was expressing no more than the dogma Pierre Trudeau has made official for the Canadian Liberal Establishment: in order to keep Quebec in Confederation, "rights" will have to be extended to Francophones across Canada by both federal and provincial governments. The simultaneous withdrawal of these rights from the Anglophones in Quebec is inconvenient but irrelevant. The potential impact of Roy's demands can be judged from the fact that the 1981 census showed 2,713,615 people living in British Columbia, of whom only 5.7% – 154,170 – professed to be bilingual and therefore eligible to enter a bilingual public service. Interestingly, the 1981 census also revealed that only 15,125 reported speaking French at home in British Columbia. An infinitesimal 1,445 were unilingual Francophones. Roy presumably claims to have 45,000 clients because that number told the census-takers that French was their mother-tongue, although this is more a measure of ethnic origin than language practice. These figures also suggest that his members comprise almost one-third of British Columbia's bilinguals, or potential provincial civil servants under a bilingual regime.

Despite recent refinements, the West's disgust with Quebec is not new. It dates back at least to the conscription crisis of World War I, and even to the Riel rebellions. To the West, Francophones have become both a symbol and a symptom of their dispossession.

The resulting antagonism is easy to caricature as racism. But the West has not yet produced anything as vitriolic as Abbé Groulx' nationalist novel *L'appel de la race,* which argued that Anglophones and Francophones were genetically incompatible, or Michèle Lalonde's more recent poem *Speak White,* described by the Toronto *Globe and Mail*'s former Quebec correspondent William Johnson as "a declaration of hate against les Anglais." And, as Parti Québécois Minister Camille Laurin said when his government's language legislation was accused of being ethnocentric, "All nations are founded on the principle of ethnocentricity." Self-affirmation is not necessarily prejudice. To the extent, however, that the discontent of the West is the stirring of a nascent nation, it will not be assuaged by the resignation of Pierre Trudeau.

There was talk of Western separatism earlier in the century, when the grain boom filled the West with a surging self-confidence eerily similar to the energy boom seventy years later. But the Depression crushed and demoralized the region. However, in its new manifestation Western separatism has already passed through the early phase of being the exclusive concern of small sects of intellectuals and activists. As early as 1971, a serious pro-separatist study, *The Unfinished Revolt,* was co-edited by the executive assistant to the Social Credit premier of Alberta. Nor is it exclusively a right-wing concern. The federal NDP's devotion to its centralist doctrines has caused it to endorse many of Ottawa's post-1980 initiatives at some cost to itself, but there are signs that the provincial parties think differently. Among the leaders of the anti-bilingual movement in Manitoba, the outstanding recent example of Western self-affirmation, were a prominent provincial NDP backbencher and a former NDP cabinet minister. In 1981, George Woodcock, who comes close to being the Grand Old Man of Canadian letters, published a book called *Confederation Betrayed.* In it he explains why, as a British Columbian, he has come to think that "separation must be held as one of our options."

Nevertheless, the form that Western separatism has taken in the last few years has been, in the context of democratic politics, undeniably right-wing, just as in Quebec, national sentiment found a social-democratic expression. This actually confirms the fundamental cultural unity of the North American nation. Western Canada's separatism is clearly in part a parallel to the American West's commitment to the American conservative movement, just as its earlier agrarian insurrections paralleled similar political developments south of the border. Western conservatism in the U.S. has been strong and long-lasting and culminated in Ronald Reagan – another suggestion of separatism's potential.

Currently, Western sectionalism is in institutional and ideological flux. Some of its leaders argue as Réné Lévesque once did in his provincial Liberal incarnation, but possibly more sincerely, that a reformed Confederation would satisfy them. Others, more pessimistic, remain outright separatists. Events in the rest of Canada will have great influence on the movement's immediate future. Western Federation's Elmer Knutson only organized his party after the Parti Québécois' 1980 referendum did not result, as he had hoped it would, in the withdrawal from Confederation of what he regarded as the malign influence of Quebec. In 1981, with Premier Lougheed in hand-to-hand combat with Ottawa over the constitution and the NEP, Knutson attended the provincial Progressive Conservative convention. The Tory Attorney General of Alberta explained that his party could not expel someone for being a separatist, although it had just evicted a Tory member of the provincial legislature who had broken ranks to support Ottawa's position on patriation.

The extent to which the Central Canadian establishment continues to brutalize Western sensibilities will be a crucial variable. Brian Mulroney's Quebec-centered political strategy and his attempt to co-opt the Liberal state leave him little room for concessions to the West, now that he has dismantled the NEP. Even before the 1984 election, he forced his party to support Liberal endorsement of the attempt to impose bilingualism on Manitoba and the imposition of official bilingualism on the Northwest Territories and the Yukon. And despite the Tory sweep of the West in the 1984 election, in Manitoba a distinctly respectable showing was made by the Confederation of Regions Party, a direct descendant of Elmer Knutson's separatist group. The COR did particularly well against one of Mulroney's more prominent supporters, Jake Murta in Lisgar.

The potential for Western disillusionment with the Tories is great. A catalytic issue could produce a further separatist surge – or the West could become the stronghold of a new party expressing national right-wing discontent with the Progressive Conservative Party's unrepresentative leadership.

"Political alienation here is total and complete," federal Liberal Party chairman Iona Campagnolo said in 1980 about her home province of British Columbia. "We're at the point Quebec was at in the 1960s." And in 1981, the various separatist groups did of course poll better in Alberta than similar groups in the Quebec provincial election of 1966. If precedents hold, all it needs is a leader – and about another ten years.

Confederation has seen the Atlantic provinces of Canada descend into true peripheral status. In the mid-nineteenth century, the Maritimes had already achieved what Ottawa now officially wants for Canada: a major and diversified role in international trade. According to economic historian David G. Alexander, ". . . the region possessed one of the world's foremost shipbuilding industries, the third or fourth largest merchant marine, financial institutions which were the core of many of the present Canadian giants, and an industrial structure growing as fast as central Canada." Of the first eleven prime ministers of Canada, five were born in the Maritimes, three in Britain and only three in Central Canada; the Maritimes also produced a future British prime minister, Bonar Law.

But some time after Confederation the Maritimes' economy began to stagnate. Its trade atrophied, and now all three provinces are heavily dependent on federal transfer payments. In 1871, Nova Scotia, New Brunswick and Prince Edward Island comprised 20.8% of Canada's population as a whole; by 1981 this had fallen to 7%. The Maritimes even lacked the political power to prevent Nova Scotia's great port of Halifax from being dispossessed of its naval heritage: during the last Trudeau government, it was announced that the headquarters of the Canadian "maritime command" would be relocated to Quebec City – a move not reversed (needless to say) by Brian Mulroney.

Maritime decline has not attracted much attention outside of the region itself, and its causes are imperfectly understood. Conventional explanations are the technological obsolescence of the traditional staples of the economy – "wind, wood and sail" – and the efficiencies to be gained in the Canadian context by the migration of industries to Ontario and Quebec. But the very similar economy of Norway adapted itself perfectly happily to the steam era and to its geographic isolation. And, unlike Norway, the Maritimes even has iron and coal. Jane Jacobs, for whom development is a complex process of dynamic inter-relation, speculated in *The Question of Separatism* that the quick profits of natural resource exploitation seduced Maritime capitalists from their shipping business which, with its deep international market, could have generated sufficient diversifications to expand the economy to a critical mass.

A more orthodox analysis would suggest that at least a part of the Maritimes' ills can be attributed to Confederation. Some emigration and a relative reduction of the industrial base was inevitable as the continent developed, and no doubt resulted in an increase in overall welfare in Canada as a whole, whatever the local effects in the Maritimes. But the decapitation of the Maritimes' elite must have been related to political unification and reorientation towards Central Canada. A case has been made, for example, that the loss of regional control over railway rate structures inhibited the growth of manufacturing. Above all, as in the West, Maritimers were deprived of the benefits of free trade. They found themselves subsidizing Central Canadian industry through tariffs on their purchases of American and other goods that would otherwise have been cheaper.

Political interference with market forces on the North American continent has left the Maritimes with a tantalizing imponderable. There is some evidence that cost levels there are not always higher than in Central Canada, and, as the industrial rise of the American South has illustrated, views on which areas are impossibly peripheral change over time – indeed, the Royal Navy chose Halifax as its main base after losing Boston precisely because of its strategic situation on the North Atlantic trade routes, an advantage from which Confederation may yet prove to have been a transient distraction.

Anglophone Maritimers have been quite deeply influenced by their Canadian experience. Some polls show them distinctly more inclined than the Québécois to place their Canadian allegiance before provincial loyalties – although observers have argued that this more accurately reflects their reaction ("terror") to Quebec separatism. Thus Robert Stanfield, who was the premier of Nova Scotia before leading the federal Progressive Conservative Party from 1968 to 1976, never openly voiced his support for continental free trade, and also deferred to Canadian Liberal elite doctrine on bilingualism. In Nova Scotia, Stanfield had also accepted Ottawa orthodoxy on the issue of what causes economic growth, joining in the Canadian game of government-sponsored industrial developments, few of which work and many of which (the Clairtone and the Glace Bay Heavy Water plant projects in Nova Scotia's case) end in financial catastrophe.

Nevertheless, it is notable that the Maritimes rejected the Liberal hegemony to the extent that by the end of the Trudeau era every

Maritime province had a Progressive Conservative government. During the Stanfield era, the federal Liberals did particularly badly in the region: in 1980 after his retirement, the nineteen seats they held of the region's thirty-two seats was their best total for many years. And this included a substantial ethnic vote from Francophone areas such as northern New Brunswick and from the Catholic enclave of Cape Breton, where Gaelic is still apt to be the second language. Despite their dependence on Ottawa and the "terror" many Maritimers undoubtedly feel at the prospect of any disruption of this relationship, their old spirit of enterprise gives an occasional twitch: "If we can work out a just and equitable confederation, I'm all for it," said Silver Donald Cameron, a prominent Nova Scotia journalist, after the Parti Québécois victory in 1976. "But if we can't, and Quebec pulls out, I'm prepared to contemplate independence for the Atlantic provinces as well."

The island province of Newfoundland, the easternmost point of North America, presents a different picture. Whereas Quebec's discontent within Confederation is primarily cultural and the West's primarily economic, in the case of Newfoundland, culture and economics combine to militate against the Canadian connection. And well within living memory Newfoundland actually was an independent state, a self-governing Dominion of the British Empire just like Canada, with its own parliament, national anthem and all the satisfactions (and problems) of sovereignty. Its current plight makes it a fascinating microcosm of the ills of Confederation, a chilling example of the well-intentioned devastation of a people.

Officially founded in 1583, Newfoundland was Britain's oldest colony. It provided the metaphysical poet John Donne with his famous apostrophe, in "Elegie: Going to Bed": "O my America! my new-found-land . . ." The Newfoundland population is a mixture of early settlers from the English West Country and later arrivals from Ireland. There has been no significant immigration for over a century. The 1981 census shows that 99.2% of the 563,750 Newfoundlanders speak English in their homes. Only 2.3% are bilingual. These are particularly impressive figures since the island also controls the vast mainland territory of Labrador, which actually borders on Quebec. And some proportion of the 1,810 individuals using French at home in Newfoundland will be the Francophone civil servants imported to meet federal bilingualism requirements. This is an ironic development for a people whose history features over three hundred

years of struggle against France, finally eliminating her last extra-
territorial fishing rights only at the beginning of the twentieth
century.

But Newfoundland's divergence from the Liberal version of Canada goes far beyond the usual Anglophone incompatibility. With its
population undisturbed and isolated in "outports" often accessible
only by sea, almost totally dependent on fishing and subsistence
farming, Newfoundland evolved like a salt-water Appalachia, producing an English-speaking culture unlike any other in North America, with a distinctive dialect rich in relict Jacobean English and
Anglo-Irish idiom. On the Canadian mainland ("upalong"), the
Newfoundlanders' singularity has made them the butt of a whole
species of "Newfie jokes" similar to Polish jokes in the U.S. On the
island, Newfoundland politics have a uniquely lurid, almost gothic
quality, rather like those of the post-Civil War American South. Many
of the usual Canadian rules are inoperative: for example, Newfoundland went solidly Tory for the first time in the federal election of
1968, despite Trudeaumania; historically, Newfoundland Catholics
have tended to vote Tory, the Protestants, Liberal. And Newfoundlanders share another characteristic with Southerners of the
post-War era: an awareness of inferiority within the polity, a pervasive
consciousness of defeat.

Some part of this must arise from the inglorious end to their
independence. Newfoundlanders had declined to join Canada in
1867 and at regular intervals afterwards. They even had a song about
it, which has exerted a macabre fascination over Canadian historians
ever since:

> Then hurrah for our own native land, Newfoundland!
> Not a stranger shall hold one inch of its strand!
> Her face turns to Britain, her back to the Gulf
> Come near at your peril, Canadian Wolf!

Newfoundland developed like Canada, as a self-governing Dominion within the British Empire. Contrary to general belief, in the
nineteenth century its reliance on fishing and farming had provided it
with a living standard comparable to "that enjoyed among working
people elsewhere in the western world," in David Alexander's words,
and despite remaining outside Confederation, its output and population grew faster than the other Maritime provinces, as foreign investors put up the capital to tap its natural resources – forest products and
minerals. But Newfoundland sold its fish throughout the world, and
the collapse of international trade during the Depression hit it even

harder than the West. It became unable to service its public debt.

Newfoundland's borrowing, largely to finance railway construction and its war effort, was not excessive on a per capita basis and other regional governments in the British Empire, such as Saskatchewan and New South Wales, were in similar trouble. But, partly because of internal political division, in 1934 Newfoundland accepted the exceptionally severe recommendation of its creditors, Britain and Canada, that democratic institutions be suspended and the island be placed under a British-appointed "Commission of Government," which ruled by decree for the next fifteen years. The point to note is that, although there was great privation in Newfoundland during the Depression, there was nothing inherently wrong with its economy. The cause of the island's collapse was not primarily economic but financial. Fortunately for Mexico and New York City, fifty years later the fashionable response to such problems was rescheduling or default.

After World War II, Newfoundland was manipulated into joining the Canadian Confederation. This is not to say that there was not support for the idea in the island, nor that Newfoundlanders had not developed considerable ties with their fellow British North Americans, nor that the local Confederationists did not have an able and cunning leader. After Confederation, J.R. ("Joey") Smallwood was to be a colorful Liberal premier from 1949 until 1971. But the key factor was the British government. It was still firmly in the grip of the passion for decanting its colonial responsibilities into convenient regional groupings which had already given the world Canada and Australia and which was to bring it, briefly, federations in the West Indies, Central Africa and elsewhere.

"Responsible government" was supposed to be restored to Newfoundland once it was self-supporting. But a Newfoundland legislature might have developed ideas of its own, so delegates were elected to a constitutional convention, carefully weighted against the merchants in the capital of St. John's who were thought to oppose joining Canada. As a hint, Britain announced that it could not guarantee aid to Newfoundland if the convention asked for responsible government. When after heated debate the convention nevertheless declined to commit Newfoundland to Confederation in advance, but instead voted for a plebiscite on a return to responsible government only, the British government chose to accede to a petition from Smallwood's supporters and include the Confederation option on the ballot. It lost, with 64,066 votes against 69,400 for responsible government and 22,311 for a continued "commission of government." But in the run-off between the two top choices, Confederation pulled ahead narrowly, with 78,323 votes to 71,334. All protests and petitions were thereafter ignored, and – after negotiations with, of course, a now pre-determined outcome – Newfoundland became a province of Canada on March 31, 1949.

The course of the referendum debate is worth study. As in the case of Nova Scotia during its nineteenth-century separation crises, Con-federation was presented by its advocates as an expression of loyalty to Greater Britain and its monarch. There was also an undercurrent of the religious antagonism that had always run through Newfoundland politics without dominating it: the island's Irish-descended Catholic minority feared – and its Orangemen no doubt welcomed – the mainland Protestants' influence, ironic in view of their complete eclipse in modern Canada. Time like an ever-rolling stream has borne away both these issues, so that important components in the original cultural basis for Confederation in Newfoundland have now disappeared.

Whether they have been replaced by a loyalty to the Canada that has concurrently emerged, reinforced by massive transfer payments as Newfoundlanders became eligible for Ottawa's extensive welfare schemes, is a vital question. It is perhaps significant that New-foundlanders, unlike any other Anglophone group, appear to be as likely as the Québécois to tell pollsters that they identify with their province rather than with Canada. In recent years there has been what University of Toronto historian Michael Bliss has described in *Satur-day Night* as an "enormous upsurge of interest in Newfoundland culture." One of the products of the prolonged struggle with the federal government over control of offshore oil has been open discus-sion of separatism, with 19% of the respondents to a 1981 poll favoring the idea if Newfoundland lost; subsequently, a small separatist party has been formed. This particularist sentiment presumably underlay Newfoundland Progressive Conservative Premier Brian Peckford's comment during the patriation struggle that he preferred René Lévesque's "vision of Canada" to that of Pierre Trudeau, an observa-tion that did his popularity in Ottawa no good at all.

The anti-Confederationists' main counter-attack in the 1948 refer-endum campaign is also significant. Led by C.A. Crosbie, scion of a leading St. John's merchant family, they argued that Newfoundland must have responsible government in order to investigate not just Confederation, but also the possibility of "economic union" with the United States. Like Confederation, economic union was an idea with a long history in Newfoundland. Versions of it had actually been negotiated in 1890 and 1902, but both times had been aborted, latterly because of opposition from U.S. fishing interests and formerly because Canada, fearful that the Maritime provinces would wish to follow suit, had compelled Britain to exercise its veto power over Newfoundland's external affairs. Ties between the U.S. and Newfoundland had been close for centuries: as long ago as 1704 a New Englander, Captain Michael Gill, had led the inhabitants of the settlement of Bonavista in the successful repulse of a French raid; traditional U.S. immigration policy had made it easy for expatriate communities of Newfoundlanders to set down roots in Boston and New York; the American servicemen based in Newfoundland during World War II had been popular and profitable, and thousands has departed with Newfoundland war brides. In the words of Frederick W. Rowe, the judicious historian of Newfoundland and also a former Smallwood cabinet minister, "the linking of 'responsible government' and 'economic union,' was psychologically, extremely clever. It represented the single greatest threat to the Confederates. . . . But for the monarchy, a clear majority of Newfoundlanders would have been induced to vote for Responsible Government."

Economic union with the U.S. has not been a favorite topic for debate in the Canada to which Newfoundland is now attached. But it is significant that the Canadian politician who raised the subject of continental free trade (both as Finance Minister and in his run for the Tory leadership), triggering a flurry of interest in a subject thought to be taboo, was the MP for St. John's West, John Crosbie, C.A. Crosbie's son.

For Newfoundland, Confederation has been a particularly agonizing paradox. Although some of its people equate independence with the economic conditions existing during the Depression, the fact is that the island would have prospered anyway in the world-wide expansion that followed World War II. However, there is no doubt that the great influx of transfer payments instantly transformed the outports, bringing them into the cash economy. "It was like getting manna from heaven," according to Premier Peckford, who himself hails from "round the bay," the collective St. John's term for the rest of the island. "In fact, Mr. Smallwood told us it *was* manna from heaven."

Ostensibly to facilitate the delivery of public services, both the federal and provincial governments launched a program of liquidating hundreds of outlying communities and resettling their inhabitants in more central locations. A drift to the towns had been evident in Newfoundland since the advent of the railway, but modern transport and communications technology might well have reversed it: in any event, resettlement caused great personal distress and effectively shattered a harsh but historic way of life. Interestingly, Roland Huntford in his survey of Sweden attributes the very similar drive exhibited by Swedish social planners to their desire for control over a dependent client constituency. Certainly, Joey Smallwood's political machine had an appreciation of the uses of patronage and coercion worthy of Tammany Hall.

The new centralized settlements, however, were hardly self-supporting. Their economics were those of distribution rather than production. What was distributed to them took the form of direct payments from Ottawa to individuals and also subsidies to a variety of local commercial endeavors.

Both federal and provincial governments have spent considerable sums on promoting industrial development in Newfoundland. The results can be fairly described as disastrous even by Canadian standards. Vast enterprises were built, suffered years of losses and then finally closed – an example being the oil refinery at Come-by-Chance, which in 1976 became the largest-ever Canadian bankruptcy.

Despite a noticeable tendency for some (although possibly not enough) of the individuals involved to move on to prison or to Panama, it would be wrong to attribute these failures entirely to incompetence or corruption. Inevitably, with governments involved, motivations were political rather than economic. The decision to subsidize the building of a linerboard mill at Stephenville, for example, was made because a major employer in the area, the U.S. air force base, was being phased out. By 1977, the mill was producing linerboard for $565 a ton when the prevailing market price was $188; the provincial government eventually closed it and wrote off an amount equal to $527 for every man, woman and child in Newfoundland.

Confederation has turned Newfoundland into a subsidy junkie. Essentially, it has allowed the province to import a larger share of goods and services from the rest of the world and pay for them with transfer payments from Canada. In the Newfoundland context, social policies designed for Central Canada often work in unexpected ways: many rural Newfoundlanders, who have been estimated to derive almost half their income "in kind" – fishing, hunting, cutting fuel – seem to have simply integrated unemployment benefits and the like into their seasonal routines. But this reliance on transfer payments is like heroin addiction. However good it feels in the short run, it has totally debauched the normal system of price signals and incentives in the economy, so that good workers have been lured into uneconomic activity, and bad workers confirmed in their dependency. It has led to a fundamental misallocation of resources – such as Smallwood's dissipation of the $40-million surplus carefully saved by the Commission of Government on illusory industrialization schemes – and in distortions so profound as to make Smallwood's claim that the island could not survive on its own, at least not without traumatic readjustment, a self-fulfilling prophecy. By 1978, according to the Economic Council of Canada, fully 80% of all spending in the Newfoundland economy was government-originated, compared with 44% in Canada as a whole.

"Don't listen to that appalling crap about separation. When you count up all the people who are getting support directly or indirectly from Ottawa, there are about 28 left," a retired Joey Smallwood told Michael Bliss in 1982, apparently with pride. Typical of social democrats of his era, Smallwood was aware only of the division of wealth, not its creation. Manna in his opinion really did come from heaven.

A comparison with Iceland suggests the price Newfoundland is paying for its heroin. Iceland (population 230,000, area 39,769 square miles) is smaller than Newfoundland (population 594,000, area 42,359 square miles – including the inhabitants of Labrador, which adds another 112,826 square miles). It is similarly situated in the North Atlantic and equally dependent on forestry and fish. Yet it has been separate from Denmark since 1918, severing its last links during World War II, just when Newfoundlanders were being prepared to resign themselves to provincial status. In 1977, Iceland's per capita income was $9,200, compared to $5,000 in Newfoundland; by 1980, Icelandic unemployment had never been above 2.4%, whereas Newfoundland's had topped 15%.

As an independent state, Iceland has had its own currency, and has been able to devalue to maintain its international competitiveness. Devaluation will not compensate for poor economic policy, but it will buy time. By contrast, Newfoundland has been unable to use this method to cut its high costs, and other countries' exchange rates have caused it persistent problems: for example, the British devaluation of 1948 priced Newfoundland fish out of an important market. Iceland's relative success is not due to any principled adherence to free-market doctrine: it is a social-democratic state which has had controls on the movement of capital and on foreign ownership of businesses. But one way or another, it has flourished while Newfoundland has floundered.

Confederation, however, has proved damaging to Newfoundland in far more specific ways. For example, the Canadian government in Ottawa has shown little interest in supporting the fishing industry.

This is partly demonstrated by its desultory attitude towards the internal organizational problems of the industry. It preferred to view these problems as a question of welfare for the fishermen, with direct government ownership always available as a last resort.

But more important is the anomaly pointed out by David Alexander: "The Canadian beaver has been flapping his tail at recent Law of the Sea conferences, but it must not be forgotten that until a few years ago, when offshore minerals began to provoke federal and corporate interest in maritime matters, the Canadian government strongly opposed any extension of territorial waters or exclusive fishing zones beyond the traditional 3-mile limit." Iceland by contrast practically declared war on Britain over the issue. The result of Ottawa's refusal to extend Canada's territorial waters was that the long-range fishing fleets of some twenty nations formed the habit of taking up annual residence on the Grand Banks of Newfoundland, mining the fish to the point of depletion right under Newfoundlanders' noses.

Ottawa's reluctance to defend the fishing industry was so extraordinary that it tends to undermine the contention that a genuine concern for national interests compelled Canada to diverge from the United States during the Law of the Sea conferences and join the "Third World" coalition advocating international control of the seabed. A more consistent explanation of Canadian behavior was what the French call a *déformation professionelle* among its foreign policy bureaucrats: they were all internationalist liberals who didn't want to be snubbed on the cocktail circuit by their fellow diplomats at the United Nations. This pattern was also observable in the U.S. State Department's vain attempts to obstruct the Reagan administration's foreign policy on the issue.

Another cause of Newfoundland distress with Confederation has been its inability to solve the province's difficulties with Quebec. Not only has Quebec simply refused to accept the court decision on the ownership of Labrador, but, by political pressure on the companies concerned, it has been able to secure for itself a good portion of the benefits from the exploitation of Labrador's minerals, most of which are shipped through the Quebec port of Sept-Iles. Even more seriously, Quebec has refused to renegotiate the 1969 agreement granting Hydro-Quebec the right to buy power from the huge Churchill Falls development at fixed prices, which with the subsequent increases in energy prices is bringing it a windfall profit of between $250 million and $600 million a year – aptly described by Bliss as "arguably . . . the worst case of profiteering by one group of Canadians at another's expense in the country's history."

Ottawa did little to rescue Newfoundland from Quebec's stranglehold, not even attempting to establish the right of provinces to transmit electricity across each other's territory in the way oil and gas are moved. But it was quick to assert its own claim over the oil and gas discovered off the Newfoundland coast. This constitutes a third Newfoundland grievance with Confederation, in many ways the most serious: although horribly expensive to exploit, the so-called "Hibernia" oilfield is a world-class find, the most important in North America since the Prudhoe Bay discovery in Alaska nearly twenty years ago. Nations have fought each other over far less.

For the Newfoundland government, oil revenues represented a unique opportunity. They could have been used as a sort of financial methadone to break the provincial economy's addiction to federal transfer payments and allow it ultimately to return to health. At the very least, they promised an Alberta-type boom. But Trudeau's Ottawa treated Newfoundland's aspirations with open contempt. The top civil servant in the federal finance ministry told the provincial government brutally that it was suffering from "delusions of grandeur" if it expected any say in offshore regulation. In Canada, mineral discoveries on provincial lands are under provincial jurisdiction. But courts have ruled that discoveries in coastal waters are in the federal government's domain. Had Newfoundland remained independent, it would have had a clear title to Hibernia. The Newfoundland government argued that this was still the case, because of the legal technicalities surrounding the province's late entry into Confederation. Meanwhile it asserted its authority over the oil companies by requiring, for example, preferential hiring for Newfoundland residents. In 1982, Brian Peckford called an early provincial election on the offshore issue. His Progressive Conservatives won in a landslide. When Ottawa moved to break the deadlock by referring the issue directly to Canada's Supreme Court, Peckford declared a "day of mourning" with unanimous all-party support from the Newfoundland House of Assembly.

By early 1984, Newfoundland was facing total defeat. The Supreme Court rejected both its attempt to break the Churchill Falls power contract and its bid to control offshore oil development. It had nothing to show for five years of delayed development, except an increased likelihood that the oil companies would shift their supply base from St. John's to Halifax if the dispute went on any longer. The

Peckford government's last hope was a new Tory government in Ottawa. And after Mulroney's election a compromise was scratched up. By this time, however, falling world oil prices made Hibernia distinctly less attractive. As the Mackenzie Valley pipeline illustrated, windows of opportunity can close as well as open.

If Ottawa regards the prospect of Western separatism with anger and Quebec separatism with anguish, it can be said to view potential Newfoundland separatism with amusement. But for another incipient separatism it has only adulation, and has actually gone some way towards institutionalizing it, although this separatism manifestly poses a threat to Canada's territorial integrity. It takes the form of land claims by Canadian Indians and Inuit – or, as they are now known in official jargon, the "First Nations."

There are about 300,000 people registered as Indians under the Indian Act of Canada, most of whom live in some 560 "bands" in some 2,200 enclaves, in addition to some 20,000 Inuit and an indeterminate number of mixed-blood "Métis." By the end of the Trudeau era, at least fourteen different native organizations had filed vast claims with the Federal Office of Native Claims. The Inuit Tapirisat wanted to carve out over 1.2 million square miles of the Northwest Territories to form a new territory called Nunavak ("Our Land"), in which there would be some 13,500 Inuit and about 5,000 whites. A coalition of Indians and Métis demanded almost the entire Mackenzie Valley, and was attempting to organize the establishment of a "Dene Nation" there. In the Western Arctic 2,139 Eskimos were also claiming 80,000 square miles, including the Yukon North Slope on the Beaufort Sea and the Mackenzie Delta. Even more disruptive, most native people lived in the jurisdiction of the provinces, south of the 60th parallel: claims filed there covered large areas, particularly in British Columbia, Quebec and Labrador.

The theoretical justification for the credulity with which the Canadian political elite listened to these ambitious and often conflicting claims was romantic, legalistic and essentially ahistorical. In 1983, the Parliamentary Special Committee on Indian Self-Government informed Canadians that the "First Nations" were "productive, cultured, spiritual, intelligent civilizations comparable to those in Europe at the time of first contact ... most First Nations have complex forms of government that go far back into history and have evolved over time ... Indian nations did not generally have written constitutions but, like England, conducted their affairs on the basis of traditions modified with pragmatic innovations." There was a more obvious reason the First Nations "generally" preferred unwritten constitutions: unlike the English, they had no form of writing. Columnist Douglas Fisher, who was once the NDP MP for the northern Ontario riding with more Indians than any other and who argues that they must be more fully integrated into Canadian life, dismissed the committee's assertion out of hand:

> The reality was rather different for most of the native people in what is now Canada. They were hardly out of the Stone Age. Most were nomads, eking a hard, brutish and brief existence. There was a score of different dialects and several languages but no writing and no really permanent communities.
>
> The relatively affluent Indians were in a few pockets, really, where food could easily be put in surplus, as through the salmon largesse on the Pacific or by the buffalo hunters on the plains (once they got horses, a European import). Medical knowledge and sanitary conditions were primitive, even before the scourge of smallpox. The wheel was unknown, and so were most metals and even anything as simple as a dependable cooking pot.
>
> If the natives had had the culture and institutions claimed by them and for them there'd have been both more effective resistance to white penetration of the continent and less readiness for guns, traps, tea, flour, rum, etc.

Native land claims were originally treated as physical token of Canada's obligation to the native peoples, to be cashed in for subsidies and services. Collective rights are not so easily extinguished, however: Cree leaders continued to argue for years about the implementation of the James Bay and Northern Quebec Agreement, concluded in 1975 to clear the way for the James Bay hydro-electricity development. And recently, the fashionable view has been that the "First Nations" should receive some form of permanent "self-government," a panacea espoused by the Parliamentary Special Committee, the federal bureaucracy, much of the Central Canadian media and many of the native leaders themselves.

On the face of it, this is an unlikely solution. The native peoples' enclaves are mostly scattered and poor with no prospect of becoming self-supporting. They are wholly dependent upon government transfer payments that seem to have produced already the social pathologies often associated with welfare ghettoes in the U.S. But with semi-sovereign legal powers, they would be strategically situated to frustrate or at least to hold hostage many of Canada's supposed national objectives, such as the development of energy reserves in the Arctic.

The basic dynamic of such political entities would inevitably be racial. As Michael Kaufman told the readers of the *New York Times* on August 22, 1983, writing about "Nunavak": "Though they carefully shun any talk of ethnic politics, it is clear that the Eskimo leaders expect that the basic demographics of the situation will eventually bring their people into the political process and into political power." This could produce an ethnocentricism even more powerful than in Quebec. Moreover, by granting what are in fact hereditary racial rights, Ottawa would be seriously impairing the principle of a society based on equality before the law, as well as establishing a disincentive to those native people who wish to leave the reserve and integrate into white society. And the whole thing is likely to prove extremely annoying to those whites who live in close proximity to the native peoples and are generally less sentimental about them than the distant elites of Central Canada are. Further friction will be created between Ottawa and the Canadian periphery.

Nevertheless, "self-government" for the Canadian native peoples' enclaves is moving ahead. As in the closely related case of multiculturalism (discussed in Chapter Eight), some insight into why this is happening is offered by "Public Choice" economics. In 1983, Douglas Fisher estimated that, leaving aside the usual pensions and family allowances, some $1.4 to $1.8 billion was being spent on the native peoples by Ottawa, and a further $400-500 million by provincial governments each year. "Over $5,000 per 'official' native!" There are approximately 6,000 civil servants in the Department of Indian and Northern Affairs alone. This amounts to a powerful vested interest which directly benefits from any attention paid to its charges. The situation is in some ways comparable to the twilight of the British Empire, where the Imperial bureaucrats actually favored colonial devolution in general (possibly not realizing how far it would go) and built successful careers – Sir Hugh Foot, Sir Andrew Cohen – by specializing in it.

Indeed, Ottawa even finances the native peoples' groups that are making claims against it. At one point, for example, it withdrew "negotiation funding" from the Mackenzie Valley Indians and Métis when they quarrelled over the details of their joint "Dene Nation" proposal – specifically to force the two groups back together to make more trouble for Ottawa. Naturally, this means that there is no shortage of professional native leaders. There may, however, be a shortage of natives. Métis leaders have been claiming for years to represent between 700,000 and 1.2 million Métis. These numbers, which implied a total of anything from 1.2 to 1.6 million native peoples, were never challenged in public and thus were widely accepted, for example, by Robert Sheppard and Michael Valpy in their standard account of the patriation struggle. But in the 1981 census a mere 98,000 Canadians reported that they were Métis and only 491,000 in total said that they were wholly or partly of native origin.

The basic reason for the uncritical reception of the native demands, however, is clearly cultural. For much of the Anglophone left, native rights are a symbolic expression of the alienation from the culture of the majority that I earlier identified as their motivating force. Not surprisingly, the NDP is deeply attracted to native causes: after the defeat of the NDP's left-nationalist "Waffle" faction a prominent member, Mel Watkins, became an advisor to the Dene Nation; during the constitutional struggle, native leaders negotiated with the federal government from a base in NDP Leader Ed Broadbent's Parliament Hill office. At times, this preoccupation has appeared so absorbing as to suggest a partial explanation for the party's loss of popularity among its traditional supporters, particularly in the West.

And Anglophone self-flagellation extends far beyond the NDP. According to Sheppard and Valpy, at the unveiling of the proposed clause that would recognize unspecified native "rights" in the patriated constitution, "with the TV cameras recording every poignant moment . . . several observers and members of the parliamentary committee [were] in tears," and there was much self-congratulatory talk about justice. Tears or not, however, Douglas Fisher has said that many politicians privately agree with his critique of native policy, but "then tell me it's too late, there's too much sympathy and too much guilt implanted in society as a whole." The power of ideas rarely can have had a more dramatic demonstration. English Canada has long ago lost the pragmatic self-confidence that enabled Goldwin Smith to dismiss its Indians in a robust paragraph:

> The race, every one says, is doomed. It has fallen into the gulf between the hunter state and that of the husbandman. Whisky has contributed to its ruin. . . . Little will be lost by humanity. The Red Indian has the wonderful powers of enduring hunger and fatigue

which the hunter's life engenders; he has the keenness of sense indispensable in tracking game: he seems to have no other gift. Ethnologists may find it instructive to study a race without a history and without a future; but the race will certainly not be a factor in New World civilization . . . [The Indian's] blood is not on the head of the British Government, which has always treated him with humanity and justice.

But Goldwin Smith was right. History, not Canada, has wreaked injustice on the native peoples. They were confronted with a civilization several thousand years more advanced. Collectively, they were overwhelmed, although individually many have benefitted. Now, however, in a curious eddy, it appears to offer them the chance of a certain blind revenge.

13

Canada and the Mulroney Answer

Hegel observes somewhere that all great incidents and individuals of world history occur, as it were, twice. He forgot to add: the first time as tragedy, the second time as farce.

– Karl Marx, *The Eighteenth Brumaire of Louis Bonaparte*

On the night of the Canadian federal election on September 4, 1984, Brian Mulroney stood on the platform at Tory headquarters in his home town of Baie Comeau, unable to make himself heard above the ecstatic crowd. His Progressive Conservatives had won in a landslide. In the new Parliament, they would have 211 of the 282 seats, well over double the 101 seats they had held after the election four years earlier. The Liberals would have a mere 40 seats, down disastrously from 148 in 1980, and the New Democrats 30, down slightly from 33. (There was one independent.) Moreover, the Tories had finally overrun the Liberal stronghold in Quebec, capturing 58 of its 75 seats. In his own riding of Manicouagan – which includes Baie Comeau – Mulroney had transformed a Liberal majority of 16,655 into a Tory majority of 20,657.

It was a scene that in its modest way was as spectacular as Alexander the Great's triumphal entry into Babylon after defeating the armies of the Great King Darius at Guagamela, deep inside the heart of the Persian Empire. Mulroney had been an MP for barely a year, yet experienced commentators like the *Toronto Star*'s Richard Gwyn were hailing him as "a truly great politician, architect of the most remarkable electoral victory in our history." Like Alexander, Mulroney's reception in this foreign land so far from his party's political home was greatly enhanced by the expectation that he would be merciful and in effect reconfirm the satraps, accepting the world

271

the federal Liberals had made and governing as their spiritual heir. The defeated Liberal MP, André Maltais, reported bitterly that his surveys showed his former constituents "really expected a lot from having a prime minister representing the riding." The crowd that cheered Mulroney in Baie Comeau was mainly Francophone. His first words to it – and Canadians watching on television from coast to coast – were in French.

Great expectations were not restricted to the Québécois, however. There was an audible sigh of relief from the whole Central Canadian Establishment. After some alarming moments, power had been transferred from the failing Liberals with no untoward accidents, and the new government was still firmly anchored in Central Canada and presided over by an acceptable Quebec leader. After quickly running the result through its political converter, The *Toronto Star* felt able to issue an editorial bulletin celebrating the unimpaired dominance of the Liberal ideological hegemony. While the electorate had been possessed by "a strong mood for change," The *Star* said, it stopped short of wanting any actual, well, *change*: "What we have witnessed is not so much a change in the basic political thinking of Canadians as a change in the political positioning of our parties . . . . The Tories were able to occupy the broad middle ground [formerly] dominated by the Liberals . . . ." It was impossible not to admire the virtuosity with which the editorial writer produced from his hat the reassuring information that, notwithstanding a Tory landslide, there was really no one here in Canada but us liberals and progressives.

The historical parallel was not all reassuring, however. As with Alexander, whether the conqueror's personal force would be sufficient to hold his disparate domain together was an open question. Mulroney would inherit the Liberals' problem as well as their power. In the future, the old divisions of culture and geography, to say nothing of the underlying crisis of the welfare state, would be reasserting themselves. Alexander, of course, was cut off in his youth at a happy juncture. In a less heroic age, Mulroney would run the distinct risk that his political career, begun so brilliantly like that of Pierre Trudeau before him, would also in the end terminate in failure.

Not all electoral landslides result in lasting political realignment, or even in re-election. Haunting the 1984 celebrations was the spectre of John Diefenbaker's very similar electoral sweep in 1958, when he won 208 of the 265 House of Commons seats then outstanding, including 50 in Quebec. But Diefenbaker completely failed to consolidate his position in the 1962 election, finally losing for good in 1963, and there were successive Liberal minority governments until Pierre Trudeau re-established the Liberal majority.

The truth is that elections, like battles, are alarmingly subject to random and unpredictable chance. Only afterwards do journalists and historians decide why the outcome was inevitable, what it means, and who should get the credit. It is easy to forget, for example, that for a brief moment after John Turner became Liberal leader in mid-1984, the opinion polls showed his party in the lead and pundits predicted his election to be an almost sure thing. There was serious speculation that Brian Mulroney, who at that time had been only a few months in Parliament and who then was in the process of failing ignominiously to recruit any prominent Francophone candidates in Quebec, would prove to be another fleeting Great Tory Hope.

Special factors hurting the Liberals in the 1984 election included: the 1981-82 recession, the worst of the post-war period; the inability of the Liberals to dispose of the blame by eliminating Pierre Trudeau (due to his late resignation and the fact that he reached from the grave to force Turner to take responsibility for controversial patronage appointments); divisions within the Liberal Party, both over the federal leadership race and between the federal and Quebec party; John Turner's rustiness, after years out of politics; the Parti Québécois' decision to revenge itself on the Liberals by providing workers and even candidates for the Tories; the support for the Tories from the remnants of other dissident Francophone factions, such as the Créditistes and the Union Nationale. Above all, the Liberals foolishly believed their own propaganda and honored the much-vaunted convention in which their leadership rotates between Francophones and Anglophones, although it is clear that Anglophone Liberal leaders do less well in Quebec (Diefenbaker's sweep came after Lester Pearson had replaced Louis St. Laurent). Thus Turner was fatally vulnerable to the remaining socially acceptable racism, exemplified when Lise Bissonette called him derisively "the perfect WASP," although in fact he is a Roman Catholic.

Brian Mulroney, by contrast, appeared to be a passable imitation of Pierre Trudeau – "the unmatchable bicultural man" – but without his character strength. Mulroney was a native-born Quebecker, a product of that small but special zone of Quebec society where English and French interact, a semi-assimilated Irish Catholic who spoke the local patois, unlike Turner whose French is Parisian.

The Mulroney family had farmed in a mixed French and Irish area just west of Quebec City since the 1840s. In Quebec, the Irish have always occupied a middle ground between the Protestant English and the Catholic French. Of all the Anglophone groups, they were the most likely to intermarry with Francophones. As a result, generations of Québécois have become used to Francophone leaders called Ryan or Johnson. Mulroney received much of his basic education in the French-language school system. So did his father, an electrician who had moved his family to the *Chicago Tribune*'s paper mill in the specially founded town of Baie Comeau in 1938, a year before the future prime minister's birth. Mulroney's law degree was from French-speaking Laval; his children were in French schools; his wife, equally neutrally, was a bilingual Yugoslav immigrant.

For Brian Mulroney, as for Pierre Trudeau, English and French Canada really have fused into one, or so he says. "I grew up bilingual. I never had any sense of there being a difference between French and English. To this day, it isn't Christmas without *la tourtière* [Quebec-style meat pie] and Irish music after Christmas midnight mass." This was not quite the message received in Quebec. Tory French-language radio advertisements hammered at the unsubtle point that Mulroney was "a Québécois, just like us." The polls showed that a substantial proportion of French-speakers thought Mulroney was indeed a Francophone. He did his best not to disillusion them.

When I glimpsed him the first time he was running for Tory leader at the Ottawa convention in 1976, Mulroney was a slim figure with very square shoulders, gliding through the endless receptions with his hand behind the elbow of his pregnant young wife, continuously moistening his lips so that his tongue appeared to flicker in and out like that of a snake. After the speeches were over, and he was sitting in his booth on the convention floor watching the even more unknown Joe Clark emerge as the candidate with the fewest enemies (a temporary condition, as it turned out), he seemed curiously vulnerable, searching the faces of the crowd as if hoping for a kind look. His own physiognomy seemed essentially amiable, reflecting neither the petulance of Joe Clark nor the ferocity of Pierre Trudeau.

"I can still see him arriving with his cardboard suitcases," reports a witness to Mulroney's arrival in 1955 at Nova Scotia's St. Francis Xavier University. "He didn't know anybody and he wanted so hard to be liked. The older kids would shove him around a bit and he'd look at them with eyes like saucers and keep trying to get accepted."

Brian Mulroney has built an entire career on trying to get accepted by people who matter. He did not suffer from defeat and deprivation in the same character-building way as did the American conservatives during the long Democratic hegemony in Washington. There were Tory governments in power both in Nova Scotia and in Ottawa when Mulroney was first engaged in student politics. His social position on campus was reportedly much enhanced by his connections with public figures. As a bilingual Quebec supporter of the party, he was a valuable commodity from an early age, achieving a personal relationship with Diefenbaker and a small but heady degree of media attention. When he left Laval, political connections got him a position with Montreal's largest law firm that probably would have been otherwise unavailable to a small-town unknown. (He specialized in labour law – making a career out of conciliation.) Later his public prominence assisted him to the presidency of the Iron Ore Company of Canada. Because the Tory Party was in such bad shape, he was able to keep his hand in its affairs without being forced to give up his career, run for Parliament and compete with his contemporaries, something he was clearly very reluctant to do.

As a backroom operator, Mulroney in a sense lived in the eye of the political hurricane. He did not have to handle direct pressure and personal attack in public. His rejection in the 1976 leadership race produced a dramatic effect. "He did not take defeat well," Martin, Gregg and Perlin report in *Contenders*:

> During the next two years, he was known to have drunk heavily on several occasions and was blunt in his assessment of the party's choice as leader. Ottawa reporters were frequent recipients of phone calls from Mulroney, reminding them that he would have been a better selection. In addition, Mulroney's behaviour at the 1976 Parliamentary Press Gallery dinner and the 1977 PC party general meeting in Quebec City, where he repeatedly criticized Clark to anyone who would listen, created a very unfavorable impression.

In a footnote they add, "By 1980, Mulroney had given up drinking and, at the time of the Ottawa convention in June 1983, had been an abstainer for three years."

During the 1983 leadership race, Mulroney showed a curious propensity to indulge in terminological inexactitude when cornered on minor issues, such as whether he ever served free liquor at his receptions or whether he had called "preposterous" the idea that a unilingual Anglophone could ever be prime minister, although he must have known that the truth could not be concealed. He also showed flashes of temper, once even announcing that he intended to sue a CBC reporter.

None of this suggests a happy warrior thirsting for brutal confrontation, which is perhaps not surprising. The personality type that flourishes in democratic politics differs from the traditional heroic conception of Leader of Men much more than is generally recognized. Professional politicians viewed at close quarters are often surprisingly indecisive, timorous and often confused, incapable of organizing an office, let alone a state. Their salient characteristics are emollience, caution and a child-like vanity. They are not really seeking power, which implies responsibility and possible recrimination, but "place" – the more honest term their counterparts in eighteenth-century England used to describe the various feudal sinecures and privileges they sought from the Crown, which brought them prestige and money but no duties. Some armies have officers who try to lead from the rear. Democratic countries have politicians who follow from the front.

Brian Mulroney's anodyne personality was highly successful because it did not interfere with forces that were converging in his favor. The Liberal order in Canada was never under any threat from him. But in the wider context of the Canadian Confederation, he faced the very different problem of dealing with forces that were fundamentally divergent – and likely to diverge further in the foreseeable future.

In coming to power, Brian Mulroney resembled Pierre Trudeau not just in his ethnic ambivalence, but also in his use of the National Unity theme to steamroller normal political debate. His biographers have written that his "vagueness on – and indeed impatience with – most issues can be traced to the fact that he believes that there is only one important issue in Canada, and that is the preservation of the country as he sees it." Other observers have advertised his "pragmatism" ("Brian is about as ideological as that coffee pot"). Mulroney chose to make the centerpiece of his collection of speeches, *Where I Stand,* a bold statement in favour of increased productivity, which hardly suggested a passionate interest in ideas – or an awareness of their force.

But no one can live without beliefs, and in fact it is clear that Mulroney's underlying assumptions are close to the Canadian Establishment consensus. St. Francis Xavier, when he attended it, was the center of the Antigonish movement, a Catholic social-activist movement with broadly left-wing sympathies, and his biographers report he emerged from law school with "nothing in his political makeup . . . incompatible with membership in the Liberal Party." This did not prevent Mulroney from successfully angling in 1983 for the support of the Tory right, which had sworn an oath that Joe Clark had to go. But it was no accident that he chose to be "vague" about issues.

The Great Mulroney Mystery, under these circumstances, is: what was he doing in the Progressive Conservative Party anyway? It helped him professionally, of course, and people who are drawn to the organizational aspect of politics often choose sides in much the same spirit as they select a baseball team to support. In Mulroney's case, however, at least part of the answer seems to be sectarianism.

Mulroney was entirely educated – apart from one year interrupted by illness – in Catholic schools. He has claimed that he went to St. Francis Xavier University because he was virtuously poor, but by 1955 Canada was enough of a welfare state to make the difference in cost of the more prestigious schools a dubious explanation. About the time Mulroney arrived there, Nova Scotia's long-time Liberal premier, a Catholic, died. The interim premier was Harold Connolly, also a Catholic, but there was general agreement in the party that the permanent successor should be a Protestant. "Then Harold, who liked being Premier, changed his mind and ran against Henry Hicks for the leadership and lost," Mulroney very frankly told L. Ian Mac-Donald, as reported in his *Mulroney: The Making of the Prime Minister.* "And all the Catholics got mad and went to [Nova Scotia Tory leader Robert] Stanfield, and that's the only reason Stanfield won." And the only reason, apparently, that Brian Mulroney went with them and became a Tory.

It's a measure of how unmentionable religion has become in the Liberals' Canada, possibly because of the historic role of militant Protestantism in uniting the Anglophones, that MacDonald doesn't seem to have understood what Mulroney was saying. He proceeds to express astonishment that in 1967 Mulroney supported British Columbia's Davie Fulton for the federal Tory leadership. This was certainly an ironic choice in view of Mulroney's later pious pronouncements about the need for a French-speaking leader; Fulton was unilingual and there was a fluently bilingual candidate in the race, Manitoba Premier Duff Roblin. MacDonald credulously accepts Mulroney's blarney that he "knew Fulton better" and "he was very nice to me." But Diefenbaker, whom Mulroney had supported in 1956, had also been nice to him; nevertheless, Mulroney worked to depose him in 1967. And Mulroney could hardly have known Fulton better than he did another candidate who was painfully learning French into the bargain: his own provincial premier, Robert Stanfield. A simpler explanation would be that Mulroney was attracted by Fulton's Catholicism – which quite possibly also brought Fulton two other young Catholic supporters, Joe Clark and Clark's subsequent lieutenant, Lowell Murray.

More recently, Mulroney has said that the American politician he most admires is a liberal Democrat, New York's Governor Mario Cuomo – an astonishing choice at a time when many Canadian conservatives are wistfully contemplating the success of Ronald Reagan. Cuomo, significantly, had made a public issue of his Catholicism.

Cronyism, on whatever basis, is intrinsic to politics. But it can have important consequences. A common religious background was one more reason for Joe Clark to stay on the ballot in the frenzy of the 1983 Tory leadership convention, ensuring John Crosbie's defeat and Mulroney's victory. And, even more than Clark, Mulroney is a stranger among the Anglophone and still largely Protestant Tories. His isolation must add an extra intensity to his fixation on Quebec, his devotion to the French connection, his deep antagonism to any right-wing stirrings in an essentially alien party.

Given his background, it's not surprising that Brian Mulroney's fundamental strategy has been to co-opt the Liberal state. This applied even to the electoral strategy he envisaged for the Progressive Conservatives. During the 1983 leadership race, Mulroney repeatedly emphasized the need to win the 102 federal ridings that he said had Francophone populations of over 10%. Conveniently, no one mentioned the alternative strategy of winning in English Canada. The result of the 1984 federal election, of course, vindicated both strategies. Once he became Prime Minister, Mulroney's celebrated pragmatism turned out to be a code-word for endorsing the Trudeauvian status quo, including political technique. During the federal election campaign Mulroney had made dramatic attacks on the Liberal government's use of patronage appointments, but his first years were spent making similar awards with such cupidity that several comic incidents occurred, including the case of one Quebec campaign worker who was named to a job about which she had not been consulted and which she didn't want. Moreover, nearly $100 million in federal projects were crammed into Mulroney's own somewhat remote riding. This crude pork-barrelling may be traditional in Quebec and parts of Atlantic Canada, but the spectacle did Mulroney no good elsewhere. And since pork-barrel politics are not noted for fine distinctions between patronage and peculation, there was an obvious potential for damaging scandal.

Apart from clearing away the wreckage of the National Energy Program, which had been undermined by collapsing energy prices, Mulroney's early moves on the economic front were basically cosmetic. His "Investment Canada" was the old nationalistic Foreign Investment Review Agency in a state of hibernation, with its personnel and powers largely intact. He bowed to Nationalist sentiment in decisions affecting the energy industry, where he facilitated Petro-

Canada's takeover of Gulf Canada's retail outlets despite the state-owned oil company's unpopularity among the West's oilmen. He showed little real interest in "privatizing" government-owned enterprises. He made no direct attack on the federal deficit, preferring to hope that a cyclically-upturning economy would resolve it in relative terms and he personally intervened to undercut Finance Minister Michael Wilson's tentative attempt to de-index social security payments.

Even more telling were the purely symbolic aspects of Mulroney's government. Despite explicit campaign promises, he zealously refused to allow the Tory right even such nominal consolation prizes as a free vote on capital punishment or an end to the Liberals' compulsory metrication program. His foreign policy was a mating dance of leftward propitiatory gestures. He refused to join Britain and the U.S. in quitting UNESCO. He not only appointed the former Ontario New Democratic Party leader Stephen Lewis as Canada's Ambassador to the United Nations, but publicly supported Lewis when he launched a vitriolic attack on the Heritage Foundation, a Washington-based think tank with close ties to the Reagan Administration. He volunteered sanctions against South Africa when the Reagan administration was fighting to keep its "constructive engagement" policy afloat. He allowed a Nicaraguan trade office to open in Toronto shortly after Washington announced its embargo. He declined to participate in the "Star Wars" Strategic Defense Initiative. Mulroney's intense preoccupation with co-opting the Liberal Establishment can be gauged from the fact that he was committing his government to the difficult task of negotiating a free trade arrangement with the U.S. – and yet would make no concessions to the susceptibilities of the most conservative American president for many years.

Conventional bourgeois politicians always have a marked tendency to minimize the policy differences between themselves and their opponents, in the hope of encroaching on their opponents' support while leaving their ideologically committed supporters no other place to go. This happens partly because the political personality dislikes arguments of all types, considering them disruptive and potentially dangerous, and partly because many political technicians are drawn from the simpler world of professional advertising, where such tactics (the "Principle of Minimum Differentiation") are standard practice. But Mulroney would no doubt argue that in Canada he especially has to moderate the Tories' image, in order to broaden its appeal to the majority of Canadians, who are presumed to be herbivorous centrists.

Ironically, in the U.S. this was exactly the argument of the liberal Republicans, from Wendell Wilkie to New York Governor Nelson Rockefeller, whom President Gerald Ford selected as his vice president. And it proved to be completely wrong. When, after a long and bitter struggle, the conservative Republicans finally got control of the party, they led it to repeated national victories by emphasizing their disagreements with what they called the "east coast liberal establishment," and by appealing to wholly new groups of voters on the basis of issues they, not the liberals, wanted to talk about. Similarly, moving the British Conservatives to the right has not hurt Margaret Thatcher. It is possible that the liberal Republicans were misled by their experiences with the peculiar politics of New York State, just as today many of Mulroney's advisors are undoubtedly extrapolating from their apprenticeships in Ontario provincial politics. But more probably they just weren't conservatives anyway – any more than Mulroney and his men.

Until recently in Canada, there have indeed been relatively few public signs of a grass-roots conservative movement comparable to the one that made Ronald Reagan possible in the U.S.. This is partly due to the absence of primaries, where such movements can make their presence felt. Many western MPs do make the free-market, rugged-individualist noises popular in the oil business and among ranchers, but they find little echo in the Toronto-dominated media. They and other ideological conservatives in Canada have no real networks of their own.

However, some groups of activists operating outside the Tory Party have begun to build single-issue movements attacking such Liberal policies as foreign aid (CFAR – Citizens for Foreign Aid Reform), bilingualism (APEC – the Association for the Preservation of English in Canada) and state incursions on free speech (CAFE – the Canadian Association for Free Expression). There is an active Canadian Libertarian Party. The Toronto-based National Citizens' Coalition has created a stir with full-page newspaper advertisements decrying various aspects of life under the Liberals and their Progressive Conservative heir, and has been active in various legal actions under the patriated Constitution. Additionally, there were unmistakable right-wing undertones in the long and bloody struggle to evict Joe Clark from the Tory leadership after the party's defeat in the 1980 federal election. In the leadership race itself, Alberta businessman Peter Pocklington's campaign was inspired ideologically and organizationally by the American conservative example, and did well enough to play a decisive role in blocking Clark's come-back attempt.

Canadian pundits and beleaguered Tory "moderates" like Joe Clark have argued that Canada's historical experience differs uniquely from that of the U.S., over such issues as Canada's allegedly stronger tradition of government activism, and that in response a native species of conservative has evolved that accepts this Canadian reality. In its highest form, representatives of this superior breed are known as "Red Tories." But to the uninitiated, Red Tories appear pretty much like liberal Republicans in America, or "wet" Tories in Britain. And in any case the argument is perfectly familiar in the other English-speaking countries. Being pronounced dead or at any rate impossible by academics and journalists is an indignity that conservative movements apparently have endured at a certain point in their historical cycle. In 1950, for example, Lionel Trilling remarked that "liberalism" – in its modern, collectivist sense – was the "sole intellectual tradition" of America. A little later Arthur Schlesinger, Jr. dismissed attempts to prove Trilling wrong as "the ethical afterglow of feudalism." By this measure, Canadian conservatives are still in their pre-Goldwater stage.

The problem with Mulroney's wholesale endorsement of Liberal policies is that such matters are not, ultimately, just a matter of taste. Policies do have consequences. There is no escaping the fact, for example, that the welfare state as it has evolved in the western world in this century has hit a brick wall – and not just in Canada. Once governments start taking more than a certain proportion of the Gross National Product, particularly when they are raising it through steeply graduated progressive taxation of personal income, enough people are affected to cause a political backlash, a dramatic increase in the underground economy and/or economic stagnation, as the incentive to work is eroded. Politicians of all parties have grown very fond of the celebrated formula: "Tax and tax – spend and spend – elect and elect." But all good things come to an end. When that formula was first enunciated by White House advisor Harry Hopkins at the beginning of the New Deal, governments were expropriating a much smaller fraction of economic output, and income taxes were paid by a small minority of the workforce. Now quite average taxpayers face the distressing marginal tax rates – the amount taken from the last dollar earned, which affects enthusiasm for earning the next – that were originally designed for the rich.

Once this limit has been reached, governments can either reduce the government's share of the economy to stimulate more growth, as happened in Britain in the first half of the nineteenth century, or overload the economy and wreck it, as in Argentina or Uruguay. And

Canada is significantly more overloaded than the United States. Canadian governments and Crown corporations take about 55% of the GNP, as opposed to about a third in the U.S.

Technically, the government share of the GNP is a more fundamental issue than the size of the federal budget deficit – unless Ottawa were to finance the deficit by printing money, which would cause inflation – but the latter has attracted most comment in Canada. And it is certainly worth noting that Canada's combined provincial and federal annual deficit is now almost three times as large in relation to the GNP as the equivalent U.S. figure. It continued to increase for three years after the 1981-82 recession ended, a sure sign of loss of spending control. Mulroney was too frightened of screams from the federal government's various client groups so he did not cut spending – bribing peripheral areas with government programs in Ottawa's basic recipe for regional peace. He had been driven to protest that he regarded social programs as "a sacred trust," even when they subsidized the rich. So the deficit problem inexorably has driven him to raising the taxes on his own middle-class supporters. It is easier, pragmatically speaking, to betray allies than to fight enemies.

However, even with tax increases and stabilized spending, the federal budget deficit projected by the time of the next election was proportionately as bad as the worst deficits run by the much-criticized Reagan administration. And that assumed continued economic growth in Canada. The pressures of Canadian politics had forced the Mulroney government to approach the budget cautiously – but this left them no room for maneuver in the event of a recession. It was a salutary reminder that the worst accidents, fiscal and otherwise, happen in the middle of the road.

Mulroney's tax decision has other serious implications. In terms of severity, the Canadian income tax system converged with the U.S. code during the inflationary 1970s, when Canadians were protected by indexation from the dramatic unlegislated "bracket creep" tax increases to which Americans were exposed. But now it is diverging towards greater harshness. This shows how far Mulroney is removed from current thinking among American conservatives – including President Reagan, who has spent much of his time in office stubbornly resisting tax increases. They view such increases as inherently self-defeating, because of the disincentive "supply-side" effects of higher marginal rates. If this is true, it suggests further relative weakening in Canada's economic performance – and, eventually, the emigration of a lot of educated Canadians.

The attempt to negotiate some form of bilateral free trade agreement with the U.S. is the Mulroney government's boldest economic policy initiative – and perhaps the most revealing. Canadians have been arguing about tariffs since before Confederation. But in recent years, the cause of free trade had become the love that dared not speak its name. Its supporters, often called "continentalists" because they were accused of favoring the integration of North America, shrank from public controversy with the regnant Nationalists, whose debating tactics tend to be rather uncouth. One example was Robert Stanfield: he did not raise the issue until his eight years as head of the federal Tory party were safely over – and then, not coincidentally, suffered the indignity of a CBC radio announcement headlining that his big speech on the subject actually opposed it.

Nevertheless, throughout Canada there was always a surprising amount of underground support for free trade. And it was constantly receiving new recruits, as successive cohorts of economics students fell under the spell of classical economic theory. If you accept standard economic axioms, the case for free trade is obvious and irrefutable. According to Dr. Michael Walker of the Vancouver-based Fraser Institute, an influential think-tank that has been a vital force in spreading free market ideas in Canada, free trade would have increased Canada's GNP by as much as 7% in any one year – and that the long-run dynamic effects could be even more dramatic, as people responded to new opportunities. But free trade had a crippling political disadvantage in Canada: its benefits would be widely dispersed, whereas the short-term dislocation costs would fall upon the obsolescent industries of Ontario and Quebec. Since these provinces between them dominated Confederation, the Canadian conventional wisdom throughout the 1970s was that free trade, whatever its theoretical merits, was just politically impossible. So when John Crosbie dared to raise the idea during the 1983 Tory leadership race, it was derided by none other than – of course – Brian Mulroney ("Free trade is terrific until the elephant twitches, and if it ever rolls over, you're a dead man. We'll have none of it".)

Nevertheless, a year after coming to power, Mulroney's government was indeed trying to have some of it – a salutary reminder of the pliability of pragmatists, and also of the volatility of Canadian politics. What had happened was that the Canadian business and government elites had been profoundly shocked by the depth of the 1981-82 recession, and by the disastrous results of nationalist economic prescriptions like the NEP. They had begun to fear that the Canadian and U.S. economies had become "uncoupled," with Canadian unemployment, productivity, growth and government financing trends deviating sharply for the worse. They had also been frightened by the increased protectionist bellowing from the U.S. Congress. Free trade advocates had been saying for some time that the Canadian domestic market was just too small and fragmented ever to offer the economies of scale necessary to compete internationally. Now there was new urgency in their contention that Canada must secure free access to a market as large as those enjoyed by its major industrial competitors, the European Community, the U.S., and Japan.

Mulroney endorsed free trade only after this elite reappraisal became safely obvious. Apart from the business community's renewed interest, bilateral free trade was a key recommendation of the Royal Commission on the Economic Union and Development Prospects for Canada, headed by Donald S. Macdonald, a former Liberal Finance Minister and himself a (belated) convert from Nationalism. another unimpeachably progressive straw in the wind was *The 49th Paradox: Canada in North America,* a favorable study of free trade by Richard Gwyn. Yet after Mulroney announced his initiative, he did remarkably little to defend free trade against the numerous enemies who instantly opened fire on it. Government documents leaked to the press suggested a deliberate low-profile policy, to the point of shunning the term "free trade" for euphemisms like "trade enhancement." And even when talking off the record to Americans, Canadian officials solemnly emphasized the need to protect Nationalist shibboleths like Canada's "cultural industries" – Ottawa jargon for subsidies to the powerful Toronto-based media industry.

Some politicians create facts and others react to them. The political culture of the English-speaking world is generally empirical and unideological, and combined with specific Canadian conditions this has in recent years produced a generation of unusually passive Anglophone leaders. By contrast, French Canada has spouted a plethora of leaders positively eager to impose their will upon even the most unpromising reality. Pierre Trudeau and René Lévesque both displayed an indifference to the cost of their policies so extreme as to amount to what might be called a form of Pol Potism, after the former (French-educated) ruler of Cambodia. In this respect, Brian Mulroney seems indisputably Anglophone. It is hard to imagine him fighting for free trade.

A clue to Mulroney's political method is his handling of the Strategic Defense Initiative. Unlike Mrs. Thatcher in Britain, he declined the Reagan administration's invitation to participate on a government-to-government basis, thus bowing to the Canadian left. However, he carefully endorsed the idea in principle, thus sneaking Washington a bone. And he magnanimously bestowed upon Canadian firms the right to bid privately on SDI contracts, which with $7000 U.S. would probably buy them one of the Pentagon's notorious coffee pots. This clever solution gave everybody something – and assumed, of course, that the Americans would continue to do whatever is necessary to defend Canada. The issue did not have to be considered on its merits. A similar pragmatically irresponsible answer to the free trade furor might see the negotiations begin, to appease free trade supporters, and fail to achieve significant results, amid Nationalist applause. But whatever happens, Brian Mulroney will be there to claim credit.

Mulroney himself, of course, would probably regard all these issues as subordinate to the cause of "National Unity," just like Pierre Trudeau before him. And the Tory victory almost certainly did ease some sectional tensions within Canada, merely because it meant the final exorcism of Trudeau, whose unifying qualities had long since been exhausted. But the Canadian Question was in one of its less pressing modes anyway. The fall in world energy prices meant that there were no "windfall profits" to be clawed from the West, but instead an expiring oil industry to resuscitate. There were no English-French eruptions to send tremors along the fault lines, like the 1970 FLQ kidnappings, the 1976 air traffic controllers' strike, or the 1983 Manitoba mutiny against the imposition of provincial-level bilingualism. Needless to say, the entire history of Canada indicates that these eruptions will recur. But the inhabitants of the rich land around volcanoes are notoriously reluctant to move.

Mulroney's attempt to repeat Trudeau's response to the Canadian Question is doomed to farce because the Tories are not the Liberals and he is not Trudeau. The Tories in the House of Commons remain in essence an unreconstructed Anglophone party, literally requiring interpreters to communicate with their many new Quebec allies, to say nothing of translating diplomatic briefings. Mulroney officially made light of this problem. Before the 1984 election, he joked with reporters that he planned to place Dan McKenzie, Tory MP from Winnipeg-Assiniboine and a rare public critic of bilingualism, in a ministry with a newly recruited Francophone Tory, on the theory that this would force them to get on together, despite not speaking each other's language. This displayed the assumption, typical of bilingualism's boosters, that opposition to the policy was simply a matter of ignorance and ill will. It also implicitly underlined the premium placed by the Trudeau system on the civil service. Without their mediation, Canada's mutually-uncomprehending masters would be reduced to gesticulation. The point remains, however, that differences in language inextricably involve legitimate differences in values that cannot be joked away.

Being shackled to an essentially Anglophone government is embarrassing enough for Quebec's Progressive Conservative contingent. Even worse is that they were in most cases personally unknown in Quebec when they were elected, and they were not backed up by any effective Tory machine at the riding level. It was partly to repair this lack that Mulroney formed a tacit alliance of convenience with the Parti Québécois government, actually attempting to assist it in the 1985 Quebec provincial election, much to the outrage of the leader of the provincial Tories. But the PQ's defeat by Robert Bourassa's Liberals meant that provincial government muscle was potentially available to help the federal Liberals, and that Mulroney would be forced to pay even more disproportionate attention to Quebec.

The sad truth is that Mulroney is miscast in the role he is attempting to play. Whatever Pierre Trudeau's faults, no one ever accused him of a promiscuous desire to please. It was only because he was such a formidable character that he was able, for a time at least, to impose his answer to the Canadian Question. Mulroney, by contrast, is the sort of politician who, when asked about his remark that Israel was one of several allies Canada had neglected, instantly and instinctively hedged: "I could just as easily have said Egypt." *Egypt?* Clowns are popularly supposed to want to play Hamlet, but this is the first recorded instance of a good-humor man trying the lead in *Tamburlaine.*

It doesn't help him, of course, that Trudeau's answer to the Canadian Question, fundamentally the same, was just as fundamentally wrong.

14

The Other Half-Sheet of Notepaper: A Prognosis

For a' that and a' that,
It's coming yet, for a' that

– Robert Burns

No man has a right to fix the boundary of the march of a nation, said Charles Stewart Parnell, the great leader of Victorian Irish nationalism. Nor even, perhaps, to predict what that march may be. In the case of Canada, however, which is emphatically not a nation, certain things seem clear.

1. Canada's fundamental contradictions cannot be resolved in the present Confederation. In the long run, Confederation must be reformed or even dissolved. But, as Adam Smith once said, there is a lot of ruin in a nation – and in a state. The Canadian Confederation could blunder on, in its convulsive and underachieving way, for a long time.

But it might not. It could be brought to a sudden stop, for example, by financial or economic catastrophe. Canada suffers from a particularly acute form of the generalized late-twentieth-century crisis of the welfare state. Its politicians apparently feel unable to respond to this problem, partly because of what they believe is the danger of exacerbating sectional and linguistic divisions by withdrawing any subsidy or privilege. If Canada's economic performance becomes terminally chronic, they may choose (or be forced) to handle the problem by seeking refuge in a closer association with the U.S., Canada's natural trading partner, just as the British elite chose to join the European Community, and Newfoundland was forced into Confederation.

287

2. Quebec is emerging as a nation. Although history does not move in straight lines, trends continue. And the evolution of the province of Quebec into a Francophone nation-state is the unmistakeable long-run message of Canadian history. It is not easy to say when the next crisis between English-speaking Canada and the Francophones will occur, or what will trigger it, but that it is coming is certain. In acquiring their own institutions, the Francophones are acquiring both the ability and the collective momentum to force change upon the Canadian Confederation. This is why Pierre Trudeau fought so hard against the *deux nations* concept, although it merely describes the developing situation.

3. English Canada will – sooner or later – recover from its post-Imperial hangover, and will increasingly assert its North American identity. This will bring it into conflict with important aspects of the Liberal state, particularly its focus on Quebec. Eventually, Anglophones will question the value of the Quebec connection. The Quebec issue in Canadian politics may become not whether Quebec will secede – but whether it should be expelled.

4. The sectional divisions within English Canada will be a continuing problem. This is particularly true of the Western provinces. They may lead some sort of rebellion against the Liberal hegemony, perhaps by supporting a right-wing, fourth party. Alternatively, individually or jointly they may one day seek a looser relationship with Central Canada, or even a closer relationship with the U.S. This would be economically logical for them, and given their North American identity, it would also be culturally legitimate and even honorable. What Parnell said about not fixing a boundary on the march of a nation applies to the 49th parallel – and to the Ontario line.

5. Brian Mulroney will almost certainly fail to create a Tory electoral coalition. But the Liberals won't find it easy to recreate theirs either. There may be a "time of troubles" in Canadian politics with no party able to gain a majority, as in 1962-68. New splinter parties may emerge.

6. Federal elections are a Canadian version of Russian roulette. One day, Confederation may get shot. In every Canadian election, there is a small but distinct chance, if everything lines up right, of something terrible happening. The most obvious possibility is linguistic polarization, in which an all-Anglophone government comes to power in

Ottawa without the French-speaking personnel to run the Liberals' bilingual state. (There already have been Francophone-dominated governments, of course, as in 1980, but by definition they need a few Anglophones to command a majority in the House of Commons.) A less obvious but quite real danger is that a sectional party, probably from Quebec but possibly from the West, could hold the balance of power in the House and demand radical reform.

"The struggle of reason against authority has ended in what appears now to be a decisive and permanent victory for liberty," wrote the historian J.B. Bury in his *History of the Freedom of Thought*. That was in 1913. It is not possible to be so confident in 1986. The twentieth century has proved bitter. The values that are common to the English-speaking peoples are in a minority in the world, and on the defensive.

Future historians might well be surprised that at this late date the English-speaking countries remain so self-absorbed, and despite their common heritage, show so little conscious awareness of their common interests. There is not much sign of "the moral federation of the English-speaking race" that was Goldwin Smith's dearest hope. Anglophone Canada seems to be in a particularly abject state of self-abasement, wallowing in its garbage-strewn alley and denying its history.

Niccolò Machiavelli was similarly distraught about the parochialism of the Renaissance city states of Italy. Their brilliant civilization had not developed a political dimension, and they were steadily falling prey to uncouth foreign powers. In the final chapter of *The Prince,* Machiavelli's cynical pose slipped and his idealism showed through in a desperate appeal to Lorenzo de' Medici to redeem their native land, quoting Petrarch's ringing invocation of their shared heritage, rendered here in Elizabethan translation:

For th' old Romane valor is not dead,
Nor in th' Italian breasts extinguished.

No one took any notice, of course, and Italy's moment passed. Perhaps the English-speaking peoples can console themselves that their art too will cause them not to be forgotten. But until the Canada Council contrives to subsidize another Michelangelo, an English Canada that remembers its past and understands its North American future would be an acceptable substitute.

Acknowledgements

I have noted with increasing distress the modern tendency of authors to compose lyrical essays acknowledging assistance received in the preparation of manuscripts. I am unable to emulate them only partly because of a journalist's professional reluctance to write one word more than absolutely necessary. For nearly fifteen years I have been questioning Canadians about Canada in (almost) every conceivable situation. Their help has been simply beyond measure. As I cannot name them all, I will name none, but my thanks are nonetheless heartfelt. I am also grateful to a number of individuals and organizations whose names do appear in the text.

I owe a special debt to a league of editors who in various ways have aided and/or tolerated this project over the appalling length of time it turned out to require: Neville Nankivell and Dalton Robertson of the *Financial Post;* Alan Abelson and Robert M. Bleiberg at *Barron's;* Robert L. Bartley at the *Wall Street Journal;* William S. Rukeyser at *Fortune;* and particularly Peter Worthington at the *Toronto Sun* and *Influence.*

Special mention must also be made of the following: R. Randolph Richardson, Leslie Lenkowsky, Roger Kaplan, Devon Gaffney. And, once again, of my brother John Brimelow, Director of International Research at Keane Securities in New York.

Thanks also to: Arnold Beichman; Conrad Black; Dr. J. Anthony Boeckh of the *Bank Credit Analyst;* Colin Brown, David Somerville and Kenneth McDonald at the National Citizens' Coalition; Robert Johnston; Hilary Childs and other long-suffering friends at the Canadian Consulate in New York; Connie Clausen and Guy Kettlehack of Connie Clausen Associates; Dennis Corrigan and Shannon Vale (and her indispensable Anthem Book Service in Toronto); Yvonne Crittenden; Barbara and Teddy Draimin; Duncan Edmonds; Paul Fromm; Michael and Zena Galway; Richard Gwyn; William G. Hammett, Joan Kennedy Taylor and Walter Olson at the Manhattan

Institute; James P. Hull; Lansing Lamont; F.A.J. Laws; Phil Lind; Dr. James Lucier; Stephen J. Markman; John O'Sullivan; Rick Archbold and other friends at Key Porter; Larry Shapiro; Sir Alfred Sherman; Dr. Michael Walker, Sally Pipes and Walter Block at the Fraser Institute.

Finally, I would like to thank my wife Maggy. Her fellow Canadian, Mrs. Lester Pearson, once remarked that behind every great man there stands an astonished woman. It is certainly true that behind this author there stands a nobly patient one.

Selected Bibliography

Abercrombie, Nicholas; Hill, Stephen; and Turner, Bryan S. *The Dominant Ideology Thesis.* London: George Allen & Unwin, 1984.

Alexander, David G. *Atlantic Canada and Confederation: Essays in Canadian Political Economy.* Toronto: University of Toronto Press, 1983.

Allen, Ralph. *Ordeal by Fire: Canada 1910-1945.* Toronto: Macmillan of Canada, 1972.

Andrew, J.V. *Bilingual Today, French Tomorrow.* Richmond Hill, Ont.: BMG Publishing Ltd., 1977.

Arnopoulos, Sheila McLeod, and Clift, Dominique. *The English Fact in Quebec.* Kingston & Montreal: McGill-Queen's University Press, 1984.

The Atlantic Council Working Group. *Canada and the United States: Dependence and Divergence.* Cambridge, Mass.: Ballinger, 1982.

Barber, Noel. *The Story of Singapore: From Raffles to Lee Kuan Yew.* London: Fontana/Collins, 1978.

Barr, John, and Anderson, Owen. *The Unfinished Revolt.* Toronto: McClelland & Stewart, 1971.

Berton, Pierre. *Why We Act Like Canadians.* Toronto: McClelland & Stewart, 1982.

Black, Conrad. *Duplessis.* Toronto: McClelland & Stewart, 1977.

Bliss, Michael. *The Evolution of Industrial Policies in Canada: An Historical Survey.* Ottawa: Economic Council of Canada, 1981.

_____ . "King of the Rock." *Saturday Night,* December 1982.

Booth, Amy. "Hints of more francization ring business alarm bells," *Financial Post,* May 7, 1983.

Bothwell, Robert, and Kilbourn, William. *C.D. Howe: A Biography.* Toronto: McClelland & Stewart, 1980.

Brimelow, Peter. "Interview with René Lévesque." *Barron's,* June 7, 1982.

Burnham, James. *Suicide of the West.* New Rochelle: Arlington House, 1960.

Cahill, Jack. *John Turner: The Long Run.* McClelland & Stewart, 1984.

Caldwell, Gary, and Waddell, Eric, eds. *The English of Quebec: From Majority to Minority Status.* Quebec City: Institut Québécois de Recherche sur la Culture, 1982.

Callwood, June. *Portrait of Canada.* Markham, Ont.: PaperJacks, 1983.

Cameron, Elspeth. *Hugh MacLennan: A Writer's Life.* Toronto: University of Toronto Press, 1981.

Carr, William N.A. *From Three Cents a Week: The Story of the Prudential Insurance Co.* Englewood Cliffs, N.J.: Prentice-Hall, 1975.

Chalmers, Floyd. *A Gentleman of the Press.* Toronto: Doubleday Canada Ltd., 1969.

Chester, Lewis; Hodgson, Godfrey; and Page, Bruce. *An American Melodrama*. New York: The Viking Press Inc., 1969.

Clarkson, Stephen. *Canada and the Reagan Challenge*. Toronto: James Lorimer & Co., 1982.

Colombo, John Robert, ed. *Colombo's Canadian Quotations*. Edmonton: Hurtig Publishers, 1974.

Commissioner of Official Languages. *Annual Reports*. Ottawa: Minister of Supply and Services, 1983.

Creighton, Donald. *John A. Macdonald: The Young Politician*. Toronto: Macmillan of Canada, 1968.

———— . *John A. Macdonald: The Old Chieftain*. Toronto: Macmillan of Canada, 1968.

Curtis, Kenneth M., and Carroll, John E. *Canadian-American Relations: The Promise and the Challenge*. Lexington, Mass.: Lexington Books/ D.C. Heath & Co., 1983.

de Gaulle, Charles. *Memoirs of Hope: Renewal 1958-1962, Endeavour 1962-* London: Weidenfeld & Nicolson, 1971.

Desbarats, Peter. *The State of Quebec: A Journalist's View of The Quiet Revolution*. Toronto: McClelland & Stewart, 1965.

———— . *René: A Canadian in Search of a Country*. Toronto: McClelland & Stewart, 1976.

Dewar, Elaine. "The New Diplomacy," *City Woman*, Fall 1982.

Diefenbaker, John. *One Canada: Memoirs of the Right Honourable John G. Diefenbaker, Volume 1: The Crusading Years 1895-1956*. Toronto: Macmillan of Canada, 1975.

———— . *One Canada: Memoirs of the Right Honourable John G. Diefenbaker, Volume 2: The Years of Achievement, 1956-1962*. Scarborough, Ont.: Signet, 1978.

Doern, Russell. *The Battle over Bilingualism: the Manitoba Language Question 1983-5*. Winnipeg: Cambridge Publishers, 1985.

Doran, Charles F. *Forgotten Partnership: U.S.-Canada Relations Today*. Baltimore: Johns Hopkins University Press, 1984.

Duncan, Sara Jeanette. *The Imperialist*. Toronto: McClelland & Stewart, 1971.

Drouin, Marie-Josée, and Bruce-Briggs, Barry. *Canada Has a Future*. Toronto: McClelland & Stewart, 1978.

Economic Council of Canada. *Newfoundland: From Dependency to Self-Reliance*. Ottawa: 1982.

Farthing, John. *Freedom Wears a Crown*. Toronto: Kingswood House, 1957.

Ferns, H.S. *Reading from Left to Right: One Man's Political History*. Toronto: University of Toronto Press, 1983.

Foster, Peter. *The Blue-Eyed Sheiks: The Canadian Oil Establishment*. Toronto: Totem Books, 1980.

_____ . *The Sorcerer's Apprentices: Canada's Super-Bureaucrats and the Energy Mess*. Don Mills, Ont.: Collins, 1982.

_____ . *Other People's Money: The Banks, the Government and Dome*. Don Mills, Ont.: Collins, 1983.

Fowler, Marian. *Redney: A Life of Sara Jeanette Duncan*. Toronto: House of Anansi Press, 1983.

Franks, C.E.S. "Borrowing from the United States: Is the Canadian system moving towards the Congressional model?" In *American Review of Canadian Studies*, Vol. XIII, No. 3, Autumn 1983.

Friedenberg, Edgar Z. *Deference to Authority: The Case of Canada*. White Plains, N.Y.: M.E. Sharpe Inc., 1979.

Fraser, Graham. *PQ: René Lévesque and the Parti Québécois in Power*. Toronto: Macmillan of Canada, 1984.

Frye, Northrop. *Divisions on a Ground: Essays on Canadian Culture*. House of Anansi Press Ltd., 1982.

Garreau, Joel. *The Nine Nations of North America*. New York: Avon Books, 1982.

Gilder, George. *Wealth and Poverty*. New York: Basic Books Inc., 1981.

Goodsell, James Nelson. "The Canadian Difference." *Christian Science Monitor,* June 12, 1983 *et seq.*

Government of Canada. *A Time for Action: Toward the Renewal of the Canadian Federation*. Ottawa: Government of Canada, 1978.

Granatstein, J.L. *The Ottawa Men: The Civil Service Mandarins 1935-1957*. Toronto: Oxford University Press, 1982.

Gray, Earle. *The Great Uranium Cartel*. Toronto: McClelland & Stewart, 1982.

Gwyn, Richard. *The Northern Magus: Pierre Trudeau and the Canadians*. Markham, Ont.: PaperJacks, 1981.

_____ . *The 49th Paradox: Canada in North America*. Toronto: McClelland & Stewart, 1985.

Hardin, Herschel. *A Nation Unaware: The Canadian Economic Culture*. Vancouver: J.J. Douglas Ltd., 1974.

Holmes, John W. *Life With Uncle: The Canadian-American Relationship*. Toronto: University of Toronto Press, 1981.

Hutchison, Bruce. *Canada: Tomorrow's Giant*. Toronto: Longmans Green & Co., 1957.

Humphreys, David L. *Joe Clark: A Portrait*. Toronto: Deneau & Greenberg Publishers Ltd., 1978.

Huntford, Roland. *The New Totalitarians*. New York: Scarborough Books, 1980.

Hyde, H. Montgomery. *The Atom Bomb Spies*. New York: Ballantine Books, 1981.

Innis, Mary Quayle, ed. *Mrs. Simcoe's Diary.* Toronto: Macmillan of Canada, 1965.

Jacobs, Jane. *The Question of Separatism: Quebec and the Struggle over Sovereignty.* New York: Vintage Books, 1981.

Joll, James. *Antonio Gramsci.* New York: Penguin Books, 1978.

Jonas, George, and Amiel, Barbara. *By Persons Unknown: The Strange Death of Christine Demeter.* Toronto: Macmillan of Canada, 1977.

Joyal, Hon. Serge. "Address to the Federation Acadienne de la Nouvelle-Ecosse." Ottawa: Secretary of State's Office, Press Release, November 13, 1982.

Kaufman, Michael T. "Socialist Alliance at Issue in Canada." *New York Times,* January 16, 1983.

_____ . "Canadian Schools Immerse the Students in French." *New York Times,* May 17, 1983.

_____ . "Canada: An American Discovers Its Differences." *New York Times Magazine,* May 15, 1983.

_____ . "Hopes for an Eskimo Territory Rise in the North." *New York Times,* August 22, 1983.

Keegan, John. *Six Armies in Normandy.* New York: The Viking Press, 1982.

Kelly, Fraser, ed. *The Canadian Voter's Guide.* Toronto: McClelland & Stewart, 1979.

Kristol, Irving. *Two Cheers for Capitalism.* New York: Basic Books, 1978.

Lachapelle, Rejean, and Henripin, Jacques. *The Demolinguistic Situation in Canada: Past Trends and Future Prospects.* Translated by Deirdre A. Mark. Montreal: Institute for Research on Public Policy, 1982.

McCall-Newman, Christine. *Grits: An Intimate Portrait of the Liberal Party.* Toronto: Macmillan of Canada, 1982.

MacDonald, L. Ian. *Mulroney: The Making of the Prime Minister.* Toronto: McClelland & Stewart, 1984.

McEvoy, Colin, and Jones, Richard. *Atlas of World Population History.* Harmondsworth, U.K.: Penguin, 1978.

MacLaren, Roy. *Canadians on the Nile, 1882-1898.* Vancouver, B.C.: University of British Columbia Press, 1978.

MacLennan, Hugh. *Two Solitudes.* Toronto: Laurentian Library/Macmillan of Canada, 1972.

McNaught, Kenneth. *The Pelican History of Canada.* Harmondsworth, U.K.: Penguin Books Ltd., 1982.

Malcolm, Andrew H. *The Canadians.* New York: Times Books, 1985.

Martin, Lawrence. *The Presidents and the Prime Ministers: Ottawa and Washington Face to Face: The Myth of Bilateral Bliss.* Toronto: Doubleday Canada Ltd., 1982.

_____ . "Most of new Quebec Tories largely unknown in province." *The Globe and Mail,* September 6, 1984.

Martin, Patrick; Gregg, Allan; and Perlin, George. *Contenders: The Tory Quest for Power*. Scarborough, Ont.: Prentice-Hall of Canada Inc., 1983.

Mathias, Philip. *Forced Growth: Five Studies of Government Involvement in the Development of Canada*. Toronto: James Lorimer & Samuel, 1971.

Meisel, John. "Where Canada and the U.S. part company." *Channels,* January-February 1984.

Mitka, Nick and Helma. *The Riel Rebellion 1885*. Belleville, Ont.: Milk Silk Screening Ltd., 1972.

Monk, Lorraine, ed. *Canada With Love/Canada Avec Amour*. Toronto: McClelland & Stewart, 1982.

Morris, Edmund. *The Rise of Theodore Roosevelt*. New York: Ballantine Books, 1980.

Mosley, Sir Oswald. *My Life*. London: Nelson, 1968.

Moynihan, Patrick Daniel, with Weaver, Suzanne. *A Dangerous Place*. Boston: Atlantic Monthly Press/Little Brown & Co., 1978.

Mulroney, Brian. *Where I Stand*. Toronto: McClelland & Stewart, 1983.

Murphy, Rae; Chodos, Robert; and Auf der Maur, Nick. *Brian Mulroney: The Boy from Baie-Comeau*. Toronto: James Lorimer & Co., 1984.

Nelles, Viv. "The Unfriendly Giant." *Saturday Night,* February 1982.

Newman, Peter C., and Fillmore, Stan, eds. *Their Turn to Curtsey, Your Turn to Bow*. Toronto: Maclean-Hunter Ltd., 1972.

Newman, Peter C. *The Canadian Establishment, Volume One*. Toronto: McClelland & Stewart, 1975.

_____. *The Distemper of Our Times*. Winnipeg, Man.: Greywood Publishing Ltd., 1968.

Osler, E.B. *The Man Who Had to Hang Louis Riel*. Toronto: Longmans Green & Co., 1961.

Penniman, Howard R., ed. *Canada at the Polls, 1979 and 1980: A Study of the General Elections*. Washington, D.C.: American Enterprise Institute, 1981.

Peyrefitte, Alain. *The Trouble With France*. New York: Alfred A. Knopf, 1981.

Phillips, Kevin P. *The Emerging Republican Majority*. New Rochelle, N.Y.: Arlington House, 1969.

Porter, Gerald. *In Retreat: The Canadian Forces in the Trudeau Years*. Toronto: Deneau & Greenberg Publishers Ltd., undated.

Powell, J. Enoch. *Joseph Chamberlain*. London: Thames & Hudson, 1977.

Pratt, Larry, and Stevenson, Garth, eds. *Western Separatism: The Myths, Realities and Dangers*. Edmondon: Hurtig Publishers Ltd., 1981.

Radwanski, George. *Trudeau*. Toronto: Macmillan of Canada Ltd., 1978.

Ravitch, Diane. *The Troubled Crusade: American Education 1945-1980*. New York: Basic Books Inc., 1983.

Robertson, Gordon. "Election to Cure Federal Ills." *Policy Options Politiques,* September 1983.

Rohmer, Richard. *E.P. Taylor: The Biography of Edward Plunkett Taylor.* Toronto: McClelland & Stewart, 1978.

Rowe, Frederick W. *A History of Newfoundland and Labrador.* Toronto: McGraw-Hill Ryerson Ltd., 1980.

Rusher, William A. *The Rise of the Right.* New York: William Morrow & Co., 1984.

Sawatsky, John. *For Services Rendered: Leslie James Bennet and the RCMP Security Service.* Toronto: Doubleday Canada Ltd., 1982.

_____ . *Men in the Shadows: The RCMP Security Service.* Don Mills, Ont.: Totem Books, 1983.

Seccombe, W.W. *A Very Private Concern.* Toronto: Nelson, Foster & Scott Ltd., 1974.

Senate Standing Committee on Foreign Affairs. *Canada-United States Relations,* Vols. I-III. Ottawa: Ministry of Supply and Services, 1975, 1978, 1982.

Senecal, A.J. "The Growing Role of the Quebec State in Language Corpus Studies." *American Review of Canadian Studies,* Vol. XIII, No. 2, Summer 1983.

Sestito, Raymond. *The Politics of Multiculturalism.* St. Leonards, NSW, Australia: Centre for Independent Studies, 1982.

Shaw, William F., and Albert, Lionel. *Partition: The Price of Quebec's Independence.* Pointe Claire, Quebec: Thornhill Publishing, 1982.

Sheppard, Robert, and Valpy, Michael. *The National Deal: The Fight for a Canadian Constitution.* Scarborough, Ont.: Fleet Books, 1982.

Sienkiewicz, Count. *Journey to America.* New York: Columbia University Press, 1967.

Simpson, Jeffrey. *Discipline of Power: The Conservative Interlude and the Liberal Restoration.* Toronto: Personal Library, 1980.

Sowell, Thomas. *Ethnic America: A History.* New York: Basic Books Inc., 1981.

_____ . *The Economics and Politics of Race.* New York: William Morrow & Co., 1983.

Smith, Denis. *Gentle Patriot: A Political Biography of Walter Gordon.* Edmonton: Hurtig Publishers, 1973.

Smith, Goldwin. *Canada and the Canadian Question.* Toronto: University of Toronto Press, 1971.

Somerville, David. *Trudeau Revealed By His Actions and Words.* Richmond Hill, Ont.: BMG Publishing, 1978.

Statistics Canada. "Highlights from 1981 Census Data." Press release, April 26, 1983.

_____ . "1981 Census of Canada 20% Data Base." April 26, 1983.

_____ . *Daily.* April 29, 1983.

Stewart, Walter. *Divide and Con: Canadian Politics at Work.* Toronto: New Press, 1973.

_____ . *Shrug: Trudeau in Power*. Toronto: New Press, 1972.

Story, G.M.; Kirwin, W.J.; and Widdowson, J.D.A. *Dictionary of Newfoundland English*. Toronto: University of Toronto Press, 1982.

Taylor, Charles. *Radical Tories: The Conservative Tradition in Canada*. Toronto: House of Anansi Press, 1982.

Thernstrom, Stephen, ed. *Harvard Encyclopedia of American Ethnic Groups*. Cambridge, Mass.: Belknap Press/Harvard University Press, 1980.

Thompson, Lovell, ed. *The Galbraith Reader*. Ipswich, Mass.: Gambit, 1977.

Trofimenkoff, Susan Mann. *The Dream of Nation: A Social and Intellectual History of Quebec*. Toronto: Gage Publishing Ltd., 1983.

Trudeau, Margaret. *Beyond Reason*. New York: Pocket Books, 1980.

_____ . *Consequences*. Toronto: Seal Books, 1982.

Trudeau, Pierre Elliott. *Federalism and the French Canadians*. Toronto: Macmillan of Canada, 1968.

Vallières, Pierre. *White Niggers of America*. Toronto: McClelland & Stewart, 1971.

Wallace, Elizabeth. *Goldwin Smith: Victorian Liberal*. Toronto: University of Toronto Press, 1957.

Wead, Doug, and Wead, Bill. *Reagan in Pursuit of the Presidency – 1980*. Plainfield, N.J.: Haven Books, 1982.

Weidenbaum, Murray L. *The Future of Business Regulation: Private Action and Public Demand*. New York: Amacom, 1979.

Westell, Anthony. *The New Society*. Toronto: McClelland & Stewart, 1977.

Winks, Robert. "An Orphaned Dominion." *The Wilson Quarterly,* Summer 1982.

Wood, Chris. "New bilingual rule brings airport turbulence." *Financial Post,* May 7, 1983.

Woodcock, George. *Confederation Betrayed: The Case Against Trudeau's Canada*. Madeira Park, B.C.: Harbour Publishing, 1981.

Zink, Lubor J. *Viva Chairman Pierre!* Toronto: Griffin House, 1977.

Other facts and figures are drawn from standard reference works such as the *Canada Year Book,* the *World Almanac* and *Quick Canadian Facts.*

INDEX